Susan McBane

HOW YOUR HORSE WORKS

DAVID & CHARLES

Preface

It is only in the last decade or so that many people are beginning to pay serious attention to other aspects of the horse than his body, what it looks like, how it functions and of what it is capable. Countless books and other treatises have been written over the last couple of thousand years about how to manage and train the horse and some of them have certainly included sections on the horse's mind and psychology. Usually, though, the emphasis has been on 'making' the horse do what humans want with little or no consideration of whether or not

he is capable of it, cut out for it or whether he actually wants to do it. Horses are very closely related to humans in that they are mammals – sentient and sensitive beings – and it is strange that this only seems to be becoming more widely accepted at this late stage in the relationship between horse and human.

It is increasingly recognised that the condition of the mind affects the condition of the body but we know much less about the horse's mind than about his body. Attitudes are slowly changing and more attention is being paid to

the psychological aspects of horse-human relationships. Formal and informal studies in several countries repeatedly indicate that the horse is far from the insensitive, unemotional, rather stupid creature many well-known figures and establishment organisations still think, and teach, him to be. In many ways, the horse's psychological capacities seem to far exceed our own.

Similarly, research into his physical functions relating to various equestrian disciplines from racing to dressage have uncovered astounding natural athletic abilities far beyond those of many other animals and certainly of humans.

Many true horsemen and women, those special, gifted few who have always had an integral bond, an almost centaur-like relationship with and understanding of horses or, as appropriate, other animals, have always known it as being the status quo that animals have spirits or souls; it would never occur to them that they have not. Yet some formal religions and other organisations large and small still maintain that humans are superior to all other life forms and that animals have no spirit or soul. In fact, one eminent churchman, only a couple of decades ago, pronounced that an animal may actually go to Heaven if a human had given it a name (Fido, Dobbin, Felix…) during its life on earth. True!

Some people believe that it must be this incredibly highly-evolved soul which gives the horse the generosity and strength of spirit to tolerate human beings. There seems to be no other rational explanation for it, especially in an animal which is not supposed to be able to think rationally for itself.

This book is dedicated to my dog
SUZIE *who is unbelievably perfect*

Acknowledgements

Although only one person's name may appear on a book as the author, each one is invariably a team effort, and accordingly I wish to thank Sue Viccars, Sue Cleave and Jane Trollope at David & Charles for their professionalism, skill and expertise during the preparation of this one. They are all extremely helpful, accommodating and a pleasure to work with.

Photographs by Kit Houghton except the following:
Bob Atkins pp97(top rt), 98(left), 108, 109, 110, 121, 152; Bob Langrish p144; Mary Evans Picture Library pp16(btm left & rt), 18–19, 20–21; Natural History Museum, London pp8/M. Long, 9; NHPA pp83/Henry Ausloos, 119/Nigel J Dennis, 124/Kevin Schafer, 125/Daniel Heuclin(left & top rt), 125/William Paton(btm rt), 127/Roger Tidman; Robert Harding Picture Library p12; Marcy & Tony Pavord pp41, 43(top left); RSPCA Photolibrary pp 87/E.A.Janes, 102/Wild Images Ltd – David Breed; Colin Vogel pp43(rt), 151(btm); Author's collection pp11(btm rt)(Photo: Peter Sweet), 15(top rt), 17, 24(btm), 52, 53, 77 (Photo: Tim Hannan), 133, 134, 146
Line illustrations by: Sally Alexander p35; Chartwell Illustrators p50; Eva Melhuish p25; Maggie Raynor p32; Visual Image/Paul Bale pp23, 26, 28, 29, 30, 36, 37, 38, 43, 45, 49, 52, 54, 56, 67, 73, 120; Colin Vogel p27,40; Author p70, 133

A DAVID & CHARLES BOOK

First published in the UK in 1999

A catalogue record for this book is available from the British Library.

ISBN 0 7153 0861 0

Book design by Visual Image
Printed in Singapore by Sino Publishing Ltd
for David & Charles
Brunel House   Newton Abbot   Devon

Contents

Section 1: Evolution and Origins

Section 2: The Horse in History, Mythology and Religion

Section 3: The Body and Its Systems

6

Section 4: The Things They Do

Section 5: Keeping Your Horse Content and Healthy

From Swamp to Plains

The horse's place

The organisms of the world are classified into sections and sub-sections for ease of identification.

Horses belong to the kingdom Animalia (Animal Kingdom), phylum Chordata (having a spine), class Mammalia, order Perissodactyla (hoofed, grazing mammals with odd numbers of toes, those with even numbers of toes being the Artiodactyla), the suborder Hippomorpha (horse-like forms), family Equidae, (all modern horses, asses and zebras), these in turn being placed in the genus Equus, modern, domesticated and feral horses (other than the Przewalski) and ponies all belonging, finally to the species Equus caballus.

Most horse enthusiasts know that the horse's first direct ancestor looked like something between a fox and a hyrax. Indeed, its first and correct scientific name, *Hyracotherium*, was coined because it was believed initially to be related to the hyrax. A later name for it is *Eohippus* as its fossils were first discovered in deposits from the Eocene epoch (about 54 to 38 million years ago), *hippus* coming from the Greek for horse.

Hyracotherium. *Its physical features, particularly its flexible spine, fitted it ideally for life in a cramped, forest environment*

Written in the rocks

Fossils of *Hyracotherium* (there were several variants) have been found in North American and European Eocene deposits but also in earlier Mongolian Palaeocene deposits, from about 65 million years ago. It was obviously widespread with characteristics which fitted it to survive in the tropical forests which covered most of the land at that time. It had a small head and primitive brain with eyes set forward in the skull and forty-four small teeth suited to browsing on leaves and fruits, grasses not having evolved. With an arched back, four 'hooflets' (rather than claws) with dog-like pads on the front feet, and three 'hooflets' on the back, its feet functioned like those of a dog without the spring-footed gait characteristic of horses. It was probably already timid (as a herbivorous prey animal) and prone to hiding as running is not feasible in dense forest.

Gradually, the horse's many ancestral types grew bigger and stronger, often existing at the same time. *Mesohippus* was a milestone in the late Eocene/Oligocene (about 40 to 26 million years ago), its toes having reduced to three, the central

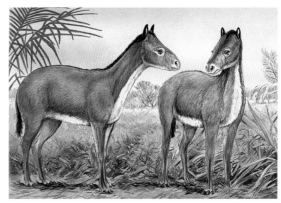

Mesohippus *was still a forest-dwelling animal although bigger and stronger than* Hyracotherium

one the largest, but it was still pad-footed. Its brain was more advanced than that of *Hyracotherium*, its teeth bigger and stronger and it was taller.

Where the forests reduced and grassy landscape developed, from about 23 million years ago, a more horse-like type called *Parahippus* appeared. Its head, brain and teeth were bigger, its two side toes bore little weight and its legs were longer, showing the beginnings of the spring-footed gait.

Merychippus in its many variants evolved from *Parahippus*, from about 17 million years ago, looking rather like a 10hh pony, with grazing teeth and eyes further back and to the sides for a wider view of approaching predators. The familiar elongated leg structure was evolving with a fused radius and ulna above the knee for strength. The side toes often bore no weight and it was a true spring-footed, fast runner.

Pliohippus appeared in the mid-Miocene from around 15 million years ago. This became a true, horse-like, one-toed grazer with several variants and was for a long time considered the modern horse's immediate ancestor but research and

Artist's reconstruction of White River, USA in the late Eocene period. (l to r) Hoplophoneus, Mesohippus, Hyaenodon, Archaeotherium, Poebrotherium, Pseudoprotoceras, Megacerops, Daphoenus, Merycoidodon, Subhyracodon

discoveries in recent years show that it probably did not give rise to *Equus* after all, this status almost certainly belonging to *Dinohippus*, the horsiest of the ancestors, which arose about 12 million years ago.

The genes of change

Any animal is the result of genes, units of hereditary material, passed on in equal numbers from both parents, some genes being more dominant in passing on their characteristics than others. Genes, however, can change naturally – mutate – producing different characteristics in the offspring.

Animals developing in a given environment have appropriate characteristics enabling them to survive there, such as long, thick coats, the ability to manage on little food, the inclination to run from danger and long legs powered by super-efficient muscles for standing starts and stamina. If *Hyracotherium*'s genes had not gradually mutated to produce a bigger head and teeth, a longer neck and legs and so on, its successors would not have evolved and we should have no horses today.

If a group of animals does not adapt genetically to changing conditions, it will die out eventually. Animals born in the wild with significant defects soon die or are killed, preventing them breeding and passing on their defects. Only those best fitted for their environment get to breed and pass on their genes.

The retreating forests and the spreading plains, steppes and tundras were, and are, environments to which horses and their ancestral types have been able to adapt ideally due to genetic change.

WE ARE FAMILY ...

Open spaces mean that the animals in them are highly visible to predators and one single animal is a clear target. Herding developed as a defence against this danger. Most horse families in wild and feral conditions are small, from two to about twelve at most, but in times of danger they sometimes join forces in one larger herd. Even a whole pack of hunting dogs or a full pride of lionesses seeks only one carcass, so the more animals there are for them to choose from the less chance there is of any one individual becoming that carcass.

Equines have no sharp teeth, claws or horns but their kicks can kill or seriously disable a large cat and a bite from an equine can easily break a leg or jaw so they are formidable prey. But their main saving graces have always been their alertness, speed and stamina, in that order. Horses are the only domestic animals which stem from wild ancestors whose first line of defence was flight.

Because they became grazers, eating tough, silica-rich grass with a high fibre and sometimes water but relatively low nutrient content, they need to eat for many hours a day to acquire enough fuel for life. With their heads down eating, they can scan visually near and far for danger. Their highly developed senses of hearing, sight and smell alert them to predators while they are still distant enough for the horses, zebras or asses to get a lightning head start and their stamina can normally keep them ahead of feline predators. Canine hunters, though, have a much higher kill rate on wild and feral *equidae* as their speed and stamina equal those of their prey.

Family Connections

Although North America is regarded as the birthplace of the horse, horse ancestors migrated over the former Bering land bridge to Asia, Europe and Africa which were once closely joined. At one time, the Atlantic did not exist and Britain and Ireland were joined to Scandinavia and north-west Europe. These land masses and bridges provided migration routes for animals and vegetation of many kinds.

From about 3 million years ago, several glaciations and major land movements created rising and falling sea levels resulting, by the end of the last Ice Age about 12,000 years ago, in today's world map. This epoch also saw the unexplained extinction of horses in America.

Equus today

Equus is represented today by many man-created types of horses and ponies and far fewer wild types of asses (Asia and Africa) and zebras (Africa only). The quagga, a type of zebra with little or no striping on the hindquarters, was hunted to extinction almost 100 years ago, the last zoo specimen dying in the 1930s. DNA tests now show that it was not a separate species but a sub-species of the plains zebra and a breeding group of the latter, with sparse striping on the hindquarters, has been assembled in South Africa to try to recreate the quagga. Although horses, asses and donkeys can breed together, many are reluctant to do so (except Jack (male) donkeys) and the offspring are almost always sterile.

Horse country

Horses are extremely adaptable and seem able to exist, in their different types, anywhere there is suitable vegetation from the Arctic Circle to the equator. Stock gradually deteriorates in humid climates, needing frequent 'fresh blood' but Australia, which never had indigenous equines, has proved an ideal environment for them.

The rare Przewalski horse is being successfully reintroduced to its former natural ranges in Asia, and also lives ferally in Europe and in reserves and zoos worldwide. The Tarpan, an influential, extinct, wild pony of eastern Europe, has been 'reconstituted' from its domestic successors and lives wild in the vast ancient forests of Poland and ferally, as 'grassland managers' on nature reserves in Suffolk, England.

The starting point

We know from rock carvings and paintings, bas-reliefs on ancient monuments and so on what natural types of horses and ponies existed before domestication. We know that there were large and small, heavy and light types with regional characteristics.

THE ADAPTABLE HORSE

Horses and ponies developed different characteristics according to the climate and environment in which they evolved. Those in cold climates developed the 'cold-blooded' features of rounded, chunky bodies to hold heat, thickish skin and a shortish neck for the same reason plus shorter legs and a low-carried tail to retain heat and reduce cold airflow round the body. Their heads are large with long nasal passages to warm incoming air and short ears to retain heat. Most obviously, their winter coats are long and thick.

'Hot-bloods' evolving in hot climes have thin skin and coats, flaring nostrils with short nasal passages, longer ears and necks and oval shaped bodies above long, slender legs, with fine tails held high.

Other features also tell where ancestors evolved: big feet probably developed on wet land and vice versa, big jaws for big teeth where the diet consisted of coarse, fibrous grasses and animals with a tendency to slower movements and reactions and to hiding behind objects were possibly forest dwellers.

The Ardennais is one of the most ancient, least altered breeds of horse in the world

The breeds nearest to natural types today are probably the Caspian (from Iran), the Akhal-Teké (from Turkmenistan), the Exmoor Pony (from England), the Shetland Pony (from Scotland), the Soraia (from Iberia) and the Ardennais (from France).

Their influence today

The modern breed we call the Arab must realistically be an amalgamation of hot-blooded, wild types probably from around Iran/old Persia and accessible regions of The Orient and not an ancient 'pure' wild type as some of its proponents assert.

What of the most famous breed in the world, the Thoroughbred, said to descend from three legendary 'Arabian' stallions imported to England in the eighteenth century? From their portraits, and descriptive practice of the times, The Darley Arabian was possibly the only Arab and clearly of the Managhi/Muniqui long-legged racing strain or type, The Godolphin Arabian, often also called The Godolphin Barb, was surely the latter, with his aquiline profile, rounded quarters and lower tail carriage and The Byerley Turk was almost certainly a Turkmene, an ancestor-relative of the Akhal-Teké and probably also of the Managhi Arab types, but he could have been a Managhi Arab himself.

These different body types are plain to see in modern Thoroughbreds – put a photograph of a lean, rangy Thoroughbred stayer next to one of an Akhal-Teké p15, an old Turkmene or a modern Turcoman and you could be looking at the same breed. Indeed, you probably *are* looking at the same genes. Even their temperaments can be the same – independent, indomitable and superior!

The old Iberian horse, descending from the indigenous Soraia pony and represented today by the Andalusian (including the Carthusian), the Lusitano, the Alter Réal and, in dilute form, the Lippizaner and Friesian, is greatly underestimated as an influence on today's breeds, yet was the mount of choice for the royalty, nobility and wealthy of Europe for hundreds of years. Taken to America by the *conquistadores*, its influence is evident in most breeds of that continent.

Finally, there are the heavy horses, the ponies and the stocky cobs (the true Great Horse of the Middle Ages) for which Europe is specially noted, with all their offshoots, such as elegant carriage horses, smart roadsters and patient, everyday workhorses. These have been the backbone of agriculture, trade and industry, warfare and transport for thousands of years and sometimes still are. They are the foundation of today's competition warmbloods and are still used for meat in some countries.

Top: *The modern Arab is an ideal example of fast, plains dwelling Equus, its more rigid spine and stable legs enabling headlong speed rather than twists and turns in escaping danger*
Above: *This lovely Andalusian stallion is a modern example of the old, interrelated Iberian breeds whose influence on other breeds is greatly under-estimated*

Domestication of *Equidae*

This is another topic scientists and historians still argue about – when was the horse first domesticated, by whom and how? Although it is generally accepted that the horse was fairly widely domesticated by about 5,000 or 6,000 years ago, some claim evidence (disputed by others) of domestication as early as 12,000 years ago in areas not affected by the receding glaciers, for this was around the end of the last Ice Age Then again, there are rock carvings thousands of years older which seem to show horses wearing some sort of headcollar.

But let's look at some of the most likely scenarios. At first, the horse was undoubtedly regarded by early man as a prey animal. Driving herds into gullies, culs-de-sac, and over cliffs were highly effective and, in this, man copied the wolf's techniques of individual roles in pack co-operation. Wolf-dogs, domesticated long before the horse, were used in hunting as our social structures and mores are the same and man learned techniques from dogs whilst using their superior senses in the chase and as guards.

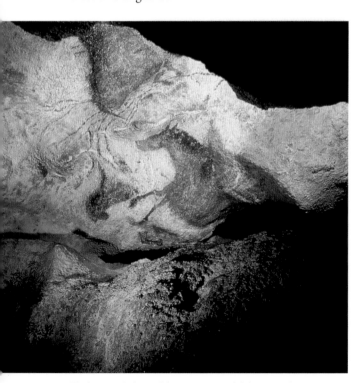

The hauntingly beautiful cave paintings left by our prehistoric ancestors, particularly in Europe (this example is from Lascaux, France), show us how important horses were at one time. They are often shown being hunted

A giant leap for mankind

Very early hominids were vegetarian like most primates but probably started scavenging and eating meat after watching other animals. As man's brain developed, he learned to hunt so he could kill animals for meat, then hide, hair, horn, bone, blood and milk. He became omnivorous and developed the hunter-gatherer lifestyle – a major step in civilisation. He later developed a nomadic lifestyle controlled by the herds' movements, a system still followed by northern reindeer-herders.

The next step would be the capture of horses (after having conquered other, more easily domesticated animals). Foals, injured or sick horses or even older ones or heavily pregnant, even foaling, mares may have been cornered and caught, and herds built up in this way. A common technique, still used today, was to tether a tamed, in-season mare within reach of a wild (now feral) stallion and let it mate her. In some areas, these tactics slowly led to a reduction in nomadism although this way of life is not obsolete even now.

Driving or riding?

Horses were probably used for pack transport before driving and riding. Perhaps a tame animal allowed equipment to be rested on its back. From here, fastening it on would be a simple step, then perhaps a child would be dandled on the horse's back and goods eventually carried, including, perhaps, a child, an old or injured person or a pregnant wife.

Man's ingenuity would soon come up with persuading the horse to drag equipment and carcasses from a simple harness, then the *travois* and sleds would be devised, and once the wheel was invented there was no turning back.

The above process could have led to riding, or perhaps younger, braver family members would dare each other as to which (unbroken) horses they could get to and sit on in the herd, perhaps skipping across their backs and/or vaulting on. But as for which came first, riding or driving, perhaps we'll never know.

The most likely peoples and locations for all this are almost certainly those of the Middle East and mid and northern Asia. Where man settled and learned to farm, some animals may also have been tethered or fenced in, stabling being a progression from this.

Near relatives

As civilisation progressed, other equines were domesticated such as asses and even onagers and zebras.

The Babylonians are the most notable people to domesticate onagers and there are carvings of them with nose rings (like cattle) which must have been horrendous for the onager and pretty useless for man as a means of control. Onagers (popularly called half-asses although they are a type of ass) habitually bite, kick and rebel (and who can blame them?) and are much less amenable to training than horses. Attempts at their domestication were fairly soon abandoned!

Zebras have often been trained to both saddle and harness. One Victorian English lady regularly hunted side-saddle and rode in Rotten Row on her zebra and a nineteenth century English aristocrat once drove a carriage and four zebras regularly around London and even to Buckingham Palace for tea, but what Queen Victoria (or the servants) thought of it is not publicly recorded.

In the 1990s, behaviourist Dr Marthe Kiley-Worthington and colleagues captured a wild zebra stallion, whom they called Zanitaye, and broke him in with kindness and patience, finding that he learned as quickly and willingly as any domestic horse (he was released afterwards) and zebras are regularly used on circuses worldwide.

Mules (horse-donkey crosses) are amply bestowed with 'hybrid vigour', being extremely strong and clever

The African wild ass species were used as foundation stock for today's humble working donkey of the Third World and British seasides, the Asiatic species being far less easy to train. Big, athletic donkeys and active, working mules have always been a feature of the American scene, as donkeys are in many areas of France and Italy, the giant Poitu breed in particular.

THE EFFECTS OF DOMESTICATION ON THE HORSE

Whilst man soon realised the benefits to himself of horse slaves, imprisoned and totally dependent on us for absolutely everything, the horse has suffered significantly from domestication. Today, the most common and troublesome conditions stemming from a stabled lifestyle are respiratory disease and stereotypies (stable vices) or abnormal behaviour patterns due to distress. Colic, laminitis and azoturia are also common, all caused by bad management.

The horse has adapted amazingly well to being stabled considering he evolved to fit a completely opposite lifestyle. We should not abuse this invaluable quality in him by causing him ill-health and psychological distress.

The Creation of Breeds

Most domestic breeds of horse or pony have been created by people for their own needs or to comply with their idea of the perfect horse, usually for a specific purpose such as riding (possibly in a particular way), agriculture, smart driving, war, pack use and so on, and this has been the case for thousands of years. Very few breeds or types of horse or pony remain which are largely unaltered from the wild types which had evolved and survived to the end of the last Ice Age.

Far-off lands

The horse and pony types which were available to early civilisations were original wild types formed by evolution to fit the environment in which they were living. Man had been using horses, as described in

The little Caspian, correctly called a horse and not a pony, is one of the oldest, purest breeds in the world

'Domestication of *equidae*', for food and other life-support purposes and as trade and travel developed, different types of horse would be taken to other regions where the native types were rather different.

People would have been quick to recognise the varying qualities of these different types and their suitability for different purposes. As people had been keeping and breeding animals for thousands of years before they domesticated horses, they were already familiar with the basic principles of stock-breeding for a purpose, and would have been keen to acquire different types of horses to breed in either their existing forms or to introduce their qualities into their own types.

The horse for the job

As they became more and more skilful at mating together different types of horse, and predicting what the offspring would be like, and also at realising how some individual horses are 'prepotent', producing stock which strongly resembles them in appearance and performance no matter what they are mated to, people became adept at creating just the type of horse they wanted, for whatever purpose. This process has continued ever since and, although horses are nothing like as indispensable worldwide for traditional roles like agriculture, heavy transport, war, rapid carriage travel and so on, they are more

A HORSE FOR AGRICULTURE AND HAULAGE

The Percheron is a hugely popular modern heavy breed, still widely used commercially and created by the French from strong native horses and cobs in the La Perche district of Normandy and mated with Arabs and other oriental types looted after the Battle of Poitiers. Further oriental booty (Arabs and Barbs) was brought in by the Crusaders. Later infusions comprised various European heavy draught breeds, including the famous Norman horse, the then new English Thoroughbred (Pur-sang Anglais) and old Iberian blood.

The French thus created a versatile, gentle, courageous and generous breed with a spread of height and strength.

With a normal height range from 14.3hh to 17.3hh and over (the tallest horse in the world today is a 19.2hh Percheron) and a range of body types, usually with blood-horse facial features and action, it is suitable as a heavy-ish riding horse (lighter in former times than today) and for short-haul road transport, particularly brewery work, forestry and agriculture.

Digging through snow for food is a common behaviour pattern in horses and ponies which evolved in northern climes

in demand than ever for leisure riding and for competitive and non-competitive sports.

Artificial versus Natural Selection

The principle of natural selection in evolution is that animals with characteristics which best fit them to a particular environment survive best in it and so breed on, passing the characteristics with 'survival value' to their offspring. Those less well suited to their environment are wiped out by environmental pressures (i.e. being unable to survive on limited water or in intense heat or cold), by disease they were unable to resist, by competition for resources and mates and, in the case of prey animals like horses, by predation they were unable to escape. The succeeding generations become increasingly strongly endowed with survival characteristics for that environment.

Artificial selection is that imposed by man, who decides which stallion will mate which mare with a view to producing the qualities man wants. Because horses are often artificially managed, they do not have to survive in a particular environment as man shelters and cares for them. This has resulted in horses which may not be able to survive if suddenly turned free in a particular place, for example Thoroughbreds in a Canadian winter or Shetland ponies in the Arabian peninsula.

A NATURAL THOROUGHBRED

The Akhal-Teké (pictured below) is associated today mainly with Turkmenistan. It is a true, ancient-type hot-blood of steppe and desert, descended, like the Turcoman of Iran (above), from a type almost surely extinct and native to what we now call the Middle East and northern Eurasia. Horses of this type are known to have existed more than 3,000 years BC and their genes must surely have been passed down to the racing Thoroughbred and other oriental types with this appearance. It is likely that the Byerley Turk, one of the oriental ancestors of the Thoroughbred, was of this type as the similarity in appearance, and of this sort of modern Thoroughbred, is undeniable. This is an excellent example of man creating from suitable raw material the kind of horse he wanted for a specific purpose, in this case racing.

The whole appearance is of an equine greyhound – spare, 'dry', long-legged, thin-skinned and hot-blooded. In temperament, it is usually arrogant, reactive, independent and rebellious yet with a sympathetic handler and rider will give its all – characteristics found in many Thoroughbreds.

History

Only two human generations have existed without dependence on the horse since it was first domesticated. In those two generations, the uses of the horse have changed to what we would call mainly pleasure or competition from a means of international survival. To the horse, of course, our demands still mean work.

Shaping the world

Civilisations from the earliest to our own have relied on control of the masses for superiority. Quality, strong, fast horses were for thousands of years kept economically beyond the price of the populace and reserved for the ruling classes, giving them the speed and mobility to cover vast areas quickly, to oversee their often vast estates, to counter rebellious crowds (still a current use) and, of course, to wage war against opposing forces. The success of armies often depended on the quality of their cavalry and other mounted units.

Famous Warhorses

Bucephalus

The first named, famous horse in history was Bucephalus, the mount of Alexander The Great. His name means 'ox-head' as he had a wide forehead and prominent eyes, rather like a bull's. It is also said he was a throwback to prehistoric ancestors, having small side-toes on each leg. Alexander as a boy managed to ride and relate to Bucephalus where experts had failed and Bucephalus carried him in battle throughout the acquisition of his vast empire, dying at the age of thirty of wounds received at the Battle of the Hydaspes (in the Punjab) in 327BC.

Babieca

The mount of Spain's knightly freedom-fighter, El Cid, was the Iberian, Babieca, a superb charger who carried his master to all his victories and even to a posthumous one. When El Cid died from a wound received during the battle for Valencia in 1099, following his death-bed instructions Babieca bore his embalmed body, strapped upright in the saddle, out of the gates of Valencia in the ghostly light of midnight at the head of his troops to terrify the Moors into defeat and finally free Spain from the yoke of Arab occupation.

Ancient Gaul warrior

An engraving of Bucephalus from the Cosmographia

Humble sacrifice

In the American Civil War, the Confederate General Forrest had no fewer than twenty-nine horses shot from under him but it was not only noble chargers who gave their all in battle but also the humble troop and transport horses. At one point, the Yankee army's requirement for horses was 500 per week, so great was their death toll. Ancient records and carvings show thousands of horses dead and dying in battle, innocent victims of man's folly and greed. In our own century, thousands drowned in the liquid mud of Flanders, not counting those killed or later destroyed from their injuries, yet they are never even mentioned at Remembrance Day commemorations.

Horses in Sport and Leisure

Racing and polo were the earliest forms of equestrian sport and entertainment. Chariot racing was extremely popular in the classical civilisations of Greece, Rome, Byzantium and elsewhere. Today, as a ridden racehorse, the British Thoroughbred is the most famous breed in the world and was used liberally to create that other breed equally famous as a harness racer, the American Standardbred.

Kincsem

The 'winningest' Thoroughbred the world has ever known did not come from the most prominent racing countries of Britain, Ireland, America or France, but from Hungary, one of those eastern European countries whose people have always had an innate flair with horses. Of that illustrious few, that crème-de-la-crème, who were never beaten, the quirky Hungarian Thoroughbred mare, Kincsem, bred from British imports (out of Waternymph and by Cambuscan who seduced Waternymph as she was on her way to be served by Buccaneer) won more races than any. Racing between 1876 and 1879 in Hungary, Austria, Germany, Romania, Poland, Italy, France and

England (refusing to travel without her cat companion), Kincsem amassed fifty-four victories, forty-one of which were against the best the world could muster in a futile attempt to topple her from her throne.

Justin Morgan

Of other breeds, probably one of the most remarkable is the American Morgan, created unintentionally from the efforts of just one phenomenal little stallion, Justin Morgan, named after one of his owners. Probably of Welsh Cob blood with oriental and some Iberian genes, he could do superbly every job from ploughing to racing, never gave up and no matter what mare he served, the foal was the image of him. The Morgan was the official mount of the US Cavalry and today is probably the most versatile and popular breed in the USA.

AFTER THE WAR ...

The two cataclysmic wars of the twentieth century changed much of the world's society, culture and economy. The development of mechanisation, force-fed by the needs of war, decimated many breeds to the point of extinction, many only being conserved through the dedicated efforts of a few devotees. Then a miracle happened: the burgeoning of the middle-classes and a more evenly spread economy spawned greater lifestyle expectations in which the horse came to play a significant recreational role in sport and leisure, one which is still his main, but not exclusive, role today.

The King's Troop Royal Horse Artillery use the same guns in their demonstrations today as they used in World War I

Mythology

Horses have bewitched man like no other animal on earth. Perhaps it is his speed, his strength, his pride and snorting, flaring nostrils, his independent spirit and his flowing mane and tail which, with his often haughty carriage, have stamped him as a beast to be coveted, admired, feared and revered for thousands of years. He saturates mythology and we have space here to relate only a few stories.

Pegasus

Probably the most famous horse in mythology is Pegasus, the Greek winged horse, wings being the only possible enhancement a horse could have. His name means 'strong' and he was the offspring of the sea god, Poseidon, and Medusa the Gorgon, only being released from her body after Perseus had severed her head, Pegasus and Chrysaor, the giant

of the Golden Sword, escaping through her neck.

With a single blow of his hoof on Mount Helicon, Pegasus caused the River of The Muses, Hippocrene, to spring from the mountain.

The mortal Bellerophon, Prince of Corinth, managed to catch Pegasus using a golden bridle. He tamed him and rode him to kill the Chimera, an evil, dragon-like monster. Drunk with success, Bellerophon flew Pegasus into the sky aiming for Mount Olympus, home of the gods, to claim a place for himself in immortality but Zeus, the

king of the gods, (whose own father, Kronos, had taken the form of a horse,) was angry at Bellerophon's conceit and ambition. He commanded a gad-fly to sting Pegasus who spooked and unseated Bellerophon. Bellerophon crashed down to earth and spent the rest of his life a blind cripple.

Pegasus himself flew on into space and became the star constellation in the northern sky which is called Pegasus to this day.

Unicorns

Sometimes horse-like and sometimes goat-like, the Unicorn is a mythological creature which travellers in past centuries to India, Ethiopia and other 'mysterious' countries actually claim to have seen although they were probably seeing the oryx, with its long, almost straight horns, from a distance.

Mentioned in early Hebrew documents, it has always been a symbol of peace, love, purity and healing. Powdered unicorn horn was a powerful medicine from ancient times to the mediaeval ages although this was, in fact, the horn of the narwhal, a type of whale.

The unicorn represented a powerful religious symbolism from early times. To purify water poisoned by the wicked serpent (the Devil), the unicorn would make the sign of the cross over it with his horn (his horn representing the horn of salvation from the House of David). He would then drink, followed by the other animals.

A nineteenth century German engraving of Pegasus carrying Perseus aloft. Perseus has the head of Medusa in his grasp

A unicorn depicted in the Cosmographia

A procession of centaurs. Centaurs were renowned for carousing and irresponsible behaviour, but there were exceptions such as the gentle and learned Chiron

that Zeus took the form of a stallion and seduced Ixion's own queen, Dia, out of revenge.

In legend, the passionate and hot-natured centaurs were not the steadiest of creatures. One revered centaur, however, was Cheiron or Chiron, who was teacher and mentor to both Jason (of the Argonauts) and Hercules. He was the product of Kronos and a mountain nymph and, so, was half brother to Zeus, ultimately becoming great-grandfather of Achilles whom he also educated, along with the children of nobles and leaders.

Being immortal in view of his parentage, Cheiron could not die after accidentally being scratched by one of Hercules' poisoned arrows. To save him eternal suffering, the gods allowed him to exchange his immortality for the mortality of Prometheus who joined them on Olympus. Zeus, Cheiron's half-brother, took pity on the centaur and allowed him to live forever among the stars where his constellation, Centaurus, can still be found along with that of Sagittarius, the zodiacal sign represented by a centaur.

19

He is often depicted resting his head on the lap of a young girl (representing the Virgin Mary) in a garden to which he has been lured (the only way he could be caught) so that the hunter (the Archangel Gabriel) can bring the unicorn (the Son) to the king (the Father). The unicorn's single horn symbolises his union with the Father and the story itself symbolises the Incarnation.

The unicorn as an ancient symbol of Scotland was installed opposite the lion in the arms of the newly united kingdoms of England and Scotland following the accession of their joint king, James, to the English throne following the demise of Elizabeth I.

Centaurs

The concept of a centaur – a creature which usually was in the form of a man down to the loins and a horse for the remainder – seems to crop up in several civilisations although mainly, as expected, in ancient Greece. During the development of riding, conquering forces on horseback must have struck terror into horseless opponents and for those who had never seen a mounted horse, the sight, blurred by terror, may well have appeared to have been half man, half horse.

In mythology, the Centaurs were a fierce Greek people, part man, part horse, living in the mountainous region of Thessaly and having beastly natures, supposedly the offspring of the king of Thessaly, Ixion, and a cloud. Ixion had abused the hospitality of Zeus, following the honour of an invitation to Mount Olympus, the home of the gods, by attempting to seduce Zeus' queen, Hera. As a punishment, Zeus formed Hera's likeness out of a cloud upon which Ixion begat Centaurus who, running with the wild mares on Mount Pelion, founded the race of Centaurs. Another version says

THE WHITE HORSES OF ENGLAND

The origin of the idea of cutting away the turf of England's chalklands to reveal the white chalk beneath, creating images of mythological figures and gods is very ancient. However, the famous images of white horses are not themselves ancient, being a very few hundred years old and carved to commemorate major victories over foreign foes. The one significant exception is the highly stylised White Horse of Uffington, which glisters enigmatically on a green hillside 30 miles north east of Bratton Down in Berkshire. Traditionally, it was said to have been carved to commemorate Alfred the Great's victory at Ashdown over Norse invaders in AD871 but is now believed to be many hundreds, and probably thousands, of years older than that, possibly older than Stonehenge and likely to represent a prehistoric religious symbol.

Its fine lines and proud bearing indicate a quality bloodhorse hard to reconcile with the chunky indigenous ponies of the prehistoric land that was much later to become England. In light of the newly realised sophistication of England's ancient peoples, we may have to revise our ideas of ancient trade and travel – and the arrival of oriental bloodstock.

Religion

Ancient civilisations and religions, like most modern ones, seem to have in common a firm belief in some kind of afterlife or other world to which the spirit travels after leaving this one. Where modern burial practices differ from ancient ones is in the provision of what are called grave goods buried with the deceased.

Everyone is familiar with the fabulous riches found in the tombs of ancient Egyptian pharaohs, the superbly crafted jewellery, tools and personal items found in Celtic and Anglo-Saxon graves and even the beautifully carved bone and horn objects, jewellery and flowers placed in Neolithic graves. Of course, it was not just goods that were buried with eminent personages for their ease in the afterlife. Servants and animals were buried with them, too. Favourite dogs, cats, horses and other animals, as well as farm animals for food and milk for the journey to the next world, commonly have been found in excavated graves. The terracotta army, with its horses, of the Emperor of China are now world famous but this comes from a time when representations of people, animals and goods were considered adequate rather than the real things. The graves of Pazyryk in Siberia held well preserved, beautifully worked saddles, bridles and bits as well as the remains of Przewalski-like horses along with the royal grave occupants.

Animal spirits

There seems to have been no doubt in the minds of the ancients all over the world that animals, like humans, had souls and spirits and that they could and would travel with their earthly owner to the next life. Not all religions today hold this view and the Christian religions are probably more backward than most in this regard, only

Top: *Castaigne's depiction of The Charge of the Persian Scythe Chariots*

Right: *A lithograph by Volleter of a Bedouin camp. The importance of the horse is reflected in the way it provides the focal point of the illustration and the attention given to it by the family*

20

recently acknowledging the beliefs and innate feelings of many of their followers that animals are simply spirits in bodies which are differently shaped from our own. 'If Heaven would not be Heaven to you without your horse,' said an Anglican vicar to a recently bereaved horse-owner, 'then he will be there waiting for you.'

Sacrificial gifts to the gods of many civilisations have usually involved the loss of life of both humans, even children, and animals to keep the deities happy and bountiful, thus ensuring the continuation of their followers on earth, and highly prized horses, the best available, were regularly included in the animals sacrificed.

The Arab Legend and the Koran
Mahommed, an astute politician and military tactician as well as religious leader, soon saw the value of horses for his campaigns and encouraged the breeding of horses among the Bedouin tribes. We can find various versions of The Arab Legend but part of it, at least, runs more or less like this:

And God said to the south wind: 'Be thou gathered together. I would make a creature out of thee.' And the wind was gathered together… And He created from a handful of wind a horse... and thus addressed him: 'I name thee Horse. I have made thee unlike any other. I establish thee as one of the glories of the earth. All the treasures of this earth lie between thine eyes. Thou shalt cast Mine enemies beneath thine hooves, but thou shalt carry My friends on thy back. This shall be the seat from whence prayers rise unto Me. Thou shalt find happiness all over the earth, and thou shalt be favoured above all other creatures, for to thee shall accrue the love of the master of the earth. Thou shall fly without wings and conquer without sword.' And God let loose the swift runner and he went on his way, neighing.

Thus, it seems, did the Koran ordain the fostering and love of horses as a religious duty but we have failed to keep God's promises to the horse in many ways.

The Zend-Avesta
The Zend-Avesta were the holy laws of ancient Persia, present-day Iran, and here, too, horses were ordained to be for both religious sacrificial and military use. 'God Himself appeared on horseback,' says the Zend-Avesta, 'and it is no mean honour for the horses that the Lord Himself has employed them in His service.'

Persian horses, usually known as Persian Arabs but probably mainly of old Turkmene genes, have,

throughout the ages, been among the highest quality and most beautiful oriental bloodhorses in existence and the ancient Persians took every advantage of this. The little Caspian, which appears on the ancient seal of the infamous King Darius, was rescued in the latter half of this century from almost certain extinction after many thousands of years of documented existence and is now in America, the UK and elsewhere, though inevitably in small numbers, and more are being bred in Iran at the turn of the millennium.

The Bible
The God of the Old Testament puts man in his place with what is probably the most famous passage ever written about horses when he exclaims to Job:

Hast thou given the horse strength? Hast thou clothed his neck with thunder? The glory of his nostrils is terrible. He paweth in the valley and rejoiceth in his strength; he goeth on to meet the armed men.

He mocketh at fear, and is not affrighted; neither turneth he back from the sword. The quiver rattleth against him, the glittering spear and the shield. He swalloweth the ground with fierceness and rage; neither believeth he that it is the sound of the trumpet – He saith among the trumpets, Ha, ha; and he smelleth the battle afar off, the thunder of the captains, and the shouting.

King Solomon is legendary for his vast numbers of horses – 40,000 stalls are quoted in his stables in I Kings – and even compared his lover, in his famous Song of Solomon, 'to a company of horses in Pharaoh's chariots.'

Ancient Egyptian chariot

Almost everywhere you look, the horse appears in most religions as a magnificent creature to be cared for and respected, a gift from God or the gods, yet one which has been and is readily abused despite holy writ.

21

The Skeleton and Ligaments

The horse's skeleton comprises about 210 bones consisting of living cells and minerals. They have blood vessels, lymphatic vessels which complement the blood system, and nerves.

No dry bones!
Bones can become diseased and injured but can repair themselves; they adjust during growth and respond to changes in stress levels caused by movement. Although it is easy to think of bone as hard and inflexible, this is not so. The skeleton evolved to suit the horse's natural lifestyle and has the ideal amount of rigidity, flexibility and ability to move, rarely going wrong in the feral horse. However, the domesticated horse's skeleton often suffers from lack of exercise which 'stiffens' and weakens it, and from the demands of excessive performance which over-stresses and injures it and its associated structures, ligaments, tendons and muscles.

What is bone?
Bone is partly fibrous, protein tissue making it tough, strong and slightly flexible, and partly minerals – calcium, phosphorus and some magnesium. Young horses' bones are about 60 per cent protein and those of old ones 60 per cent or more minerals, making them more rigid but brittle.

Cartilage is a rubbery, fibrous substance containing collagen (a type of protein) and carbohydrate. Strong and flexible, it covers the ends of bones, greatly helping to reduce concussion and friction in joints. Young horses' skeletons are high in cartilage which is gradually replaced by bone.

Bone growth
Long bones grow at their ends from the epiphyses or 'growth plates', where cartilage gradually gives way to bone. The membrane surrounding bone, the periosteum, makes bone from cells called osteoblasts, increasing the circumference of the bone during maturing or a fittening programme. Bone contains channels for blood and lymph vessels and nerves which all help maintain and develop bone.

Types of bone
There are two main types of bone:
- Dense or compact bone, such as the hard bone found in the long bones of the legs.
- Cancellous or spongy bone as at the ends of long bones and in short bones – a fine network of bony threads lining the dense bone and filled with marrow.

Both can be found in differing proportions in one bone. For example, the shaft of the cannon bone is a tube, the outer part being dense bone covered by the periosteum and the inner part cancellous bone.

The purpose of the skeleton
- It gives a supporting framework to the body.
- It protects vital organs: the skull protects the brain, the spine protects the spinal cord running down the internal channel formed by the individual vertebrae, the shoulder blades and ribcage protect the heart and lungs and the pelvis and sacrum (croup) protect the urinary and internal reproductive organs.
- It provides locomotion because the joints enable bones to act via muscles as levers.
- It stores calcium, phosphorus and magnesium which can be laid down in or removed from the bone as needed.
- Red and white blood cells and also platelets (used in blood clotting) are made in the bone marrow.

Different types of bone
Bones are classified according to appearance:
- Long bones are the largest with a roughly cylindrical shaft (diaphysis) and two extremities (the epiphyses) from which they grow. The long bones function as levers in support and movement, examples being the leg bones.
- Short or cuboid bones which absorb concussion have no marrow but a spongy bone inside, examples being those of the knee and hock.
- Flat bones are thin, flattish and for protection and/or muscle attachment, such as those of the skull which consists of thirty-seven fused bones, and the shoulder blade.
- Sesamoid bones are mainly involved with tendons, muscles and the reduction of friction, acting as pulleys as tendons run over them. Examples are the navicular bone, the patella or kneecap and the fetlock sesamoid bones.
- Pneumatic bones contain air spaces or sinuses, such as those in the head.
- Irregular bones are the vertebrae of the spine. Of different shapes, they protect the spinal cord, provide support and form a base for muscle attachment.

Joints

There are various types of joints in the body – moveable, slightly moveable and fixed.

Moveable joints comprise

- Hinge-type joints allowing movement in one plane only such as the elbow and fetlock.
- Ball and socket joints; e.g. the hip. (Normally giving more directional movement, this is restricted in the horse which finds sustained sideways movement of the hind legs, such as when being shod or if bracing the hind legs during transport, uncomfortable, even painful.)
- Pivot joints such as those between the skull and two top neck vertebrae which allow the horse to turn his head.
- Gliding joints where bones glide over one another, such as the knee, hock and patella.
- A typical moveable joint comprises two cartilage-covered bone-ends, lubricated by synovia or joint fluid produced by the inner lining of the joint sac or capsule surrounding the whole joint. In addition, bands of ligament tissue support and bind together the joints and bones.

Slightly moveable joints

These comprise those joints between vertebrae. There are thick pads of cartilage between them for protection; as each can move a little, the spine is slightly flexible.

Fixed joints

Joints which have fused together, such as those of the skull and sacrum (croup). There is a thin layer of fibrous tissue or cartilage between them.

Ligaments

Ligaments are strong bands, cords or sheets of fibrous tissue which lash the skeleton together, particularly at joints and support the whole framework.

A special arrangement of ligaments and locking mechanisms in the bones and joints of all four legs permits the horse to sleep standing up so that he can take off in an instant should danger threaten.

23

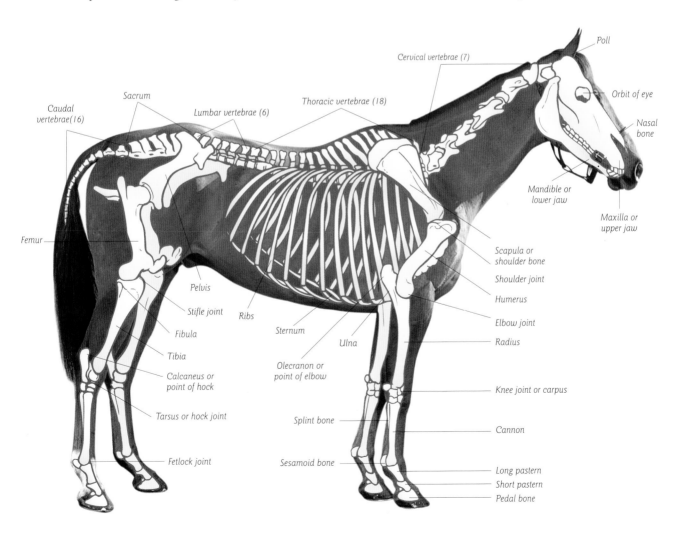

Poll

Cervical vertebrae (7)

Orbit of eye

Thoracic vertebrae (18)

Nasal bone

Sacrum

Lumbar vertebrae (6)

Caudal vertebrae(16)

Mandible or lower jaw

Maxilla or upper jaw

Femur

Scapula or shoulder bone

Shoulder joint

Humerus

Pelvis

Elbow joint

Stifle joint

Ribs

Radius

Fibula

Sternum

Ulna

Tibia

Olecranon or point of elbow

Knee joint or carpus

Calcaneus or point of hock

Cannon

Tarsus or hock joint

Splint bone

Long pastern

Fetlock joint

Sesamoid bone

Short pastern

Pedal bone

Dentition

Fossils of *Hyracotherium* show it to have had forty-four teeth but the number has reduced during evolution to *Equus*. Now, adult male horses normally have forty teeth and females thirty-six. Like other mammals, they come in two sets – deciduous (baby, milk, first or temporary) and permanent (second) which are bigger and stronger. The deciduous teeth begin to shed when the youngster is about two-and-a-half years old and the permanent ones should all be in place, but will not be fully developed, by the time the horse is about five years of age.

Caps

When the deciduous teeth are being shed they sometimes become jammed on top of the permanent ones growing through underneath them and have to be removed by a vet or equine dentist, otherwise the youngster's mouth will be extremely uncomfortable and he will not be able to eat properly, with obvious results. For this reason, youngsters should have their teeth examined about every three months and a careful watch kept on how they are eating.

Right: The strength and size of a horse's teeth make them a formidable weapon when backed up by the powerful muscles of his jaw and neck. Stallions are on record as having torn off their grooms' arms

Below: When the 'baby' or deciduous teeth become jammed on top of permanent teeth erupting underneath them, they are known as 'caps'

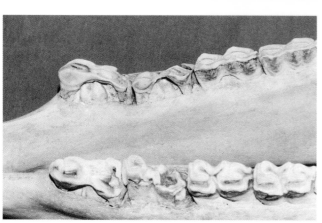

Types of teeth

Adult horses have six front, incisor or cutting teeth at the front of the top and bottom jaw – twelve in all. These are for gripping and cutting or nipping off grass and leaves. Males have, just behind them, the remnants of canine teeth called tushes, two in each jaw, making four; in earlier horse-types they will have been bigger and used for fighting. Occasionally, mares also have tushes, usually smaller. There is then a gap or diastema which developed during lengthening of the head during evolution; conveniently, this is where the bit can go. Then come the cheek or grinding teeth, called premolars (the first three sets, making twelve) and behind them the molars (the second three sets, making another twelve). These are reinforced by infoldings of very hard cement for grinding up the horse's natural fibrous, silica-rich grass diet.

Sometimes, vestigial premolars, popularly called wolf teeth for some reason, appear in front of those in the upper jaw which sometimes cause bitting problems and have to be removed. Some experts feel they are a primeval remnant and others that they are a development in the horse's continuing evolution as a grazing animal.

Structure

The part of the tooth above the gum is the crown (the modern horse having high-crowned teeth), the part surrounded by the gum is called the neck and there is a root embedded in a socket in the jaw. Except in very old horses, the teeth have a cavity filled with sensitive pulp with blood and nerve supplies to nourish the hard structures of enamel (the outer covering), dentine (the softer inner material) and the extremely hard cement in the cheek teeth evolved to cope with grass.

Growth and development

As the teeth develop, the crown height increases and the roots extend deeper into the jaw until about age seven. From then, the teeth erupt outwards from the root (rather than actually growing) to compensate for wear.

In very old horses, the crown may have worn

away and, as the roots keep erupting, the horse will be eating on his softer roots and may not be able to cope with tough, fibrous feed any longer. By the mid-thirties, the root will have erupted completely, leaving the horse no means of eating, and he will die of starvation (unless given a soft, nutritious diet) or be killed by predation, if feral.

From birth to adulthood

A newborn foal will have his four central incisor teeth and may have his six pairs of temporary cheek teeth, which will have appeared by four weeks of age, anyway. By four weeks, he will also have his four lateral incisor teeth next to the centrals. By nine months, he will have his four corner incisor teeth next to the laterals and his first four permanent molar teeth immediately behind his temporary cheek teeth. By eighteen months, the next four permanent molars will have come through.

At two-and-a-half years, the temporary central incisors will shed and be replaced by the permanent ones, and the first two pairs of temporary cheek teeth will shed and be replaced by two pairs of permanent ones called premolars (because they precede, in position in the mouth, the molars).

At three-and-a-half years, the temporary lateral incisors will be shed and replaced by the permanent ones and the third pair of premolars will replace the corresponding temporary cheek teeth. In males, the permanent tushes (there are no temporary ones) will come through.

At four-and-a-half to five years, the temporary corner incisors will be replaced by the permanent ones and the final and hindmost permanent molars will be present, giving the horse his 'full mouth'.

Chewing in action

Because the horse's lower jaw is narrower than the upper, as the teeth grind the inside edges of the lower cheek teeth and the outside edges of the upper cheek teeth can become worn sharp, cutting the tongue and cheeks respectively. The bit may also press the tongue and cheeks on to these edges, depending on its type and how it is used, which can cause further injury, with obvious results.

Hooks can also develop on the fronts of the upper cheek teeth and the backs of the lower ones, causing chewing difficulties and even preventing the mouth from closing properly. These problems can be corrected by any vet or competent equine dentist and the teeth should be inspected every six months, more often in young and old horses, to check their condition.

Teeth can also become diseased and broken

which calls for veterinary treatment. A missing tooth will not be there to wear away its opposite number, which will have to be rasped down frequently so that the chewing motion is not interfered with.

If the top incisors extend further forward than the lower ones, this is termed parrot jaw. If the reverse is the case, the teeth are said to be undershot. Mild cases of this may not interfere with grazing but more pronounced malformation will prevent the horse grasping and nipping off growing food so he will have to be fed extra in other ways.

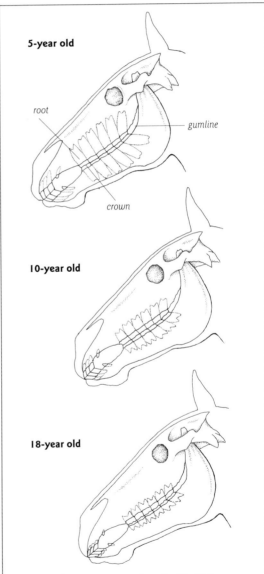

5-year old

root

gumline

crown

10-year old

18-year old

A horse's teeth continue to erupt throughout its life to compensate for the wear caused by chewing. The roots diminish as the horse ages until eventually there is no 'growth' left and the teeth wear smooth and low so the horse cannot cope with any but soft foods. Feral and wild equidae die mainly from predation or (if they live long enough) the wearing down of the teeth resulting in starvation

Muscles and Tendons

Muscle forms the flesh of the animal body, as opposed to the fat or other tissues. It is the part of the animal which is eaten (other than the liver and kidneys), is very high in protein and is the most abundant tissue in the body. Horses are mainly kept as athletic animals for work, so their muscle condition is very important.

Muscle types

We usually think of the muscles which move the body but there are three types of muscle tissue:
- Skeletal muscle which moves the bones. This is also called striated muscle because it appears striped when seen under a microscope. Also known as voluntary muscle because it is under the horse's control; he decides whether or not he is going to move apart from during sleep.

- Smooth muscle has no striations when seen under a microscope. It is found in the walls of hollow organs of the body such as the digestive tract, the bladder, the arteries and the uterus. It is also called visceral muscle because of these locations and involuntary muscle because the horse cannot wilfully control its actions. The muscular contractions of the digestive tract (called peristalsis) are an example of muscle movement over which the horse has no control.

- Cardiac muscle is special and only found in the walls of the heart. It is actually striated but the cells are branched so it has a different appearance under a microscope. Cardiac muscle never tires and its contractions are very rhythmic although capable of rapid changes of speed according to the body's needs.

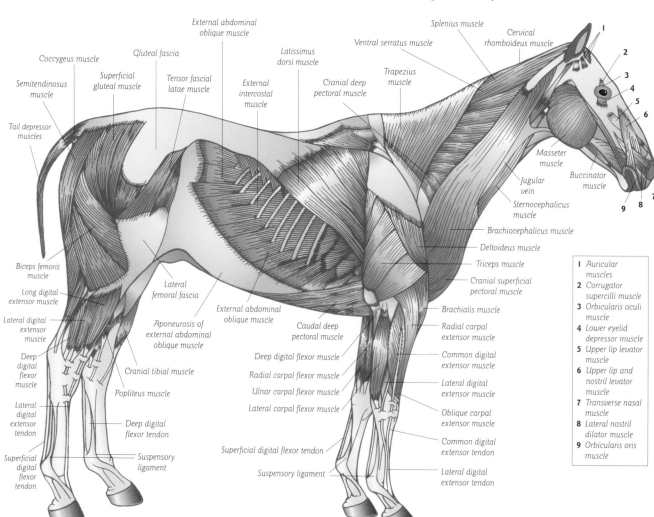

Coccygeus muscle
External abdominal oblique muscle
Gluteal fascia
Latissimus dorsi muscle
Splenius muscle
Cervical rhomboideus muscle
Ventral serratus muscle
Semitendinosus muscle
Superficial gluteal muscle
Tensor fascial latae muscle
External intercostal muscle
Cranial deep pectoral muscle
Trapezius muscle
Tail depressor muscles

Masseter muscle
Buccinator muscle
Jugular vein
Sternocephalicus muscle
Brachiocephalicus muscle
Deltoideus muscle
Triceps muscle
Cranial superficial pectoral muscle
Brachialis muscle
Radial carpal extensor muscle
Common digital extensor muscle
Lateral digital extensor muscle
Oblique carpal extensor muscle
Common digital extensor tendon
Lateral digital extensor tendon

Biceps femoris muscle
Long digital extensor muscle
Lateral digital extensor muscle
Deep digital flexor muscle
Lateral digital extensor tendon
Superficial digital flexor tendon

Lateral femoral fascia
Aponeurosis of external abdominal oblique muscle
Cranial tibial muscle
Popliteus muscle
Deep digital flexor tendon
Suspensory ligament

External abdominal oblique muscle
Caudal deep pectoral muscle
Deep digital flexor muscle
Radial carpal flexor muscle
Ulnar carpal flexor muscle
Lateral carpal flexor muscle
Superficial digital flexor tendon
Suspensory ligament

1	Auricular muscles
2	Corrugator supercilli muscle
3	Orbicularis oculi muscle
4	Lower eyelid depressor muscle
5	Upper lip levator muscle
6	Upper lip and nostril levator muscle
7	Transverse nasal muscle
8	Lateral nostril dilator muscle
9	Orbicularis oris muscle

MUSCLE FUEL

Muscles have a rich blood and nerve supply which is why muscle injuries and disorders such as azoturia can be very painful. They can store energy for their own use as glycogen (a form of glucose). They also store oxygen (for the 'burning up' of fuel to produce energy) as myoglobin so they can work instantly without waiting for supplies.

Energy is produced by a basic chemical reaction in which oxygen combined with glucose produces energy and the waste product carbon dioxide. If there is insufficient oxygen such as when the muscles are using up oxygen faster than lungs and heart can supply it, lactic acid or lactate is formed in the cells which is toxic and can significantly injure the muscle tissue.

The blood also brings fuel and oxygen to the muscles for storage or use and removes waste products created by work, whether it is winning the Grand National or wandering about the field. Skeletal muscle tires due to lack of glycogen and the build-up of waste products which can actually injure muscle tissue, causing fatigue and pain. Muscles also suffer when a horse is dehydrated or when they have to work in an unnatural way as when travelling or compensating for pain elsewhere, for example in lameness or a badly fitting saddle.

Muscle Structure and Function
Skeletal muscle

Muscle is about 60 per cent water and so is heavy. Muscles are powerful, sensitive structures operating often in particular groups.

The muscle cells are long fibres controlled by the nervous system. The fibres are arranged in bundles and the bundles are, in turn, bound together by a membrane of fibrous connective tissue. Each muscle fibre is composed of smaller myofibrils again arranged into bundles within each fibre.

Muscles can only contract or shorten; they cannot stretch themselves but can be stretched by the action of opposing muscles. Muscle fibres can grow in size with appropriate work and nutrition but their numbers cannot be increased. A horse may have a predominance of aerobic fibres (which work with a free supply of oxygen) and will be suited to endurance work such as steeplechasing, endurance riding, hunting and so on, or anaerobic fibres (which can work with little or no oxygen) and will be more suited to short, sharp, fast work such as sprinting, show jumping at speed, polo and so on. Exercise and appropriate fitness training can

change the main type of muscle fibre a horse has to some extent.

Cardiac muscle

Cardiac muscle has several unique features.

The heart is a hollow pump consisting mainly of muscle. There is an outer membrane only one cell thick called the epicardium, a middle layer of muscle called the myocardium and an inner membranous lining, again one cell thick, called the endocardium. Surrounding the whole structure is another membrane called the pericardium.

The myocardium or heart muscle consists of many cells which are not, however, distinguishable one from another as single cells. They are all joined together and so function as one unit called a syncitium. This structure and function is so that the heart can contract and relax, and so perform its crucial pumping task, on its own (a state called myogenic). It does not require nervous stimulation from the nervous system, like skeletal muscle, and is the reason a heart removed from a living body will continue to beat if kept in a suitable environment. The heartbeat starts in one part of the heart by means of an electrical impulse and will be sent all over the heart by all these cells working as one.

Tendons and Movement

Muscles responsible for movement of the skeleton are attached to a stable bone at one end, and to a different bone at the other by means of a tendon which is a strong, slightly elastic cord of adapted muscle tissue. In between the two ends is a joint.

When nerve messages reach the muscle fibres, the myofibrils contract or shorten, pulling on the tendon which must then move the bone to which it is attached, flexing the joint in between and causing movement. As an instance, when one set of muscles contracts to bring the leg backwards, an opposing set then contracts whilst the first set relaxes, bringing the leg forwards again, and so on. The opposing muscle groups maintain a slight tone or tension which helps counteract the movement of their partners and normally prevents over-extension of joints.

Tendons have a slight elasticity which, through a process called elastic recoil, helps the limb to spring back again after bearing weight, which takes no energy and so is an economical aid to movement.

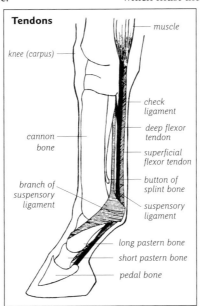

Tendons

- muscle
- knee (carpus)
- check ligament
- deep flexor tendon
- cannon bone
- superficial flexor tendon
- button of splint bone
- branch of suspensory ligament
- suspensory ligament
- long pastern bone
- short pastern bone
- pedal bone

27

Feet

Structure

The hoof is formed around three bones. The bone which gives the hoof its crescent shape is the pedal bone, semi-circular in the front feet, more oval in the hind. The bottom of the short pastern bone forms a joint with the pedal bone and extends above the top of the hoof to form a joint with the long pastern bone. The small bone behind the pedal bone which forms a joint with it and the short pastern bone is the navicular or distal sesamoid bone. This acts as a pulley to lessen friction on the tendons running over it (from muscles high up the leg) which attach to the pedal bone.

The hoof horn grows down to form a tough case around the internal structures – the tendons, ligaments which bind the bones together, the blood vessels, nerves and sensitive tissues. It grows from the coronary band which forms a ridge around the top of the wall and is equivalent to the cuticle of our nails. The wall is longer and thicker at the toe, decreasing in height and thickness and becoming more flexible as it goes round to the quarters (sides) and heels. Very roughly, the horn at the toe will take a year to grow from coronet to ground. The inner surface of the wall comprises hundreds of horny leaves or laminae which interlock with sensitive, blood-filled laminae lining the surface of the pedal bone. This bond is immensely strong and is what supports the weight of the horse. He is not standing

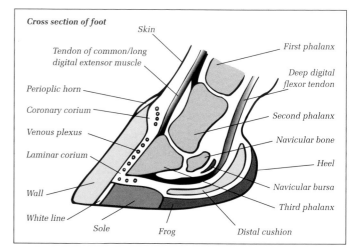

Cross section of foot

Skin
Tendon of common/long digital extensor muscle
Perioplic horn
Coronary corium
Venous plexus
Laminar corium
Wall
White line
Sole
Frog
First phalanx
Deep digital flexor tendon
Second phalanx
Navicular bone
Heel
Navicular bursa
Third phalanx
Distal cushion

on his feet so much as in them!

Underneath the foot, the wall turns inwards at the heels forming the bars, bordering the rubbery, triangular frog. Between bars and frog are two grooves and the frog has a central cleft. The frog is the remnant of the foot-pad in horse ancestors.

The horny soles arch slightly for strength, which also helps prevent bruising. Between the sole horn and the ground or bearing surface of the wall horn can be seen, in the unshod, freshly-trimmed foot, a

The horse's hoof is perfectly capable of withstanding the natural wear it experiences in the wild and will grow and shape itself according to a horse's individual conformation and action, as well as the ground surface

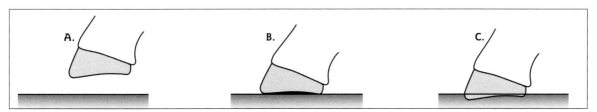

line of softer, white horn called the white line. It can 'give' a little in action and represents the point where the insensitive and sensitive laminae interlock. Therefore, the farrier will normally aim to keep his nails outside this line and in the bearing surface.

Above the sole and frog inside the foot is sensitive tissue and, at the heels, a pad of insensitive, fibrous, springy tissue called the digital cushion.

Rising from ends or wings of the pedal bone inside the foot are the lateral cartilages, made of cartilage and fibrous tissue. They lie vertically, one on each side of the digital cushion, their tops protruding above the coronary band at the heels where they can be felt.

Foot function

Horses' feet have been a source of fascination for hundreds of years and despite centuries of experience and study, we are still not certain of how they work. Various theories about foot function, relief of concussion (which is considerable) and the movement/pumping of blood within the foot abound. Generally, it has been believed that as weight is put on the foot, transmitted via the short pastern bone, the heels expand slightly and the foot flattens a little, the insensitive digital cushion is squashed and the blood vessels in the sensitive tissues throughout the foot are squeezed, forcing the blood out of them up the leg. As weight is released, the vessels reopen, admitting fresh blood. This combined action both absorbs concussion and encourages blood circulation.

American research

Scientific research is progressing in various centres but a particularly interesting piece of work has been done by Professor Robert Bowker at Michigan State University College which indicates that the blood system in the hoof may function in a similar way to that of air-, gel- or liquid-filled running shoes.

Moving liquids are excellent at dispersing energy and absorbing concussion and Professor Bowker feels that much of the blood in the hoof fulfils this purpose as well as providing nutrients and oxygen and removing waste products.

Researchers placed energy measurement devices into digital cushions and found that, while the hoof is in the air it registers zero pressure but when it hits the ground, instead of registering positive pressure,

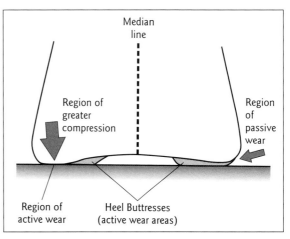

The feet of feral horses are often found to wear quite unlike the standard, level trim most farriers carry out. In particular, the toe often wears square and the quarters (sides) wear, too. Some farriers now purposely trim and shoe horses in this way

the readings are actually negative. Professor Bowker suggests that the negative pressure is caused by the outward movement of the hoof cartilage as the hoof expands under weight. The movement creates a vacuum action which sucks blood from under the pedal bone into the back of the foot. 'As the blood moves to the rear of the hoof through microvessels in the lateral hoof cartilage, it dissipates the energy caused by its impact on the ground, much like fluid-filled running shoes do,' he said.

The team also found that horses with good feet have more blood vessels in the lateral cartilages than those with histories of foot problems, and their digital cushions tended to consist more of cartilaginous material than of elastic, fibrous tissue.

Environmental factors

The traditional view has been that, in general, horses' feet function best on ground with a moderate amount of 'give' in it, despite the fact that thousands of horses worldwide live in hard-ground areas and have tough, healthy feet.

Interestingly, Professor Bowker and his researchers found more cartilaginous digital cushions in horses from the hard-ground Rocky Mountains area whereas horses from areas with softer ground mainly had digital cushions of elastic tissue. He expressed the belief that the latter horses had a greater chance of developing internal foot problems.

Conformation

We read and hear a lot about the importance of good conformation or how a horse is constructed and many people find it a difficult subject to get to grips with. After all, there are so many different breeds and types of horse and pony: breed characteristics and formal breed society standards, not to mention the nuances of that inexplicable quality called 'type', particularly where it relates to specific show-ring categories, confuse the issue – and the student of conformation.

However, there is a very simple way of working out whether or not an animal has good or poor conformation, which is applicable to almost any horse or pony. There are other systems, and refinements to this one, but if you grasp the essence of this it will help you to develop an eye for a horse, well or poorly conformed, and to go on and understand more detailed schemes.

A good fit

The essence of good conformation is to look for balance so that the horse looks as though he fits himself and is all of a piece. Your first impression of overall symmetry, which you will absorb in a couple of seconds, will probably be correct if you have developed any feel for horses at all. If he first strikes you as ungainly and out of proportion, he probably is.

Faults cause problems

A fault in one part of a horse can produce not only injury to that part but undue compensatory stress and strain elsewhere. Badly conformed horses seem prone to more 'mysterious' unsoundnesses than others because of this and they find it harder to balance themselves in work, either under the weight of a rider or manipulating a vehicle. This in turn produces too much stress on his physical structure and can lead to sprains and other injuries.

Horses' bodies do learn to compensate for this stress and strain, either by the part concerned becoming stronger or some other part taking extra stress due to the failing of the faulty part. Another vital point to remember is that no horse is perfect: they all have something wrong with them. It is often only when that something is pronounced that it becomes significant during athletic work. Light hacking or similar easy work can be performed by almost any sound horse, no matter what he looks like.

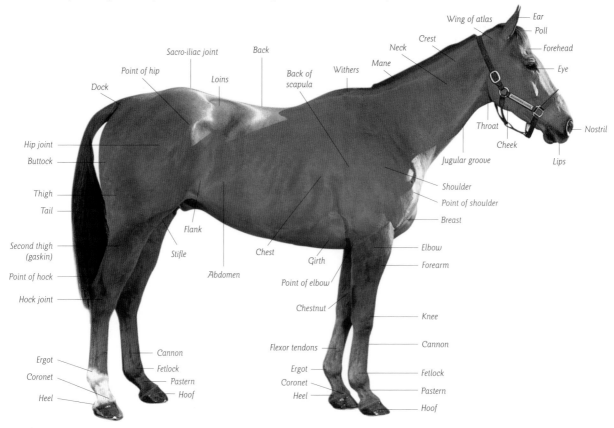

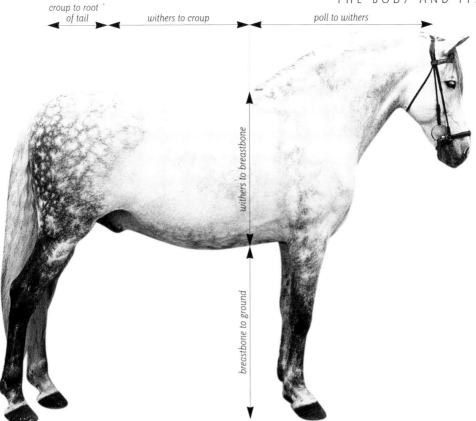

croup to root of tail | withers to croup | poll to withers

withers to breastbone

breastbone to ground

A simple blueprint

It helps to take a clear photograph of the horse you want to assess so that you can mark the following measurements on it, but you can use this method by careful visual assessment. The measurements marked on the photograph above are not meant to be followed pedantically but to a close approximation.

- Following a horizontal line, the length from the poll to the highest point of the withers should be about equal to that from the withers to the croup and that from the croup to the root of the tail should be about half that.
- Following a vertical line, the distance from the highest point of the withers to the girth or breastbone should be at least half that from the withers to the ground.

These basic proportions ensure a well-balanced framework. Additional pointers are:

- The length of the head, taken as a straight line from poll to upper lip, should fit into the neck length, again using a straight line measurement from poll to withers, one and a half times.
- The breastbone/belly line should run parallel to the ground for its length, then the belly should slope slightly upwards just in front of the stifles. In very fit horses, the belly will be fined down and slope up before this point.
- You should be able to fit the width of your hand between the horse's last rib and his hip (which is actually the wing of the pelvis). Too much space

here could mean the horse is probably too long in the back (known as slack in the loins) which could indicate weakness: too tight a squeeze can indicate a very short back which may cause over-reaching and forging.

- For riding, a 'well sloped' or 'well laid back' shoulder is required for a good 'feel'. Follow the line of the shoulder (the spine of the shoulder blade) to check this. If unsure, look at the point of the elbow and run your eye straight up to the withers. The point of the elbow should lie noticeably in front of the highest point of the withers on this line. For driving, a more upright shoulder is looked for as this makes it easier for the horse to push into the collar.
- The highest point of the withers should be level with or just higher than the point of the croup for a level feel in the saddle.
- The horse should carry his muzzle naturally at a point about midway between the point of the shoulder and the withers or slightly lower.
- From behind, visualise a vertical square with its top line running across the croup, its lower line through the points of the hocks and the two side lines touching the hips and thigh muscles. If your horse fits snugly into this square he will have good hindquarters.
- From the front, the barrel should look well rounded and not flat (slab-sided) and be just visible at the sides of a chest of good width.

Action

The Gaits

We normally think of horses as having four natural gaits – walk, trot, canter and gallop – and, with schooling, they can exhibit variations within them. For example, there are working, medium, collected and extended versions used in schooling and in competitive dressage, and the walk on a loose rein is called the free walk. The horse also has 'reverse' (rein-back) which a highly schooled horse can perform in walk, trot and canter, but we perhaps don't count this as a gait.

The horse normally starts any stride (a stride comprising any sequence of four footfalls starting with one foot and ending with the same foot) with a hind leg because his hindquarters provide his propulsion, pushing him along from behind.

The walk is a four-time gait in which three feet are always on the ground and there is no period of suspension. The horse moves both legs on one side first, then the legs on the other side; for example, the sequence is near hind, near fore, off hind, off fore. A horse who naturally over-tracks (places his hind hoof well in front of the print left by the preceding fore hoof) has a good walk – normally a sign that the other gaits will be good.

The trot (jog in Western riding) is a two-time gait in which only two feet are on the ground at once and there is a period of suspension in which all feet are off the ground. It is called a diagonal gait as the legs move in diagonal pairs. For instance, the near hind and off fore move forward together during the suspension phase, they land, then the horse springs off them up into the air for the next suspension phase during which the off hind and near fore move forward in the air ready to land, and so on.

The canter (lope in Western riding) is a three-time gait. If the stride begins with the near hind foot, the footfall sequence will be near hind, off hind and near fore together, off fore – then suspension. Although the near hind began this stride, the foot which landed last, the off fore, is called the 'leading leg' as this is how it looks to the human eye and is why this would be called 'right canter' or cantering with the 'off fore leading'. Human logic!

The gallop is the horse's fastest gait and is four-time. The change from one gait to another in all the other three is quite noticeable (but should be smooth) but the change from canter to gallop involves no distinct change – the gallop can be

The walk

The trot

The canter

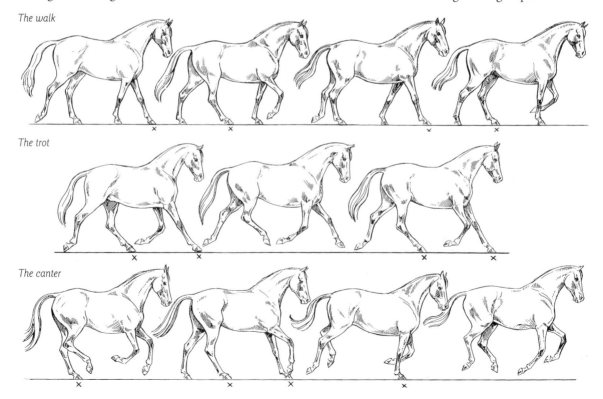

The horse begins a stride with a hind leg. The hoof hits the ground, force travels up the hindleg and is transmitted via the pelvis to the spine. The hindquarters, in this way, push the horse forward. His forelegs come forward and hit the ground to take the weight of his forehand. Force travels up the supporting forelegs and attached shoulder blades and is largely absorbed by the soft tissues connecting them to the ribcage. The head and neck act as a balancing device

regarded as a fast canter with an extended footfall sequence – near hind, off hind, near fore, off fore (leading!), then suspension.

Most well-conformed, Thoroughbred-type horses have a top sustainable galloping speed *under saddle* of very roughly 30mph which, for a big, heavy animal with only one suspension phase to the stride, is excellent. They can reach their top speed from a standing start in less than five seconds – one of their most valuable survival mechanisms. (In informal tests some years ago, a wild Somali Wild Ass was clocked by Land Rover in the desert at 40mph over short bursts.)

The fastest predatory animals, such as the greyhound and the cheetah, have two suspension phases, which makes them faster for their size than the horse. (The endangered cheetah is our fastest land animal with a top speed of about 65–70mph.) Their suspension phases are at the end of the stride sequence, as in the horse, but also in the middle between the two hind footfalls and the two fore footfalls, made possible by their much more flexible spines, particularly in the cheetah.

The ground has a braking influence on the gait: every time a foot hits the ground the resistance slows the animal down, so the more time the feet can spend in the air, at any phase of the gait, the faster the animal can go.

Artificial Gaits

Some horses have other gaits both natural (despite being termed 'artificial') and learned. The most familiar is the *pace* which looks like the trot until you realise that the two legs on the same side are moving together. This is called a lateral gait which can be easy and comfortable for long-distance journeys (as was its slow version, the *amble*, in former centuries) and very

fast for harness racing (as fast as the gallop and slightly faster than the racing trot) because the suspension phase is longer than in trot. It does, though, put greater stress on the horse. Horses using this gait are often born with it (the foals often move with a natural, lateral version of walk and trot in the fields) and it is developed by training and special harness. Harness racers using it are called pacers, others trotters.

Other artificial gaits, used in some working horses in the Americas and particularly in north American showrings, are as follows:

The slow gaits

- The *running walk* and *stepping pace*, 'slow gaits' and a collected form of the fast rack (q.v.), these are very similar four-beat gaits in which the feet come down individually and the horse's body has a gentle, side-to-side, swinging motion very comfortable to sit.
- The *fox trot*, a slow, shuffling trot, smooth and comfortable for the rider. The horse walks with the front feet and trots with the hind, the hind feet stepping into the fore prints and sliding forwards. (The horse's head nods and the teeth clack together in rhythm with the footfalls.)
- The *amble*, a slow version of the pace, in which the lateral footfalls do not contact the ground simultaneously but have a slight pause between them, more exaggerated in the *broken amble*.

The fast gait:

- The *rack* or *single-foot*, a fast, four-beat, flashy gait with individual footfalls and much elevation of the legs.

In American showrings, the three-gaited horse shows walk, trot and canter; the five-gaited horse shows these plus one of the slow gaits and the fast rack. However, the Tennessee (Plantation) Walking Horse does not show the trot but the walk, slow gait and canter. The breeds which are most commonly 'gaited' are the Saddlebred, the Tennessee Walker, the Fox Trotter, the Paso Fino and the Peruvian Paso.

Performance Factors

To a horseman, there are few more beautiful and exhilarating sights than a horse in perfect health, comfort and high spirits tearing around a huge open space, revelling in his own speed and strength and power, the sound and feel of the air rushing around his ears, in and out of his nostrils and lungs, through his mane and over his body, and the sense he must experience of being master of himself, doing what horses have been born to do for millions of years.

To a horseman, too, there can be no more ecstatic sensation than being on that horse, at one with him stride for stride, sharing his power and the virtual immortality of the moment, for it never leaves you. The thrill is just the same if horse and rider share in perfect comfort and harmony the intricate movements of High School, the thrill of the chase or competition or an ideal, satisfying hack. It all depends on your preferences.

But how often does all this really happen and how often is it marred because the horse, unable to tell his perhaps not very perceptive rider or handler in ways he or she will absorb, that there is something wrong with him, that he feels unwell, that some part of his body is painful, that his tack is really uncomfortable or that the rider is riding so badly that he or she is the cause of the horse's problems and is actually preventing him from creating one of those special moments?

Pain and discomfort

Everyone experiences discomfort and pain at some time. Anyone who has experienced the very real pain of, for instance, a badly sprained ankle, wrenched shoulder muscles or a 'bad back' well knows how exhausting and disabling not only the pain itself can be but also the physical effort needed to move in unaccustomed and abnormal ways to avoid inflicting more pain on the injured part. Such movement, in turn, places unnatural stresses on other parts of the body not used to moving in such ways or to bearing such weight or force – and they, too, may become injured. It is exactly the same for the horse. Unfortunately, many horses are so stoical that they do not complain when we arrive with tack for work (even a light hack is work of a kind to the horse). They have learned that it is pointless to 'say' anything because humans don't take any notice. They are still made to work and may be punished in various ways (not only, or necessarily, by whipping

Bad riding is the cause of much poor performance!

but by harsh, insistent aids and strong verbal exhortations) if the horses object or do not move normally.

Most people recognise if a horse is noticeably lame and will rest him and possibly call in the vet. In cases of slight pain and discomfort, however, very many people just keep on and on expecting the horse to work, pushing him to do so however badly, not accepting or considering that he could be ill or in enough pain or discomfort to affect his energy levels, his movement and, just as important, his willingness.

Physical discomfort or pain will cause the horse to try to avoid it. Badly fitting tack or harness frequently produce resistance or poor performance and many owners are reluctant to consider this, partly because tack (especially a saddle) is expensive to keep replacing but also because people find it difficult to amend old and perhaps ill-considered ideas of how it should be fitted and used.

It is increasingly recognised that pressure and friction from badly fitting saddles is a major cause of 'unexplained' lameness, stilted action, resistance and poor work. Another cause of such reactions is girthing up far too tightly; this is compounded by badly designed girths which, among other faults, do not spread pressure evenly, do not 'give' enough, if at all, or do so in an uneven and uncomfortable way (for example having an elastic insert on one end only).

Many, indeed most, people still hoist bits far too high in the horse's mouth, even curb bits, without giving a thought to how they would like it, how very uncomfortable it must feel and how badly this must affect the horse's attitude and work. Sadly and, to the author, unfathomably, this current fashion is usually taught as correct in the UK.

Effects

What are the effects on the horse of tolerating, long-term, any discomfort or pain whether from tack, bad riding, painful feet, an injury which has not healed fully or even badly fitting clothing which causes bruising and friction injuries?

Attitude

In the short-term, unless the horse is an absolute saint his attitude to work and possibly to humans must be affected. Depending on his temperament, he may become unwilling, resistant and either nervous or aggressive. Longer-term, the aggression may become worse or the horse may become dull and withdrawn.

Physical injury

Physically, one injury can lead to another. The discomfort of compensating for pain in one part of the body by moving unnaturally and so over-stressing another has already been pointed out. This new technique of moving can become a habit or, if the original injury is constantly, if slightly, exacerbated, unavoidable. The new way of going may be quite unsuitable for the horse's job; for instance, a show jumper who can't tuck up his hind hooves has a problem and so has a dressage horse

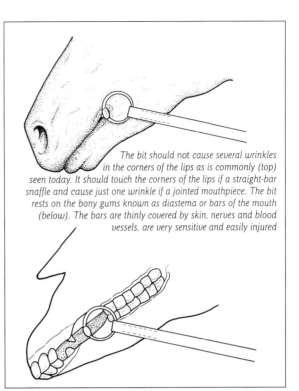

The bit should not cause several wrinkles in the corners of the lips as is commonly (top) seen today. It should touch the corners of the lips if a straight-bar snaffle and cause just one wrinkle if a jointed mouthpiece. The bit rests on the bony gums known as diastema or bars of the mouth (below). The bars are thinly covered by skin, nerves and blood vessels, are very sensitive and easily injured

35

whose back is so warped that he can't or won't move straight despite his rider's strongest aids.

Injured soft tissue such as muscle, tendon and ligament tends to repair to a level slightly below its former status and this can be made worse if the original injury has been poorly managed and not allowed or encouraged to heal properly, and if adhesions have been allowed to form unchecked. Scar ('replacement') tissue is always weaker than the original particularly in areas without a good blood supply such as tendons, ligaments and connective tissue. The part will, therefore, be more likely to be re-injured under less stress than that which caused the original injury – and every time it is re-injured the repair will be less and less good.

This is, for example, why racehorses or eventers who have 'broken down' (sustained serious tendon injuries) rarely race or event successfully again, if at all, or for very long. They may 'retire' to less demanding disciplines but old injuries never die, they just keep coming back unless the new owners are extremely careful.

If we want to hold on to that picture painted in the first two paragraphs, it will pay us never to ignore even a slight change in a horse's attitude, behaviour or action, to give him the benefit of the doubt, to keep a close eye on him backed up by a perceptive, understanding brain and to be prepared to investigate properly any problems which may arise rather than keep hoping that they will go away.

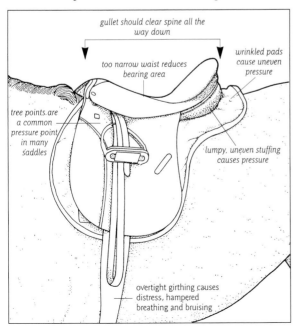

gullet should clear spine all the way down

too narrow waist reduces bearing area

wrinkled pads cause uneven pressure

tree points are a common pressure point in many saddles

lumpy, uneven stuffing causes pressure

overtight girthing causes distress, hampered breathing and bruising

Fitting a saddle

Blood Transport

A simple way of understanding the circulatory system is to think of it as being like a railway system. The heart is the station, the blood vessels are the major and minor tracks and the blood is the trains. An efficient transport system is essential to life for delivering oxygen and nutrients to the body tissues and for taking away toxic substances. It also carries hormones to wherever they are needed, and certain drugs and other substances administered to the horse.

The Heart

The heart is a hollow pump which pumps blood around the body, made mainly of cardiac (involuntary) muscle. It is divided vertically by a muscular wall (the septum) into two parts with no connection between them after birth. It is formed into four chambers – upper right and left atria (singular: atrium) and lower right and left ventricles.

The atria and ventricles have valves between them to prevent backflow of blood and keep it moving on. The atria receive and collect blood and the ventricles pump blood out around the body.

Blood vessels

There are two main types of blood vessels – *arteries* which carry blood away from the heart and *veins* which carry blood to the heart.

The arteries and veins reduce in size (then being called arterioles and venules respectively), becoming smaller and finer till they meet in an extensive, complex network of microscopic tubes whose walls are only one cell thick, called the capillary network.

Arteries have thick, strong, elastic walls of smooth (involuntary) muscle, and a small lumen (internal space) through which blood travels at high pressure. They have a recoil mechanism which keeps pushing the blood along. As the blood pressure has greatly

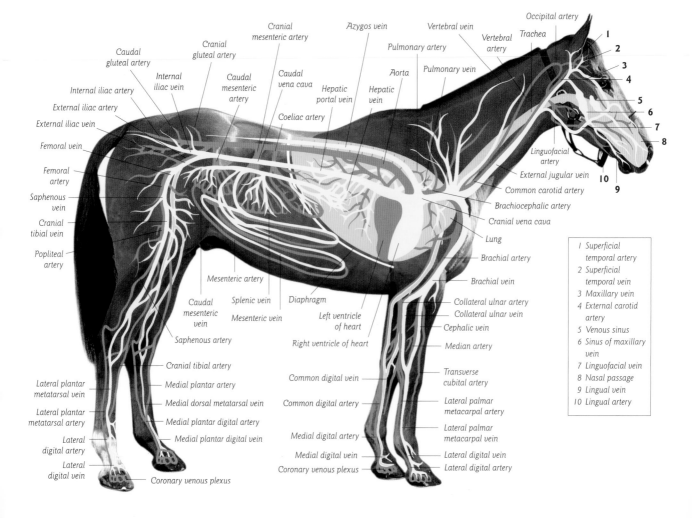

1 Superficial temporal artery
2 Superficial temporal vein
3 Maxillary vein
4 External carotid artery
5 Venous sinus
6 Sinus of maxillary vein
7 Linguofacial vein
8 Nasal passage
9 Lingual vein
10 Lingual artery

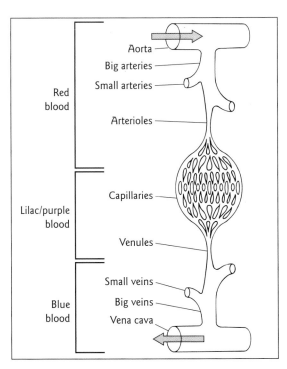

Red blood

Lilac/purple blood

Blue blood

Aorta
Big arteries
Small arteries
Arterioles
Capillaries
Venules
Small veins
Big veins
Vena cava

Capillary network and the direction of blood through it

reduced by the time the blood is on its return journey in the veins, their walls are much thinner but some have valves to stop backflow of blood. They actually can act as partial blood reservoirs during periods of rest.

The *capillaries* are crucial to metabolism and, therefore, to life. Substances can pass through their walls, both ways, when they are 'delivered' and 'collected' but capillary lumens are only large enough in diameter to accommodate a single red blood cell at once.

The walls are selectively permeable: that means they allow movement out of the blood into the body's cells of substances such as oxygen, glucose, protein, water, vitamins, minerals and so on and movement in from the cells to the blood of waste products such as carbon dioxide, urea and others. This is how the blood provides its transport function.

How the system works
The left side of the heart deals with blood containing oxygen (called oxygenated and bright red), the right side with blood depleted of oxygen (called deoxygenated and a dark, bluish red).

Blood picks up oxygen in the lungs from where it is carried in the large pulmonary vein (pulmonary meaning lung-related) to the left atrium of the heart. When full, the muscular wall of the atrium contracts and pushes the blood down into the left ventricle, the valve between them preventing backflow. The

left ventricle has the thickest, most muscular wall as it has to pump the blood all the way round the body and to the head via the main artery, the aorta.

The arteries become smaller and thinner (arterioles) until the arterial capillaries meet the venous ones, meshing together almost all over the body. Here, the 'good' substances pass out and the 'bad' ones pass in, as described. The venous capillaries become venules, then veins which take the deoxygenated blood back to the heart in the main vein, the vena cava, which empties its blood into the right atrium of the heart.

When full, the right atrium contracts, pumping the blood down into the right ventricle which pumps the blood via the pulmonary artery to the lungs. In the air sacs of the lungs, which are wrapped around by capillaries, carbon dioxide in the blood is exchanged for oxygen in the air sacs in a vital process called *gaseous* exchange. The reoxygenated blood then travels again via the pulmonary vein to the left atrium, beginning the continuous cycle again.

ABOUT BLOOD
Blood has three main components – plasma, cells and platelets.

Plasma This comprises serum and a protein called fibrinogen instrumental in clotting blood, mainly to repair injuries. Serum is the fluid part of blood and is 92 per cent water plus 8 per cent dissolved substances, mainly nutrients.

Blood cells There are two types of cells:
- Red cells (erythrocytes) are made in the bone marrow and contain an iron-containing pigment called haemoglobin, the main function of which is to pick up and transport the oxygen breathed into the lungs. Once the oxygen has attached to the haemoglobin, it is called oxyhaemoglobin. Unlike other body cells, red cells have no nucleus or control centre, so are short-lived, their lifespan being three or four months.
- White (colourless) cells (leucocytes) of five types which help the body fight disease and repair dead or damaged tissues. They also are made in bone marrow and in the lymphatic system. As their main function is protection of the body, they are part of the immune system. Some attack bacteria, some attack viruses and some are involved in allergic responses, so help to protect the body in their different ways. They have nuclei and live much longer than red cells. For every white cell, there are about 500 red cells.

Platelets: These are disc-shaped cell fragments circulating in the blood which gather at sites of injury and work with fibrinogen (by giving off various products) to clot blood and provide temporary repair while new tissues form.

The System in Action

Many people are unaware of what a superb athlete the horse is *even when unfit*. Relatively speaking, his cardiac system easily outperforms ours. A human athlete's heartbeat increases about three-fold during peak exertion whereas a horse's increases by about six-fold.

Tailor Made

The horse's circulatory system is ideal for a grazing, running animal which needs to perform standing starts to the gallop to evade predators or, in domesticity, to do fast, strenuous work.

Capacity

Horses have about 40 to 50 litres (10 to 12 gallons) of blood in their bodies and, in a fast-galloping horse, one blood cell will take about five seconds to travel right round the body. We all know that the harder a horse (or human) works the faster the heart beats: this is to increase the speed of the bloodflow and carry extra oxygen and nutrients to the muscles and to remove toxins, but as well as beating faster the amount of blood the heart pumps through with one beat (called the stroke volume) increases greatly, particularly with 'fittening'. Therefore, as the horse grows fitter, the heart can pump through more blood with fewer strokes or beats than for the same amount of work in an unfit horse.

Adaptation to work

Work increases the heart's size by up to about one third in response to the stress of a fitness programme. It can enlarge in response to any condition which requires it to work harder than normal in order to keep up its 'service levels' such as COPD, a heart murmur or equine influenza.

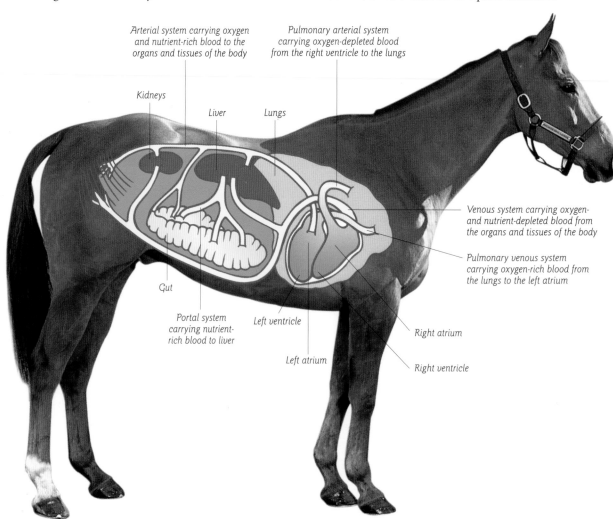

Arterial system carrying oxygen and nutrient-rich blood to the organs and tissues of the body

Pulmonary arterial system carrying oxygen-depleted blood from the right ventricle to the lungs

Kidneys

Liver

Lungs

Venous system carrying oxygen- and nutrient-depleted blood from the organs and tissues of the body

Pulmonary venous system carrying oxygen-rich blood from the lungs to the left atrium

Gut

Portal system carrying nutrient-rich blood to liver

Left ventricle

Right atrium

Left atrium

Right ventricle

The normal at-rest pulse or heart rate is about 36 to 42 beats per minute. Young and unfit horses have a higher rate and old and fit ones a lower rate: a fit horse's at-rest rate may drop as low as about 26 beats per minute. During peak work, though, the rate can rise to about 240bpm.

PCV

As well as the action of the spleen, the body responds to work by producing more red cells. The proportion of red blood cells can be established by measuring them relative to the blood as a whole to arrive at the horse's packed cell volume (PCV) or haematocrit. Blood is placed in a test tube and spun in a centrifuge so that the cells separate from the plasma in the bottom of the tube.

The usual at-rest PCV is 35 to 50 per cent but this can rise by at least 15 per cent in very fit horses. Excitement, distress, diseases and disorders such as dehydration, azoturia, colic and grass sickness can also cause a rise; a drop will be occasioned by such conditions as haemolytic jaundice, anaemia, infections involving fever and severe blood loss. Performance-wise, then, blood volume can be increased and therefore the number of red cells and the haemoglobin content and oxygen-carrying capacity of the blood.

To support these factors, the capillary network actually increases in response to the stress of work, so there is more 'track' on which the extra 'trains' can travel from their extended 'station'.

All these factors mean the horse can greatly increase the effectiveness of the blood supply to his tissues, particularly the muscles during work, and he can sustain those effects much better than most animals.

Heart Abnormalities

Significant heart abnormalities are fairly uncommon in horses. Not least because of their low-fat, vegetarian diet (notwithstanding the odd few ponies who pinch ham sandwiches at picnics), horses rarely have 'coronaries' (heart attacks) as do humans and carnivores. Although defects do occur, many can be easily lived with and may not affect a pleasure horse used as a family pet, hack or even one used for active hacking or light hunting.

Every horse should have an annual check-up including a check on his eyes, heart and wind and most wise purchasers will have a horse 'vetted' before purchase. During checks like these, the vet will auscultate (listen to) the heart sounds through a stethoscope and give information and an opinion on any abnormal sounds detected and how they might affect a horse's potential for work. More

BLOOD RESERVOIR

The horse's spleen helps him meet the body's demands for extra oxygen quickly during hard work by releasing stored red blood cells (stimulated by the hormone adrenaline). The spleen both breaks down erythrocytes and manufactures them. It is also involved in the production of lymphocytes, a type of leucocyte or white cell. Therefore, although the body makes over 35 million red blood cells every second of every day, extra supplies can be obtained from the spleen, when needed.

precise information can be gained from examination by means of various electronic instruments.

Aneurysm

An aneurysm is the 'ballooning' of an artery wall which is nearly always caused by an accumulation of worm larvae. Regular worming reduces this risk. The wall, so weakened, may burst at any time and cause the sudden death of the horse.

Arrhythmia

This is an irregular heartbeat or rhythm. Sometimes popularly called 'dropped beats', these are not uncommon in resting horses if the body detects that requirements are being met and the heart can take a very short break. The normal rhythm will be restored when the horse is more active and alert.

A more common problem is a rapid, shallow beat which will mean that the heart is not putting through enough blood and not pumping it strongly enough. This results in insufficient oxygen and nutrients being delivered to the tissues and imperfect removal of waste products, resulting in an unhealthy, weak horse.

Murmurs

Many owners are shocked when a vet first tells them that their horse has a heart murmur but insignificant murmurs are fairly common and barely affect a horse in light to moderate work, depending on their nature and severity. Others are more serious.

Murmurs happen when the valves in the heart do not close properly so that there is some backflow of blood; this creates a rushing sound picked up by the stethoscope and can be easily distinguished by an experienced owner who checks his or her horse regularly. The poor flow means less oxygen and nutrients being delivered and fewer toxins being removed, with the expected results.

How Blood Fights Disease

The Immune System

The body has an excellent system for fighting disease, even though it can often benefit from our outside help. It is the circulatory system which enables the *immune system*, as it is called, to work because, along with the lymphatic system, it transports defensive structures and substances to the parts requiring them.

The immune system's job is to defend the body from antigens, foreign materials, usually proteins, such as bacteria, viruses, organ transplants and blood components (as in blood transfusions) and others. It works in two main ways:

- Via the skin and mucous membranes, which form an effective physical barrier to the entry of antigens unless breached by cuts, parasite bites, abrasions or disease.
- Internally, where white blood cells both engulf or 'eat' invading micro-organisms and also produce antibodies and antitoxins.

  Antibodies are proteins produced in response to the presence of specific antigens which they recognise and to which they bind selectively, enabling other components of the immune system to dispose of them.

  Antitoxins are substances which neutralise toxins by combining with them.

Types of Immunity
Non-specific immunity
This is a general resistance to disease provided by:

- Genetic factors such as species or breed resistance (for instance, horses and humans are susceptible to tetanus but dogs almost never get it).
- Environmental factors such as the surrounding temperature, quality of ventilation, nutrition, hygiene, quality of exercise, etc.
- Age and sex (some diseases only occur in certain age groups or are sex-specific).
- The skin and mucous membranes which are good, general barriers to the entry of pathogens or 'germs'.
- Acid secretions in the stomach which kill many pathogens.
- The cough, sneeze and blink reflexes, the first two bringing out much disease material from the lungs and head and the second, along

---

THE IMMUNE RESPONSE

This is an essential element of the horse's immune system. As described, pathogens invading the body stimulate the production of antibodies by the lymph nodes. These are released into the lymph and blood and circulate round the body, if the disease is systemic (present throughout the body), or go to wherever they are required (if the infection is local as in an infected wound).

Antibodies are also produced in infected tissue, skin, fat and some muscle tissue. This production of antibodies or 'soldier cells' is called the immune response.

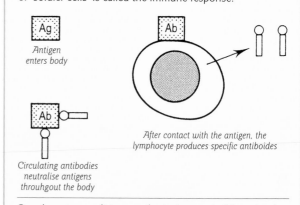

Antigen enters body

After contact with the antigen, the lymphocyte produces specific antiboides

Circulating antibodies neutralise antigens throuhgout the body

---

Complementary medicines mostly aim to promote this process by stimulating the body's own immune system so that more self-healing takes place. Orthodox medicine tends to provide 'back-up' to the body via vaccinations and/or synthetic drugs

---

with the eye's natural saline tears, clearing the eye of debris and germs.

Specific immunity
This can be natural or artificial:

- Natural immunity can be passive (such as that gained by a foal from its dam's colostrum which contains antibodies) or active (which comes from exposure to disease-causing micro-organisms, stimulating the body to produce its own antibodies).
- Artificial immunity can be passive (when the horse is given antibodies via antiserum – serum containing antibodies taken from another horse and purified in a laboratory) or active (administered by vaccination which stimulates the horse's body to make antibodies against the appropriate disease).
- Acquired immunity (that acquired from

colostrum, exposure to disease or vaccination) has a limited period of effectiveness. Once the body senses that the relevant germs are no longer a threat, it stops producing appropriate antibodies and the horse's immunity to that disease reduces. Should the disease recur and the horse be exposed to it, he may become infected which is why it is recommended that vaccinations be kept up to date even in the face of very low risk. As immunity takes a little while to develop, vaccinating the horse once the disease has recurred may be too late.

The Lymphatic System

The lymphatic system is a network of thin-walled vessels throughout the body which carry a clear, slightly yellowish fluid called lymph, derived from blood. It is not a true circulatory system as there is no heart and the channels are blind-ended but it is linked to the blood circulatory system because it empties into it near the heart and has capillaries which mesh with the blood capillaries, working with them.

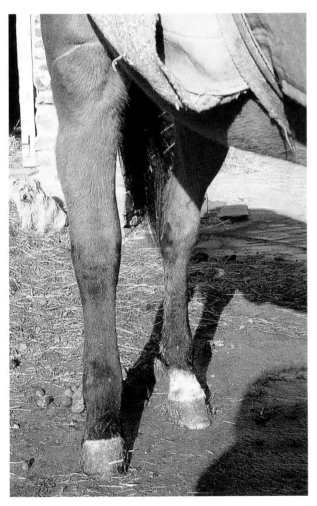

Lymph

Lymph consists of water, protein, fat and a small quantity of lymphocytes. As there is no true circulation, lymph can accumulate in the limbs and other areas due to lack of exercise, resulting in 'filled legs'. The vessels have no valves, as do veins, so the movement of lymph depends on the channels being constantly squeezed by muscles and other tissues during movement. The system is an essential aid in regulating the body's fluid balance, draining excess fluid in tissues, in the blood and being involved in the fluid transport system and the defence mechanism against disease. It also 'cleanses' and nourishes tissues with no blood supply such as cartilage, horn and the cornea of the eye. Frequent, ample exercise is essential to its optimal functioning and, therefore, to the horse's general good health. (The traditional hour or two, once a day, is inadequate.)

Lymph nodes or glands

These occur in various places round the body (such as beneath the jaw and throat, near the ear, in front of the shoulder and in the groin – although there are many more) and can be easily felt if they become hot and swollen due to disease. If glands are swollen, it means that they are actually doing their job but they can become 'overloaded' and may abscess and burst, most familiarly in strangles (in the jaw/throat area) and lymphangitis (in the legs, usually the hind and sometimes only one). The glands produce antibodies, act as filters for germs and debris and contain many lymphocytes.

Lymphangitis, characterised by hard, hot, painful swelling of one leg, can be caused by infection, injury which blocks lymph channels or overfeeding and insufficient exercise. Fluid escapes from blood and lymph vessesl into surrounding tissues causing 'filled leg' which 'pits' on pressure from the finger

41

The Breath of Life

Strictly speaking, we should call the respiratory system involving the lungs, airways and their functions the pulmonary system (pulmonary meaning 'lung-related') because there is another type of respiration – that which occurs in the body cells and involves the metabolic processes by which cells break down carbohydrates, amino acids and fats to produce energy, which is called cellular respiration. However, everyone connects the above title with the lungs so we'll stay with it.

Purpose

The main purpose of the respiratory system is to supply oxygen to the blood and remove carbon dioxide from it. The removal of carbon dioxide, a toxic waste product of metabolism, is the driving factor which tells the heart how fast and strongly to beat. This is one reason for the increased heart rate in respiratory disorders which adversely affect not only the supply of oxygen but also the removal of carbon dioxide. It is interesting to note that air breathed in is 79 per cent nitrogen, 21 per cent oxygen and only 0.03 per cent carbon dioxide whereas that breathed out is 80 per cent nitrogen, 16 per cent oxygen (which surprises most people) and 4 per cent carbon dioxide.

Other functions of the system are:

- The regulation of the acidity or alkalinity of body fluids, the correct balance of which is vital to optimal functioning. The carbon dioxide content of the blood just means the amount of carbonic acid and bicarbonate in the blood.
- Body temperature control, as heat passes out with exhaled air.
- Elimination of water, as water vapour is also exhaled.
- Voice production, when air is pushed across vocal cords made to touch by muscular action, causing vibration.
- Operation of the sense of smell as the horse sniffs in smells for identification.

Structure and Function

The system begins and ends with the nostrils as it is almost impossible for horses to breathe through their mouths.

The chest cavity is separated from the abdominal cavity by a strong, dome-shaped sheet of muscle and tendon, the diaphragm, which is attached to the ribs, the cartilage of the sternum or breastbone and to the lumbar vertebrae. (It has three openings to permit the passage through it of the aorta (the main artery), the oesophagus or gullet and the posterior vena cava (the main vein).)

The diaphragm works with the intercostal muscles (between the ribs): it contracts and flattens back and down towards the abdomen and the intercostal muscles contract, lifting the ribs up and out, the joint result being the expansion and increase in size of the chest cavity. This sucks air into the lungs at the nostrils like bellows, it travels through the air passages in the head and over the pharynx or throat; here, there is a 'lid' at the entrance to the trachea, the epiglottis, which is down during breathing to allow the passage of air but flips up during swallowing to prevent fluids and food getting into the trachea and lungs.

The air passes on through the larynx or voice box into the trachea or windpipe, a tube held open by C-shaped rings of cartilage or gristle. The trachea branches

The flat racehorse needs to make maximum use of his lungs during fast work. Living in polluted areas with poor air quality plus not being kept on a clean-air régime (dust-free bedding, feeds and hay/haylage/ forage feed) significantly reduces their efficiency

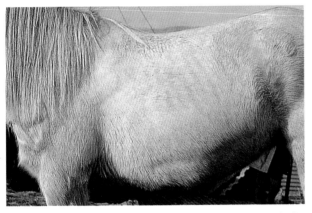

Due to constantly making a muscular effort to force air out, this broken-winded horse has developed the muscles around the ribs (chest) to the extent that they form what is known as a 'heaves line' ('heaves' being another name for broken wind or COPD) along the flank

Right: *Greatly enlarged photograph of cilia lining the mucous membranes of the respiratory tract*

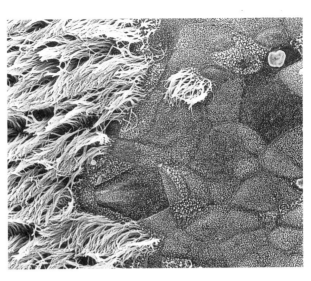

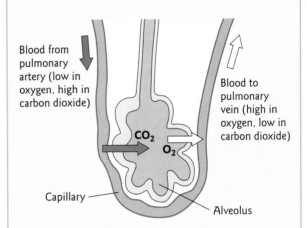

Blood from pulmonary artery (low in oxygen, high in carbon dioxide)

Blood to pulmonary vein (high in oxygen, low in carbon dioxide)

CO_2

O_2

Capillary

Alveolus

into two further tubes, the bronchi, one each passing into the left and right lungs. The bronchi divide again and again (when they are called bronchioles), to end in tiny air sacs (alveoli) which are like tiny, hollow bunches of grapes, wrapped round by capillaries.

The expression 'lung tissue' covers the alveoli, bronchioles and the lower end of each bronchus. Lung tissue is elastic and is stretched by the intake of air. When the horse breathes out, unlike the operation of bellows he needs to make no physical effort if his lungs are healthy. The elastic lung tissue recoils and the diaphragm and intercostal muscles relax which forces the air out.

Horses with COPD (see page 45) have lost much of this tissue elasticity and use muscular effort to exhale, including the abdominal muscles, to push up and forward against the diaphragm. This eventually produces the characteristic 'heave line' running diagonally down the flank or lower edge of the ribcage, created by muscular development.

For our convenience, we divide the respiratory system into the upper respiratory tract (the nostrils, nasal passages, pharynx and larynx as far as the trachea) and the lower respiratory tract (comprising the trachea to the bronchi, into the bronchioles, ending as the alveoli).

Clearing the Pipes

The respiratory tract is lined by hair-like projections called cilia which give a velvety appearance. They move in a 'Mexican-wave' fashion to carry mucus and debris (bacteria, viruses, dust etc.) up to the throat for swallowing (to be dealt with by the acid environment of the stomach) or to be coughed, sneezed or blown out of the nostrils.

GASEOUS EXCHANGE

The crucial process of the exchange of oxygen breathed in for carbon dioxide to be breathed out is called gaseous exchange and takes place in the alveoli.

Carbon dioxide is dissolved in the plasma of the blood returning to the lungs in higher concentrations than that of the air breathed in. It diffuses through the thin capillary and alveolar walls into the air space and oxygen breathed in passes the other way into the capillaries surrounding the alveolus, to be picked up by the red blood cells.

The horse breathes out the carbon dioxide, and the oxygen in the now reoxygenated blood is carried on all round the body.

It is clear that anything which interferes with this process can, ultimately, place the horse's life at risk and certainly his health. Tight nosebands or any means of restraint around the nostrils or throat, poor air quality inside the stable or out, lack of exercise to keep the respiratory system 'on the go' and disease or any disorder which results in malfunction of the sensitive lung tissue, and so on, are all normally avoidable with good riding, handling and general management.

Hampering the System

As stressed in The Breath of Life, anything which interferes with the normal working of the horse's respiratory system can place the horse's health and even his life at risk. Horses have particularly sensitive lungs and airways and, obviously, their evolution has fitted them to a life outdoors in clean, oxygen-rich air, not exposed to high levels of toxins such as carbon dioxide or ammonia given off by soiled, rotting organic matter such as dirty bedding or to the fungal moulds, spores and dust of artificially dried forage (hay) or bedding (straw, shavings and shredded paper). They would not encounter significant levels of these items during a natural life.

There are more respiratory disorders in today's horses than ever before, and some experts believe this is partly due to deteriorating air quality due to planet-wide pollution, so whether our domesticated horses are inside or out they are beginning at a disadvantage. (This problem also applies to ourselves and other animals, of course, and is believed to be one reason for the increased number of asthmatic children.)

The respiratory system seems, at present, to be the only one which cannot be improved or enhanced by training. Whilst the muscles and other tissues can be increased, strengthened or improved in performance by fitness training, the respiratory system cannot: the best we can do is to enable it to work optimally. In other words, the horse has the respiratory system he was born with and nothing we can do can enhance its function. We can simply make conditions as favourable to its operation, and as near as possible to nature, as we possibly can so that we are not hampering the horse's chances from the start. This will be dealt with more fully in Section 5. For now, let us look at some conditions which can hamper the efficient functioning of the respiratory system.

Equine Influenza

This is a highly infectious disease of the lower respiratory tract which usually can be effectively prevented by vaccination.

The horse will have a fever, the temperature rising to about 39–41°C or 102.2–105.8°F, a watery nasal discharge, a persistent harsh cough, inflamed and sore throat, loss of appetite, shivering and considerable dullness as the horse feels very ill.

The influenza virus attacks and injures the lung tissue and it is not always realised that unless the horse is completely rested for about a month (depending on veterinary advice) after apparent recovery, the permanent damage to the lungs can adversely affect the horse's work potential for the rest of his life.

Following influenza, strangles (a bacterial infection) and, more commonly, COPD (an

Most owners now realise that the safest plan is to soak or thoroughly wet all hay, no matter how 'clean' it seems, to swell the fungal spores found on it to a size too big to be inhaled into the tiny air spaces in the lungs. Currently, we are advised to soak for no longer than thirty minutes, and many nutritionists recommend a thorough dunking for only five minutes. Hang it till it has stopped dripping then give it to your horse. Do not let it dry out, though, as the spores will then shrink again and cause trouble (see also pp130, 141 and 147.)

allergic condition) are possible sequels, both of which, again, can permanently hamper the functioning of the respiratory system.

Chronic Obstructive Pulmonary Disease

This increasingly common allergic condition affects the lower respiratory tract and is familiar to most people these days. In most yards of more than a very few horses there will be one or two 'windy' horses who need special care.

COPD is an allergic reaction to fungal spores on organic material, usually hay and straw, even clean-looking samples. The spores are breathed down into the airways where, if the horse has a sensitivity to them – and many do – they stimulate the production of histamine by special cells called mast cells, the results of which have already been explained.

Horses affected by COPD obviously cannot breathe properly. They have particular trouble breathing out but the damaged lung tissue also adversely affects gaseous exchange so their respiratory systems cannot work properly.

Fortunately, COPD can be effectively treated these days both from a management and veterinary point of view. At one time, it was believed that the condition could not be reversed but, although the sensitivity may remain, horses can be returned to athletic work with appropriate management and treatment.

Whistling and Roaring (Laryngeal hemiplegia)

These terms indicate the noises made by horses suffering from partial obstruction of their larynx during inhalation due to a defect of the recurrent laryngeal nerve (a branch of the vagus nerve in the head and neck) which causes paralysis of the muscle controlling the (usually) left vocal cord. Then, instead of the vocal cord being pulled back by the muscle to allow the passage of air, it collapses into the airspace of the larynx, partially blocking it, and causing air turbulence which accounts for the variety of noises heard. This interferes with the clear flow of air, producing a reduced oxygen supply and compromised performance.

Surgery which permanently ties back the vocal cord is moderately successful (although it prevents the horse using his voice) but, even if not treated, many horses are suitable for less demanding pursuits.

Epiglottal Entrapment

This condition is also believed to result from a defect in the recurrent laryngeal nerve. The

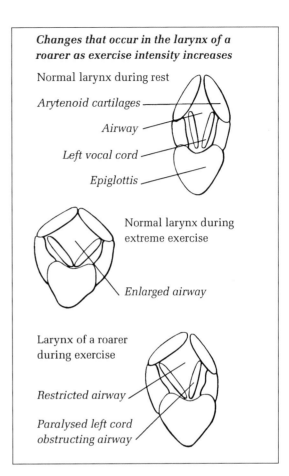

Changes that occur in the larynx of a roarer as exercise intensity increases

Normal larynx during rest
Arytenoid cartilages
Airway
Left vocal cord
Epiglottis

Normal larynx during extreme exercise
Enlarged airway

Larynx of a roarer during exercise
Restricted airway
Paralysed left cord obstructing airway

45

epiglottis becomes displaced from its normal position and becomes wrapped in the membrane from its own lower lining and from the throat which traps it in an abnormal position obstructing the entrance to the trachea. This obviously reduces the amount of air which can be taken in and, so, the amount of oxygen, with the usual results.

It usually happens at the gallop and can right itself when the horse slows down but sometimes the epiglottis becomes permanently displaced (which also interferes with swallowing). Affected horses may make noises during work and may cough and appear to choke. It can sometimes be treated surgically and some horses can put up with it if not worked fast.

Soft Palate Displacement

Popularly called 'swallowing the tongue', this happens at peak exertion during a fast gallop, when the horse will make gurgling noises and slow right down. The condition then usually rights itself and the horse can continue. It is caused by abnormal muscular action causing the horse to, in fact, make a swallowing action during work which blocks the airway. There are varied causes and treatments and the matter should be investigated by a vet if the horse is required to work at peak speeds.

The System in Action

The two main purposes of the respiratory system are (1) to provide the body with oxygen for living and work and (2) to remove waste products, mainly carbon dioxide. Horse owners normally have horses to perform athletic work at some level and most realise the importance of getting their horse athletically fit and conditioned to the required level.

Oxygen, toxins and muscles

Muscle fibres (cells) are of two main types called slow-twitch and fast-twitch. Slow-twitch fibres contract slower than fast-twitch fibres and are those mainly used during rest and relaxation and for slowish, steady work such as hacking, dressage but also demanding driving and endurance riding involving long time periods. Fast-twitch muscle is used for power-burst activities like sprinting, polo, show-jumping, shying, bucking and getting away from predators. The type of fibres of which a horse has most (they all have differing proportions of each) will largely dictate the type of work for which he is best suited.

Muscle is also classified according to its ability to use oxygen and energy. Slow-twitch muscle uses oxygen very efficiently so is called high oxidative muscle. Fast-twitch muscle can be high oxidative (used for middle- to long-distance work at speed like racing over jumps, cross-country competition, hunting and the like) or low oxidative which works rapidly and requires little oxygen (used for getting away from starting stalls, Quarter Horse and two-year-old Thoroughbred flat-racing, escaping predators, dangerous objects and for twists and

turns over short periods, like show-jumping and polo).

Those muscle fibres which need and efficiently use oxygen (slow-twitch and high oxidative fast-twitch) are said to work aerobically (in the presence of oxygen) and the type which can work rapidly without much oxygen (low oxidative fast-twitch) works anaerobically (without oxygen).

Skeletal muscles tire because they run short of oxygen and, therefore, energy because the oxygen is needed to oxidise or 'burn up' the fuel stores in the muscles (glycogen) to convert it to energy. This process also creates carbon dioxide, and sometimes lactic acid in anaerobic work, waste products which must be removed in order for a healthy working environment in the muscle to be maintained.

One main purpose of fitness training (other than in sprinters) is to adapt the muscles to use oxygen and glycogen as efficiently as possible and delay the build-up of toxins by delaying the point at which anaerobic muscle function and the production of lactic acid (which creates pain and fatigue) takes place.

Gearing Up For Work

The horse's body is alerted for work by the hormone adrenaline which 'fires up' the whole system and gets him ready to go. At rest, a fit horse's respiration rate is approximately between eight and sixteen breaths per minute. Even the sight of a human with tack will produce adrenaline which begins to hype up the horse, increasing the heart rate and respiration slightly in an initial boost of oxygen and nutrients.

Depending on the horse, his warmed-up rate after walking and trotting before fast work, will be about 60 to 80 breaths per minute (in and out counting as one) which further supplies the muscles with oxygen and nutrients, and during fast work the rate can easily increase to about 120 breaths per minute.

Air flow

Athletic horses need the facility for good air movement in and out. Large nostrils and a wide space between the lower jawbones have been found

Racehorses with a high proportion of fast-twitch fibres will make good sprinters but the leaner, wiry type, like this horse, usually have more slow-twitch fibres and make good middle and long-distance racehorses, steeplechasers and point-to-pointers

to relate to airflow efficiency, reasonably enough, but a point not taken on board by many riders of performance horses is that, when working in fast gaits, the horse needs reasonable freedom of head and neck, otherwise the airflow channel is cramped at the throat, interfering with the intake of oxygen and offloading of carbon dioxide.

Capacity

The many millions of alveoli in the lungs are tiny which creates a vast surface area for gaseous exchange. If you could spread the lung tissue out flat it would cover a football pitch. The following figures may be of interest:

- An at-rest horse will breathe in and out about 6 to 10 litres (23 to 38 gallons) of air per breath, depending on the individual horse's physique.
- The maximum amount of air the horse can move in one breath at peak exertion is about 30 to 40 litres (8 to 11 gallons).
- The respiratory rate can increase about eight-fold at peak exertion.
- The maximum amount of air the lungs can hold after the deepest inhalation is about 42 litres (11 gallons).
- After a deep exhalation, there will still be about 12 litres (3 gallons) of air left in the lungs, and after a normal, at-rest exhalation about 24 litres (6 gallons).
- The peak rate a horse will usually breathe at will be about 120 breaths per minute.

Quarter horses have a high proportion of fast-twitch fibres. Their highly developed musculature is evidence of their ability to sprint and cut cattle – note the completely loose rein

BREATHING IN STEP

In canter and gallop, the horse's respiratory rate is tied to his footfalls, which is another restrictive factor as to how effectively he can breathe. Basically, as his forelegs hit the ground he breathes out and as they leave it and the moment of suspension in the gait occurs, he breathes in. In addition to the muscular action in breathing already explained, two other physical features are involved in this phenomenon.

Firstly, there is the head-and-neck 'balancing pole' or cranio-cervical pendulum created by the head and neck being suspended from the trunk by the strong, elastic *ligamentum nuchae* which extends roughly from the poll to the withers and which, with the help of neck and shoulder muscles, creates an up-and-down, swinging movement in time with the gait.

Secondly is the visceral- or gut-piston effect involving the back-and-forth movement of the abdominal contents, again in time with the gait. Very simply, as the forelegs hit the ground, the head and neck swing down and out, (helping to extend the stride and balance the horse,) and the abdominal contents (mainly the intestines) lurch forwards, pushing against the diaphragm and helping to force air out of the lungs. As the forelegs lift and the suspension phase of the gait occurs, the head and neck swing up and back and the guts shift back, helping the expansion of the chest cavity and the in-rush of air. Some researchers and physiologists in practice have quoted a possible peak respiratory rate of about 180 breaths per minute (obviously higher than the 120 quoted above), dependent on the individual horse's stride rate.

47

Endurance horses have a high proportion of slow-twitch fibres in their long, lean muscles. This type of horse benefits from correct dressage training as well, to encourage proper engagement of the hindquarters and counteract the tendency of the back muscles to become flat and stiff with restricted function

The Nervous System

The horse's nervous system works closely with his endocrine or hormonal system in supplying his 'control centre' or Central Nervous System with information so that it can issue instructions to the body on how to function. This task is obviously essential to the horse's survival and the nervous and endocrine systems work closely to give the horse the near-instantaneous reactions he needs to evade danger and also the slower, longer-lasting processes needed to maintain life in general.

The Somatic Nervous System

The nervous system operates very rapidly and has two main divisions – the Central Nervous System and the Peripheral Nervous System – together called the Somatic Nervous System and responsible mainly for voluntary actions (those under the control of the horse's will). There are three principal roles of the Somatic Nervous System:

HOW IT ALL WORKS

Reacting to pain

If the horse leans against a barbed wire fence or treads on a sharp stone, he receives a stimulus which tells him he is feeling discomfort or pain. The PNS then sends sensory messages about this along the appropriate sensory ('feeling') nerves to the CNS. The CNS assesses the information and sends back instructions along the motor ('action') nerves of the PNS to move the stimulated (painful) part of the body away from the stimulus (the barbed wire or the stone). Result – the horse jumps back from the fence or snatches up his foot.

Reacting to heat

If the horse's skin senses hot surroundings or a rise in the body's internal temperature due to hard work, a fever or hot surroundings, chemical messages go to the CNS via the PNS. The CNS assesses these and sends back instructions to dilate or widen the blood vessels in and just under the skin so that they can carry more blood (which, itself, transports heat) near the surface of the body. This heat can then pass out through the skin and escape, helping to lower the body temperature.

The tiny erector muscles at the base of the hairs will be told to relax and flatten the coat so that the warm-air layer next to the skin is reduced, and the sweat glands will be told to send out heat-containing sweat (liquid) which will evaporate away outside the body, taking heat with it.

- An information, sensory ('feeling') role, being stimulated, through the horse's senses, by conditions inside and outside the body (the weather, a predator, thirst, hunger, pain, irritation, heat, cold etc.). It sends messages – chemical substances and electrical impulses – to the brain and/or spinal cord, informing them of the situation.
- A 'director' role. The Central Nervous System assesses these messages and makes a decision, conscious or otherwise, on what to do about them.
- An 'executive' role. It has a motor or 'action' function, putting any action decided upon into effect. Signals or return messages are sent out to the part of the body concerned, with instructions on how to respond to the stimuli.

The Central Nervous System (CNS)

The Central Nervous System is composed of the brain and the spinal cord. The brain is made of soft, pinkish-grey tissue (hence the expression 'grey matter') and protected by the cranial cavity ('brain case') in the skull; the spinal cord runs from it down the central tunnel formed by the individual bones (vertebrae) of the spine or backbone. The brain and spinal cord consist of nervous tissue which receives information from the body and sends back instructions as to how the body must react.

The Peripheral Nervous System (PNS)

This is a very complex system of cord-like nerves comprising a collection of nerve fibres which transmit impulses between a part of the body and the CNS. The nerves of the PNS run out from the spinal cord, through spaces in the vertebrae, and branch out all over the body.

The PNS is extremely complicated.

- Its sensory function has two types of nerve cells which sense conditions, one type for external conditions and one for internal.
- Its motor or action function has a voluntary section which causes the horse to perform actions of his own free will, such as deciding whether or not to shy at that plastic bag, pass that pig farm, jump that ditch, go for a drink or lie down and have a roll.
- It also has an involuntary section over which the horse has no control, concerning functions such

as the workings of the digestive system, circulatory system, reproductive system and so on. Sometimes this system can be partially over-ridden; for instance, the horse can decide whether or not to hold his breath for any reason, exactly how to breathe when sniffing something, and so on, but generally the involuntary function of the PNS is outside his control.

The Autonomic Nervous System

The involuntary part of the PNS is divided into two more parts – the parasympathetic system and the sympathetic system, together called the Autonomic Nervous System responsible for involuntary processes over which the horse has no control. They work antagonistically against each other.

● The parasympathetic system prepares the body for relaxation and is concerned with obtaining and retaining energy. For example, it slows down the heart and constricts the airways as the horse 'winds down' to rest; it stimulates the horse to feel hungry and eat, and stimulates gut movement (taking in energy), and tells the horse he is tired and should sleep or rest (conserving energy).

● Its opposite number, the sympathetic system, prepares the body for action and is involved with the using up of energy. For instance, it stimulates the horse to flee from a mountain lion or a human carrying tack. It may warn the horse to be alert for danger and on guard rather than eating or resting, to protect, control or discipline a youngster or to respond to its rider's requests to gallop after those hounds or round a cross-country course. It will even control a lazy amble over to the water trough or a casual nip at a fly on the horse's flank. It accelerates the heart and slows down gut movement as blood is diverted to the muscles for work and dilates airways for the intake of more oxygen and the removal of more carbon dioxide.

49

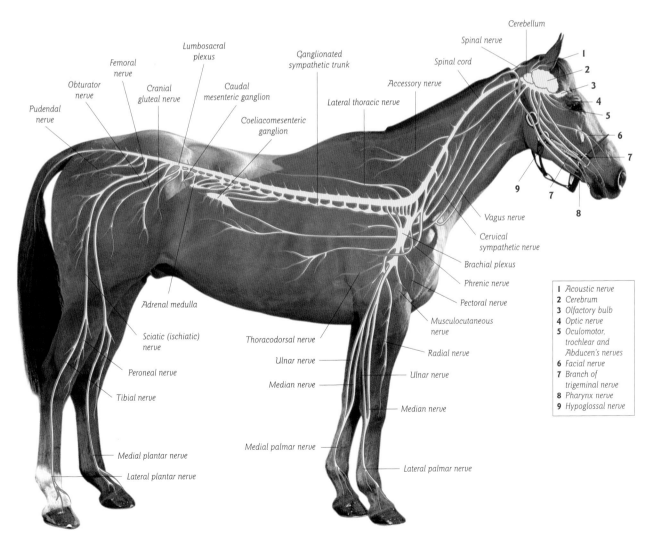

Lumbosacral plexus
Femoral nerve
Obturator nerve
Cranial gluteal nerve
Caudal mesenteric ganglion
Ganglionated sympathetic trunk
Coeliacomesenteric ganglion
Lateral thoracic nerve
Accessory nerve
Spinal cord
Spinal nerve
Cerebellum
Pudendal nerve
Adrenal medulla
Sciatic (ischiatic) nerve
Peroneal nerve
Tibial nerve
Medial plantar nerve
Lateral plantar nerve
Thoracodorsal nerve
Ulnar nerve
Median nerve
Medial palmar nerve
Vagus nerve
Cervical sympathetic nerve
Brachial plexus
Phrenic nerve
Pectoral nerve
Musculocutaneous nerve
Radial nerve
Ulnar nerve
Median nerve
Lateral palmar nerve

1 Acoustic nerve
2 Cerebrum
3 Olfactory bulb
4 Optic nerve
5 Oculomotor, trochlear and Abducen's nerves
6 Facial nerve
7 Branch of trigeminal nerve
8 Pharynx nerve
9 Hypoglossal nerve

The Endocrine System

The endocrine system is one of those vital functions of the horse which is generally out of sight and out of mind as far as most horse owners are concerned. Horse breeders pay more attention to it because it determines when, and whether or not, mares come into season, stallions feel in the mood and, therefore, whether or not their entire enterprise, and maybe their living, is going to succeed or fail, but for most owners it seems of little importance. The endocrine system works with but more slowly than the nervous system and its effects are longer lasting, from minutes in the adrenaline-maintained flight-or-fight response to months or even years in the maturing and ageing process.

Whilst it is the horse's nervous system which senses danger and electrical impulses act almost immediately to tell him to flee, it is his endocrine system with its hormonal messages from the adrenal glands near the kidneys which pump out the adrenaline, keeps up his fear level and keeps him galloping and hyped up for some considerable time after the danger has passed or the exciting situation has ceased. Once the horse is upset, as we all know, he can remain so for not merely the rest of your ride but maybe the rest of the day, according to his temperament.

What Is It?

The endocrine system is one of the systems of control and information: it consists of glands sited at various points in the body which produce hormones, chemical messengers which control the horse's emotions and behaviour (unless he and/or we override

the latter) as well as such processes as maturing and ageing, the reproductive system and the digestive system. There are *many* different hormones, each having its own functions and often working with others to bring about extremely complex chains of events or cycles in the body. A hormonal imbalance, even a slight one, can have mild effects on the horse or can throw out of kilter an entire complex process causing fatal ill-health or simply abnormal behaviour.

Glands

The glands which secrete hormones are termed endocrine or exocrine.

Endocrine glands secrete hormones internally directly into the blood or lymph system for transport around the body to a target area or organ. Some examples are the adrenal glands near the kidneys, the liver, the ovaries and testes, the thyroid gland and the pituitary gland.

Exocrine glands secrete their substances towards the outside of the body and include the mammary glands in the udder, and the sweat, sebaceous, tear and salivary glands.

The pituitary gland and hypothalamus

The pituitary gland is called the master endocrine gland because it controls other endocrine glands. It itself is controlled by a small but crucially important part of the brain called the hypothalamus to which it is connected by a stalk. The different centres of the hypothalamus have many functions, both somatic and autonomic; it secretes various hormones itself, including those called releasing and inhibiting factors which induce or prevent other hormonal processes.

An Example

A good example, familiar to many owners, of how hormones affect and control a horse, in this case on a cyclical basis, is the mare's oestrus cycle or seasons. Precise noting of the stages involved in this cycle are vital to breeders, but many non-breeders also are only too aware of it.

This being 'in season' business often irritates owners: horse magazines in spring, summer and autumn regularly feature letters from mare owners wanting to know how they can stop their mares being 'difficult' and 'naughty' for a few days every three weeks (when in season) throughout the most active riding months of the year for most people. A vet friend of mine replied to such a query in one

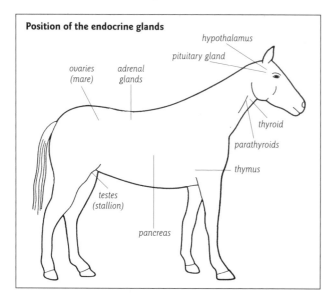

Position of the endocrine glands

hypothalamus
pituitary gland
ovaries (mare)
adrenal glands
thyroid
parathyroids
thymus
testes (stallion)
pancreas

The old saying 'you discuss matters with a stallion, you ask a mare and you tell a gelding' is often overlooked by mare owners. Sensitivity and tact are needed to cope with some in-season mares

magazine: 'If you can't stand mareish behaviour, buy a gelding!' Such owners do not realise the irresistible effects of the hormones responsible or that the mare is not being difficult or naughty but simply the female that nature made her. So in the interests of understanding and empathy, let's see how it works.

The oestrus cycle

It is spring or summer. The mare has had about seventeen days of normal behaviour, in other words non-oestrus behaviour – she has not been in season during that time. In order to bring her to that heady state again, the pituitary gland releases follicle stimulating hormone (FSH). (A follicle is a fluid-filled sac which develops round an egg in the ovary.) FSH acts on the ovaries to stimulate several follicles to enlarge and produce the hormone oestrogen. It is oestrogen which brings the mare into season with all the accompanying soppiness, kicking, squealing, tail-raising, vulva-winking, urinating and outrageous flirting with any horse, animal or human in the danger zone. Broodmares usually stand gladly for the stallion towards the end of this period. But if your mare is not a broodmare – tough – she'll still fall in lust with any substitute.

The oestrogen produces a negative feedback on the pituitary which produces less FSH but, as oestrogen levels rise, releases instead luteinising hormone (LH) which causes one follicle to mature and the egg to be released. Ovulation has occurred.

A corpus luteum or yellow body forms in the site of the ruptured follicle and secretes the hormone progesterone which, after about five giddy days, causes your brazen hussy to come to her senses and go out of season. Woe betide any stallion who tries it on with her now! Progesterone is known as 'the pregnancy hormone' and stops the mare coming into season. The owner can breathe again.

If the mare was served towards the end of her season, fertilisation of the egg by the stallion's sperm may occur and pregnancy ensue. Otherwise, her uterus, recognising that there is no fertilised egg inside it, will secrete the hormone prostaglandin F2α (PgF2α) which tells the corpus luteum to stop producing progesterone so that everyone can have another go at getting the mare pregnant. Out of work, the corpus luteum withers and 'dies' (regresses) there are no visible follicles developing in the ovary and the secretion of progesterone ceases. This allows the pituitary gland to once again start producing FSH, the whole cycle restarts and your mare once again becomes anybody's. It takes about twenty-one or twenty-two days from beginning to end.

If you think this is complicated (and it is, though elegantly devised), consider the complexity of the hormonal control of digestion, pregnancy, lactation, sleeping and waking, fleeing or relaxing, developing from fertilised egg to elderly horse and the many other intricately linked functions going on in the horse's body all the time. That's quite an animal you have there.

51

OESTRUS CYCLE

Length of oestrus cycle	days	21±2	Depends markedly upon body condition
Duration of oestrus period	days	6±3	Varies according to time of year
Length of dioestrus period	days	15±5	As above
Ovulation	hours	48±12	Before the end of the oestrus period
Optimum time before covering period	hours	48±12	In the period 48 hours before the end of oestrus up to the end of oestrus
Gestation period	months	11±1	Varies considerably between mares, but each individual is generally much the same from year to year
Foal heat	starts	8±3	Days post foaling. Not always evident but often causes diarrhoea in foal

Table courtesy Tony Pavord

The Common Integument

The title of this section is the name given to the skin, hair and horn combined. Integument means husk or covering and although the expression relates mainly to the skin, the hair and horn are obviously involved. Between them, they cover and protect almost the entire body apart from the eyes (and even these have eyelids for the job).

Skin, hair and horn are all 'related' by being made mainly from a hardened, fibrous protein called keratin although in the case of skin the keratinised layer is just the outer, insensitive layer which flakes off. Feed supplements abound which claim to improve the quality of, in particular, hoof horn and users of those that work notice that their horse's hair – and skin if they look that far – are also in tip-top condition. Nutrients which benefit one benefit all.

Skin – the multi-purpose protector

The skin forms an elastic, tensioned protective covering for the sensitive tissues underneath. It is essential to the regulation of body temperature, excretes waste products in the sweat and provides information by means of nerve endings which sense pressure, pain, heat and cold. It can repair itself, is important in the formation of vitamin D when exposed to sunlight, protects the body from toxins, pathogens, excess moisture or dryness and minor injuries.

The dermis contains the sweat glands, oil glands which secrete sebum to lubricate skin and coat, the nerve endings, hair follicles and a capillary network. It also contains the colouring agent, melanin, which has a practical, strengthening effect on the skin, making coloured skin less sensitive than pink (non-coloured) skin to sunburn, mud fever, parasites and allergies.

Skin has two main layers, the outer layer called the epidermis and the sensitive under layer called the dermis. The outer layer constantly wears away or flakes off and forms the dandruff in a horse's coat and at the roots of the mane and tail. Live cells from the dermis replace them and are constantly being formed, most effectively in the young horse. In older horses (and humans!), skin loses its elasticity and body due to the gradual breakdown of two proteins called elastin and

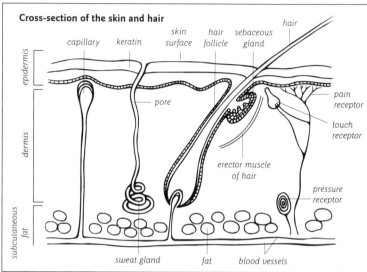

Cross-section of the skin and hair

epidermis

dermis

subcutaneous fat

capillary | keratin | skin surface | hair follicle | sebaceous gland | hair

pore

pain receptor

touch receptor

erector muscle of hair

pressure receptor

sweat gland | fat | blood vessels

collagen which give the skin its resilience, elasticity and 'tone'.

However, the horse doesn't appear to suffer from wrinkles!

Skin is generally thicker over the top half of the body to protect against the elements and thinner on the underparts and legs where more sensitivity is needed. It is also true that pony and cold-blooded types have thicker skin than hot-bloods – overall a range of from about 6mm (almost ¼in) to 1mm (⅟₂₀in) can be found in different breeds.

A short, smooth summer coat can help make a horse look his best. This Thoroughbred has a very short coat. 'Cold-blooded' types will always have a slightly longer coat even in summer

The almost furry winter coat of breeds whose ancestors evolved in cold climes offers excellent protection against their environment

The Coat

The hair of the horse's coat, mane (including the forelock) and tail can certainly be his crowning glory or make him look totally tattered. Foals can look particularly comical when their baby fuzz is coming out, often leaving them with smooth 'spectacles' round the eyes and odd patches of fuzz and grown-up coat.

Domestication has brought many varied colours from the primeval dun/yellow/brown colours evolved for camouflage. The white stallion of Hollywood tradition would not stand much chance in the wild where he would stand out to predators like a sore thumb.

The coat protects the skin from grazes, insect attacks to some extent and the weather. It casts (moults) in spring and autumn according to the climate and day length – long, warm or hot days need a short coat but short, cold ones need a longer, thicker coat.

Built-in blanket

The hair provides a neat insulation system. The roots in the dermis each have a tiny erector muscle which contracts to pull the hair outwards when the horse feels cold and relaxes to allow it to flatten when he warms up. In addition, hairs are hollow. This dual quality creates an adjustable, warm-air layer next to the skin particularly effective in winter due to the greater overlap of the longer hairs, creating a thick, high-tog duvet. Some really cold-climate breeds have a soft, almost furry underlayer as well. Although prolonged rain can flatten this layer, breeds meant for that kind of climate seem to cope. In addition, the long hair, called 'feather', on their lower legs protects against cold and wet.

The mane and tail hair do not cast like the body hair although they come out easier at casting times. They are long and flexible, protective and

CHESTNUTS AND ERGOTS

The horny chestnuts on the insides of the legs are believed to be a remnant of a toe in ancestral types, but there are none on the outsides and no signs of a former bone under them. They have a distinctive smell often useful to rub on your hands if you want to take a horse's mind off something.

The ergot, the little horny lump on the point of the fetlock, is also thought to be vestigial hoof horn, again without evidence.

Both chestnuts and ergots can often be peeled off to keep them short but in some animals they are tough, grow long and have to be clipped or cut off, often by the farrier.

particularly helpful to swish against insects at ' fly-time'. Their quality varies from wiry, wavy and very tough to fine and almost silky, in cold-blooded/pony types and hot-bloods respectively.

An important type of hair frequently overlooked, indeed purposely removed, is the whiskers or vibrissae round muzzle and eyes. These perform important sensory functions and it is sad that many people persist in clipping them off for supposed neatness whereas horses so treated simply look deprived. Fortunately, some enlightened, humane breed societies now insist that animals be shown with whiskers intact.

Horn

Obviously crucial to the health, work potential and comfort of the horse, the hoof horn protects the sensitive structures of the complicated foot structure inside the casing it forms. It grows down in tubules from the coronary band above it like our nails from their cuticles, an injury to the coronet often producing cracked or grooved horn, maybe permanently.

It takes a hoof wall about a year to grow down from coronet to ground at the toe, less at the heels. The horn is thickest at the toe, gradually thinning towards the heels. The sole and frog also consist of horn, thinner and more rubbery respectively. The whole wall is protected by a thin varnish-like layer which extends about two-thirds of the way down the hoof. Horn is slightly permeable to air and moisture, helping to create a healthy horn consistency; obviously, the application of ordinary hoof oil, fortunately now understood to be detrimental, destroys this quality.

Hearing

It is likely that the horse's sense of hearing, above all others, is responsible for much of the 'strange', unexplained behaviour horses are sometimes prone to. Apart from having a sense of hearing vastly improved upon our own, they rely on it much more than we do and, being natural prey animals, react to what they hear. If we cannot even hear what they are hearing, let alone put an equine interpretation on the sounds we can both hear, how can we possibly understand or judge what seems on the surface like untoward behaviour?

Structure and Function

The most obvious part of the ear is the outer ear, funnel part or pinna, made of cartilage, which the horse can move almost 180° from front to back. In addition, because of the great mobility of his head and neck, he can easily hear (and see) all around him without moving a foot – a great survival feature. The outer ear runs down as far as the ear drum or tympanic membrane which seals off the outer ear and receives the soundwaves funnelled down to it by the pinna.

The middle ear, begins with an air-filled cavity behind the ear drum containing three small bones, firstly the hammer (malleus), then the anvil (incus) and finally the stirrup (stapes). The hammer touches the eardrum and transmits the soundwaves vibrating it to the anvil and finally the stirrup which, in turn, vibrates against one of two membrane-covered windows between the middle and inner ear, which is actually inside the skull.

Inside the inner ear are fluid-filled tubes – a curled structure called the cochlea concerned with hearing and three semi-circular canals, set at three-dimensional angles to each other, concerned with balance. Sound waves can pass through air, fluid and solids and the vibrations of the stapes against the window set the fluids moving. The cochlea detects this by means of sensitive hairs and nerve impulses are sent to the brain for assessment. This all happens in a mini-fraction of a second.

Practical Implications

We know horses can pick up soundwaves from a much greater distance than humans, and can also hear at frequencies much higher and lower. This obviously means their information bank is constantly bombarded with all sorts of input we don't even know exists.

Some years ago, a major point of interest to members of The Equine Behaviour Forum (see Useful Addresses) was that of tonic or catatonic immobility. Behaviourists normally state quite categorically that this state is one of paralysed fear, of the horse being rooted to the spot totally unable to move. This is not the condition EBF members noted. They all, without exception, described a condition where their horses were certainly rooted to the spot and extremely alert, but calm with ears pricked to the distance, eyes gazing afar off as if receiving something from another dimension and obviously quite in control of their faculties, but no matter what the humans did nothing but nothing

Horses can hear sounds above and below our range despite all land mammals having similar auditory equipment. Feral horses rely greatly on their ability to pick up sounds from several miles away and make good use of the horse's ability to turn each outer ear

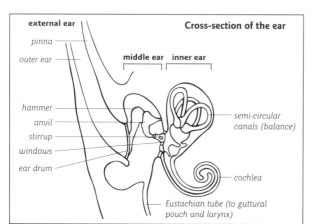

external ear

Cross-section of the ear

pinna

outer ear

middle ear   **inner ear**

hammer

anvil

stirrup

windows

ear drum

semi-circular canals (balance)

cochlea

Eustachian tube (to guttural pouch and larynx)

could shift the horses till they decided to move. They were oblivious to everything else. Eventually, they snapped out of it and went on, unconcerned, as if nothing had happened.

Extra-sensory perception was the most fancied explanation among members for this phenomenon – where they ventured an explanation, and it was interesting that the scientist members did not – but I feel sure (it happened regularly to my Anglo-Arab gelding) that such horses are hearing something fascinating which we cannot pick up, and simply ignore us till they are satisfied. Readers are welcome to write to the EBF on the matter.

Noise pollution

Horses are certainly highly susceptible to noise and, contrary to popular opinion, most do not like radios constantly playing in stable yards. (There is

always the odd exception.) Loud, heavy music, from rock to Wagner, greatly upsets most horses but short spells of soft, soothing music calms them down. And horses living in noisy environments, depending on their temperaments, are known to be more stressed than those living in quieter places. Aircraft noise is almost certainly responsible for abortion in mares living beneath flight paths or near airports.

All this must be quite understandable when we consider the much greater amount of aural information bombarding the horse's brain compared with our own. Anything we can do to reduce all noise to a minimum must help them. Shouting has long been regarded as the sign of a rank amateur, as has babbling.

Many owners report problems on windy days. 'It's the wind under his tail', some say! It is much more likely to be the fact that the wind is bringing even more sounds to his ears and, what is worse, is distorting them so the horse not only does not

MAKING SOUND WORK

Apart from trying to maintain a reasonably quiet environment for horses, the old ploy of stuffing cotton wool in the horses' ears during times of unavoidable noise can help a lot.

When speaking to horses, it's best to keep the tone and level of the voice down as well as keeping to a set vocabulary of short, easily-recognised noises (words) which the horse can readily associate with whatever you want him to do and how you are feeling (pleased or cross). It is important to be consistent in the exact way the words are said, too. Horses differentiate minutely between sounds and even giving a request in a different accent from the one the horse is used to can result in confusion, doubt and sometimes fear as the horse, being anxious to please, may worry about what you are asking.

Other sounds are readily recognised, such as the feed-room door, buckets, car engines, rustling tit-bit bags, polythene bales being split open, different people's voices and so on. Horses pay much more attention to their sound environment than we do and it's as well to try hard to look at (or listen to) things from how the horse is perceiving them and to try to understand the effect it could all be having on his state of mind and behaviour.

know where they are coming from but is worried by the warped unfamiliarity of all this extra information. No wonder he flips!

Imported horses are quick to learn new accents and languages: of course, verbal commands are just sounds to them with no meaning till they begin to associate them with a particular action or happening.

Undue noise during travelling is also probably responsible for much of the so-called bad behaviour of horses during this stressful process. Rattling horseboxes and trailers, engine noise, doors and ramp slamming shut, the cab radio and the altered soundwaves inside the vehicle are all upsetting to many horses. Tree branches scraping the vehicle can be particularly terrifying and not often considered.

Sight

If we woke up one morning with the vision of a horse – the focusing technique, the visual field and the colour perception – we'd probably think we were hallucinating!

The horse's eyes are placed like those of a prey animal: his head is long to accommodate grass-grinding teeth and the eyes are placed high up on it to front and sides so, with his head down eating, his eyes are raised above the ground and so placed that he can see almost all round him. To obtain 360° vision, he only has to turn his head slightly, not even his neck. His natural grazing motion, with the head moving repeatedly from side to side, and the minor obstruction created by his thin legs, means that he surveys the full circle around him every few seconds – another brilliant survival mechanism.

Structure and Function

Images enter the eye because of light rays reflecting off objects in view entering the pupil: horses can see in the dark better than we can despite their eyes taking longer to adjust, but no creature can see in total darkness. The rays pass through the lens and are focused – upside down – on a sheet of nerve cells called the retina at the back of the eye. The optic nerve transmits the images to the brain for reversal and assessment.

The horse's eye is slightly flattened from front to back. The tough, white, outer layer is the sclera, made of connective tissue and cartilage. The next layer is the choroid, its generous blood supply nourishing the eye. It contains an iridescent, light-reflecting layer called the choroid tapetum or tapetum lucidum, common to nocturnal animals, which reflects light back on to the retina, making double use of it. The final layer is the retina at the back of the eye. At the front of the eye, there is a hole in the eye wall, sealed by the clear, very sensitive cornea. The edges of the lens are obscured by the coloured iris surrounding the pupil. The iris contains muscles allowing it to enlarge or diminish the pupil to let in or exclude light, according to external conditions. In bright light, the pupil is

drawn horizontally narrow and in dim light it is larger and more nearly circular. On the upper edge of the iris above the pupil can be seen what some owners worry are growths, brown bodies or corpora nigra which are part of the pigment material of the iris and which are believed to act as built-in sunshades for this outdoor animal.

Behind the iris, the choroid extends and thickens into the ciliary body made of muscle and

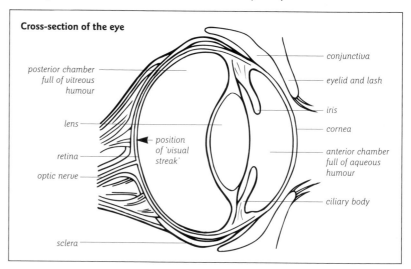

Cross-section of the eye

posterior chamber full of vitreous humour

lens

position of 'visual streak'

retina

optic nerve

sclera

conjunctiva

eyelid and lash

iris

cornea

anterior chamber full of aqueous humour

ciliary body

processes which provide attachment for ligaments supporting the lens. The muscles change the shape of the lens which helps the horse clearly to focus incoming light rays on to the retina. This structure divides the eye into front and back chambers – the part in front of the lens is filled with a watery fluid called aqueous humour and the part behind with a more jelly-like substance called vitreous humour.

Now We Know Better!

There are traditional beliefs which recent research has scotched, about the horse's ability to focus on objects near and far and about his ability to see in colour, although the latter topic is still a subject of uncertainty.

The rampless retina of the horse

Most horse enthusiasts have heard of the ramp(ed) retina theory. This says that the lower part of the back of the eye is flatter than the upper part so the lower part of the retina is nearer the lens than the top part – in other words, ramped. This is believed to be why the horse has to alter the position of his head to focus on near or distant objects, so that the

56

light rays will fall on the appropriate part of the retina.

When focusing on close objects, the horse arches his neck, draws in his muzzle and tilts his head on one side. For distant objects, he raises his head and extends his muzzle. Researchers in Australia have found that the bottom part of the retina is only 1mm closer to the lens than the upper part which would make a minimal difference to focusing ability. They also found that the horse has a very wide but vertically narrow, intense horizontal strip of high cell density in the lower part of the retina, called the visual streak, meaning it sees in a very wide, narrow field unlike our small, round one. The horse can, by moving his eyes and head as described earlier, see all round him within this field. The visual acuity ('sharpness') outside the streak is not good so the researchers believed it 'completely unlikely' that the horse would tilt his head to use very low acuity retina: instead, he may be doing so to fix on a close object and bring it within the visual streak.

Binocular vision

The researchers also found that the binocular overlap used for distance vision is about 100° (wider than believed) but is directed down the nose towards the ground with a blind area straight ahead. So, the horse has to raise his head high and point his nose up and forwards to point the binocular field forwards to see distant objects – like predators or jumps. If the rider 'takes a firm contact' and brings in the nose, or rides 'on the bit', he is purposely, if unintentionally, depriving the horse of forward vision – not a good idea, especially when the horse has to assess an obstacle over which he is expected to jump safely!

Colour

Everyone used to 'know' that horses were colour blind and some still think so. There are several studies going on in this area which suggest that horses do see colour but maybe not in the way we see it. Studies in America and Scotland suggest that horses can see red and orange well, yellow poorly, green as white

(imagine white grass) and blue and purple well. 'Ordinary' horse owners are often poorly regarded as sources of hard evidence by the scientific community which tends to disregard their observations as 'anecdotal evidence' and, because not scientifically proven, not to be taken seriously (which does not mean they are inaccurate, of course).

The more open minded are interested and might try to find out why, then, horses often balk at yellow objects and vehicles, including yellow, but not white, road lines, also why different horses react to different colours, why bright colours and shiny objects (including water) elicit the strongest reactions and why horses also react strongly to sharp contrasts such as black and white. These features of equine colour vision were clear from many questionnaires completed for Carol Hall, an Equine Behaviour Forum member researching the topic, and are known to many owners.

Fortunately, the horse still holds many mysteries for us yet to solve.

Horses with a pale, blue-ish iris are called 'wall-eyed'. They do not necessarily have worse eyesight than horses with brown eyes. Usually, only one eye is affected

Smell

The sense of smell, as with most other things about the horse, is much better developed than our own which is another survival mechanism enabling early detection of predators – who, therefore, soon learn to approach from upwind.

It is said that a stallion can easily smell a mare in season from a mile or more away if the wind is in the right direction and from about 200 yards or metres on a still day. Racing yards which habitually have mixed groups of horses normally arrange their work strings with entire colts in front, then either geldings or females not in season, with in-season mares and fillies bringing up the rear. This does not entirely solve the problem of sexually distracted colts but helps a little, at least!

Structure and Function of Olfactory System

The nostrils are very mobile in the horse, able to change from slits to round, wide openings. They lead to nasal passages in the head which contain tightly coiled bones (turbinate bones) covered in moist mucous membrane well supplied with blood. These coils increase the surface area for detecting odours: there are olfactory nerve cells in the mucous membrane each covered in tiny hair-like projections containing the actual sensory cells that detect smell.

Odours are physical things. They consist of minute particles of varying sizes which land on the moist mucous membranes in the nasal passages and dissolve in the fluid environment. The sensory cells can then assess the type of smell involved and pass an appropriate message to the central nervous system, which will tell the horse whether or not it is interesting, frightening, acceptable or otherwise.

Practical Implications

As with the sense of hearing, we should not be too quick to condemn horses who seem to be behaving strangely for no apparent reason but who are really receiving some important smell and, obeying their survival instinct, investigating it and where it could be coming from. It is usually fairly clear from the horse's exact posture and actions what is going on. Snorting and blowing, a raised head and flared nostrils all indicate the sense of smell (as well as others) being brought into play in an information-gathering exercise.

Feeding

Changing feeds over gradually is good practice to accustom the digestive system to it but also because if we introduce something completely strange-smelling the horse may not eat it. It is obvious that horses do not find attractive the same smells as we do (which is why the more fastidious often refuse supplements smelling strongly of herbs, much to their owners' dismay). It is a case of trial and error as far as smell and also taste are concerned with such horses.

Even good eaters usually have the sense to refuse food that is 'off' but you cannot rely on this. When

FLEHMEN HORSES!

To make the process even more definitive, there is an organ known as the vomeronasal organ or Jacobson's organ, in the form of a longish sac, towards the top of the nasal passages, which horses use to investigate any particularly unfamiliar or intriguing smell. It is a familiar sight to see horses extending their noses upwards and curling their top lips and it always makes observers smile. Of course, the horse is not trying to entertain us but to savour even more closely some particular smell, perhaps something someone has offered him, a new hairspray or feed or the smell of a new horse in the yard on a groom's hands or clothes. The horse sniffs in the smell, raises his head and curls up his top lip. This closes off the nostrils, at least partially, to avoid interference from other smells coming in, giving him a chance to let his Jacobson's organ fully assess the smell he is interested in. The horse may do this two or three times before he is satisfied with his new information.

grazing, horses very selectively pick out plants they want. Many believe they have a self-medication ability and although they may have nutritional intuition it is not foolproof as shown by the number who eat poisonous plants.

Identification

Horses living together develop a 'herd smell' composed of all their individual scents mixed together. The field rolling patch is covered in this smell and they all use it as a bonding process. When a new horse is introduced, therefore, his unfamiliar smell will certainly create some initial squealing if you are lucky, but maybe kicking and biting as well. This is natural, instinctive behaviour, and why newcomers must be introduced carefully and to the most accepting existing herd members first.

Marking territory with droppings and urine is also connected with smell. Stallions or the many geldings who show stallion-like behaviour often dung on top of each other's droppings or urine patches, or those of favoured companions, mares in season and so on, to demonstrate 'ownership'. Horses nearly always stale on fresh bedding for this reason.

Although horses greet each other with nostril-to-nostril blowing and sniffing (almost always followed by a squeal and maybe a strike-out, too), humans

Equines set great store on others' body smells which they use in individual recognition and, in stallions, to gauge a mare's likely receptivity to mating attempts

who try this often end up with 'facial surgery' or at least seeing stars. There is obviously a right and wrong way to do it and the horse, sensing their inadequacy, takes the natural rejecting or dominating action with his teeth.

Breeding

The pheromones (smells) given off by mares and stallions in and out of breeding condition change accordingly. The stallion is best-qualified to decide, through smelling her, when a mare is just ready to mate: when she 'goes off', her pheromones change and he is no longer so interested. And she certainly isn't no matter how sexy he smells.

Individual smells are also vitally important between mare and foal for the essential bonding process which will determine, in the wild, whether the foal is accepted and lives or rejected and dies. A bereaved mare may be eventually induced to accept a foster foal if it is covered in her dead foal's familiar-smelling skin. Sometimes, a little strong-smelling substance such as an anti-congestant nasal ointment (Vick, UK) is smeared in her nostrils to confuse her and disguise the smell of the new foal coming through.

Taste

Partnered by the sense of smell, the horse's sense of taste plays a great role in generally keeping him safe from harm in the form of toxic substances he may wish to experiment with or actually eat. However, as pointed out in the section on smell, it is not foolproof and horses do eat poisonous things (not only actual food) with serious or fatal results.

Structure and Function

The horse senses taste by means of tiny projections or papillae of sensitive tissue, his 'taste buds', mainly in the tongue but also in the throat and on the palate.

The taste of a substance or object is sensed by the nervous receptor cells in the taste buds which have hair-like projections just protruding through pores in a membrane covering the tongue and, therefore, in direct contact with whatever he takes into his mouth. Nerve fibres then send this information to the gustatory or taste centre in the brain for assessment, and information flies back, telling the horse whether the taste is sweet or salty (both of which horses like) or bitter or sour (which they don't) or a combination of these four tastes between which horses can discriminate.

Practical Implications

Horses' salivary glands are not stimulated by the anticipation of food or by, for example, familiar sounds connected with preparing food. True, horses

Horses and ponies first investigate anything new by sight, then by smell

60

become excited at the sound of the feed-room door, the buckets and the sight of feeds, hay or haylage being brought round, but saliva is only secreted in significant amounts when the taste buds are actually stimulated by the taste of the food.

Feeding

Like smell, taste is best distinguished in a moist environment and although the inside of the mouth is usually moist, damp feeds are more comfortable and pleasant for the horse to eat and probably tastier than dry foods, although horses will obviously eat dry foods. Their natural food, vegetation, is rarely dry but has a fair water content so the old idea of not damping food because it dilutes the saliva and inhibits digestion does not hold water. (The saliva does no actual digesting; it is alkaline and simply softens the food making it easier for the teeth to chomp it up ready for digestion to begin in the stomach.)

Because horses are known to have a sweet tooth, commercially compounded feeds usually contain a fair degree of a sweet syrup, often molasses, to tempt horses to eat them and, it follows, their owners to buy more; but nutritionists encouraged us all not to feed too much refined (as opposed to raw) sugar. It was as bad for horses, and their teeth, as for us, they said, and is not a natural food for horses.

True enough, so many commercial feeds now contain far fewer gooey additives like molasses and more palatable light oils and syrups. A little extra sweetness, though, goes a long way towards disguising anything unpleasant, such as worming granules or phenylbutazone powders (although you can get rid of the bitter taste of 'bute by keeping the powders in the fridge or freezer).

The titbits most owners give their horses are sweet and mints seem by far the favourite although most horses seem to like chocolate, too. Competition horse owners, however, have to be careful that their horses are not given anything containing menthol (some mints) or caffeine (all chocolate) as these are prohibited substances even though you would have to feed an awful lot to stimulate the performance of an animal as big as a horse.

Electrolytes, so beloved of competition horse owners but often not their horses, are mineral salts and, therefore, taste salty. Horses usually sense when they need them but those who consistently refuse them can be given restorative minerals by offering them the water in which sugar beet pulp has been soaked, maybe with commercial electrolytes added. This water is a sweet-tasting source of such minerals and widely under-estimated as such. Soaked sugar beet added to feeds is a fair taste-disguiser of 'doctored' feeds, too.

POISONOUS PLANTS

We are told that most of these taste bitter. Presumably the chemists have found this out because few of us want to try them. In any case, because the sense of taste is species specific (what human likes the taste of grass, yet horses go mad for it?), perhaps we can never really know how the horse perceives what we believe to be bitter.

Most well-fed horses and ponies will not experiment with poisonous things: this usually only happens when horses are extremely hungry. Sadly, though, a few do develop an acquired taste for presumably nasty-tasting plants, some of which, like ragwort, can kill them fairly slowly and others, like yew, within seconds.

Breeding

One of the most natural things for a stallion to want to do is lick all around his potential mate's vulva, absorbing not only her inviting pheromones but the taste of her. He will then usually perform the flehmen action. This all helps the bonding between the two (something which is unfortunately denied to many mares and stallions today) and, therefore, the mating process. Wild mating *equidae* are seen to spend long periods of time touching, smelling and licking each other which shows how important it is to them.

Like the sense of smell, the sense of taste plays an important role in bonding between mare and foal. The mare licks the foal dry and frequently licks him as he matures, as a familiarity-enhancer, an expression of affection and of bonding. The foal soon absorbs the taste of his dam's teats and milk which helps him recognise her, although he will drink from any mare who lets him. Few will, though.

Touch

It is sometimes difficult for animals like us, who are manually-orientated, to understand that other animals' senses of touch are as important to them as ours is to us or as well developed. The horse's equivalent to our hands and fingers is his muzzle. This area is extremely well-supplied with nerve endings, the skin is very thin, the mouth and nose, and so the senses of smell and taste, are here and the whole apparatus is greatly assisted by the presence of the antennae whiskers or vibrissae (which grow around the eyes, too) which have extremely sensitive root areas to warn the horse, mainly in the dark, of what is immediately near his vital head.

Structure and Function of Nerves

The sense of touch obviously depends on the nerves which sense stimuli such as touch, pressure pain, heat and cold transmitting messages from one part of the horse to another. Nervous tissue consists of cells called neurones which form a network of nerves connecting each part to another, all around the body.

Neurones have a cell body with a nucleus and two or more processes or appendages which may be very short (dendrites) which carry messages towards the cell body and typically branch out in tree-like processes or longer than a metre (axons) which carry messages away from the cell body and which branch at their ends, as dendrites, to form synapses – tiny gaps or junctions – with other nervous tissue or body parts.

Imagine you have touched your horse on the side whilst grooming to ask him to move over. The dendrites in his skin sense the pressure and an electrical impulse (message) is sent to the cell body. Another impulse is passed from the cell body along the axon. At the synapse, the impulse is converted to a chemical neuro-transmitter released at the end of the axon which diffuses across the synapse and

LEFT A BIT, RIGHT A BIT, AAAHHH!

Touch can obviously be as enjoyable to the horse as it can be torture. Horses habitually 'mutual groom' each other along the neck, withers and back and derive great pleasure from it. It can be just as enjoyable when a human does it, provided it is done properly, and you will soon get to know where the horse wants rubbing or scratching as he moves under your hand or points with his muzzle to an itchy place.

Horses exhibit pleasure from touch by raising their muzzles, and tensing and twitching their top lips with half closed eyes. You'll know you've got the right spot when they do this!

Horses' skins are very sensitive. The muzzle is particularly sensitive and used to investigate objects which the horse cannot see, being directly below his head

attaches to receptors on the neighbouring dendrite. This sets up another electrical impulse – and messages are passed around the body, to and fro. Your horse 'gets the message' and is told by motor nerves passing information messages back, that you are pressing or touching his side. Note that they don't tell him to move over. Your training means he associates a touch on this spot with your desire for him to move over. Whether or not he does so is up to him because this is a somatic function (remember this from The Nervous System) which his will can override.

'White noise'

The problem with us and our schooling and training methods is that we often stimulate the horse's dendrites in ways which lessen their sensitivity. Nerve endings can, after a few stimulations in rapid succession, such as kicks in the ribs, yanks on the bit or thumps on the neck or quarters prior to an injection, 'tire' or 'deaden'. They do not respond so well or so quickly and so the horse becomes less conscious of the stimulus.

Riders who ride with their legs constantly pressing or rubbing against the horse's sides, sometimes to the extent that they wear bald patches in his coat, or keep up a bit contact of several pounds or even kilos of pressure which deaden the nerves in his bars, cannot expect to have horses with light sides or mouths who are sensitive and a pleasure to ride. And the horses doubtless get even less pleasure from the experience.

The injection, however, will be less painful. The vet's thumping two or three times before pushing in the needle will mean that the dendrites have

Rolling is extremely important to horses who obviously derive great pleasure from it. Giving the back a good scratch is only one of its functions

already discharged and received several times and need a little time to recharge and restore their previous sensitivity. Of course, the feeling does not go entirely except in the case of nerve damage, but the process is less effective.

Inner feelings

There is an inner sense of feel which senses pain and discomfort, hunger, thirst, lameness or illness. The horse also 'feels' the need to urinate, defecate, mate, move around, roll, lie down and get up. Sensory nerves detect swelling which causes pressure on and stretching of nerve endings. The sensory function also tells a horse when he has what we call colic but he cannot describe the exact type of feeling he has and we can only diagnose it by careful observation of how he responds to his feelings and physical signs like the passing of droppings and so on.

THE MESSAGE IN THE EARTH

If you are in the habit of watching Western films, you will at some point see someone, usually a scout or tracker, put his (it's always men) ear to the ground (a metaphorical practice useful in commercial and professional networking!) to feel the vibrations or even hear the soundwaves created by galloping horses' hooves. Horses are said to be able to feel such vibrations through their feet and legs and can even feel when someone or some horse colleague is approaching from the rear. Some people say their horses do this all the time. Maybe I've been unlucky with mine!

Body Temperature

The horse's body is made to function within a fairly narrow range of temperature, his norm being about 38°C or 100.4°F, always taken in the rectum. The 'shell' temperature of the skin and extremities is lower than the rectal temperature, easily rising and falling which helps keep the 'core' temperature constant. Although a rise to about 41°C or 105°F is normal during strenuous exercise, a rise at other times of only one degree Celsius or two degrees Fahrenheit, or less, is cause for concern.

The two main groups of animals are homoeotherms (warm-blooded animals like mammals and birds) and poikilotherms (cold-blooded ones such as fish, amphibians and reptiles).

Homoeotherms

Homoeotherms (the group into which horses fall) can keep their temperature constant by generating heat via the body's metabolism, to balance the heat loss to the environment. Heat moves from a warm object to a colder one which is why it is easier to warm our bodies up than to cool them down. Homoeotherms must eat to provide enough energy to create heat to balance that lost and so keep their temperatures steady, the need

normally being to keep the temperature up rather than lower it.

Heat regulation

Heat regulation is one of the functions of the hypothalamus in the brain: it involves balancing the body's heat loss and gain mainly by the regulation of respiration, skin temperature and sweating. Some heat is lost through exhalation and the passing of urine and droppings, but the skin is the main means of losing heat. As blood passes through the hypothalamus, its temperature is sensed and messages are sent out to regulate it as needed, by various means.

The animal's body type is a great help in this: horses whose ancestors evolved in cold climates have different physical features from those evolving in hot climates. They have thicker skin (with an insulating fat layer beneath) to prevent heat from the blood vessels escaping too easily, thicker, longer coats which increase the warm-air layer, big heads with narrow nostrils and long nasal passages to warm incoming cold air and they do not sweat readily. Their bodies are rounder as it is more difficult for heat to escape from this shape than from a thinner object, the legs are shorter to reduce cold-air flow around the body and, for the same reason, their thick tails are held low to protect the thin-skinned area between the buttocks.

Animals from hot regions are just the opposite with short heads, flaring nostrils, long, fine necks, oval-shaped bodies and long legs. Their skin is thinner with blood vessels nearer the surface so they can readily dilate and let out more heat. They sweat readily so heat can be lost as the hot sweat evaporates. Their coats are shorter and finer and the mane and tail hair sparse and fine, with the tails held out from the body.

These features help horses and ponies to respectively retain heat well or lose it effectively – but they do not explain why so-called cold- and hot-blooded horses often have temperaments to match their physical type. Has anyone any ideas?

A feral pony in the New Forest in England. There is plenty of shelter here but the ponies often go short of food, which is essential for them to keep up their body temperature

A Horse's Year

The whole of a horse's biological life is geared to the survival of the species. Nature is unconcerned with our plans: she will carry on regardless of what we want, manipulating horses' minds and bodies, largely through hormonal control, so that they can survive individually in order to procreate as a species.

The horse is a photoperiodic animal, one controlled by the changes in day length throughout the year, and a long-day breeder, producing young during the longer days. The mare's oestrus cycle has been described elsewhere. Let's look at what happens to both females and males on a natural, year-round cycle.

Winter

In winter, many plants and animals are dormant, hibernating or operating on a minimal level, waiting for spring to raise the sap and bring everything to life again. Horses now have and need their full protective winter coats which will have been 'set' since the end of November. Food is scarce and the sodden, frozen vegetation they can scrape up has little or no feed value: they will be living mainly on the body fat they accumulated during kinder seasons.

As the Winter Solstice passes (the shortest day of the year around 21 December in the northern hemisphere) the horses' brains sense that the days are, just, getting longer. Less and less melatonin is produced, a hormone which suppresses breeding activity, the winter coats begin to think about casting and the horses slowly gear up for reproduction.

Spring

By spring, these changes are evident as the hormones in both mares and stallions rampage around like the horses. Stallions fight for territory, supremacy and mares and in-season mares may fight for their stallion's attention. Last year's foal, now a yearling, will be chased away should he still try to suckle. The winter coats shower out and the smooth summer versions will be set by May. The growing grass, high in nutrients, restores weight to thin bodies, provides fuel for the production of mares' milk and nourishment for foals. The warm, unchallenging days are just what they need to grow and develop.

Summer

The mares' oestrus cycles continue in full swing – if they did not conceive again at the 'foal heat' (the first season after foaling), and many don't in nature, there is plenty of time for them to try again, or have a year off to recharge.

The grass now takes a dip in nutritional content but the horses will have made up their winter losses and the foals got off to a good start, so this is not critical. Everyone is now at their plumpest and glossiest, concerned with mating and nurturing the next generation. But summer sees another major turning point in the year – the Summer Solstice or longest day around 21 June in the northern hemisphere. Once again, the brain senses the reduction in the amount of daylight entering the eyes and, very slowly, the horses' internal pendulums begin to swing back.

By the end of the breeding season, feral herd stallions are often in poor body condition due to expensive pursuits like fending off rivals, courting and mating mares, retrieving straying females and having little time to eat and rest

Autumn

Now, the hormones reduce as melatonin rises, the summer coats are gradually cast and the horses lose both their bloom and their interest in, and capacity for, sex. Oestrus cycles stop and there is a surge in the carbohydrate content of the grass to enable the horses to stock up on body fat for the coming winter – which is where we came in.

From Teeth to Tail

The horse's digestive system is unique in the animal world. He has a single stomach and small intestine similar to those of a human or a pig and a hind part similar in function to that of the first part of a ruminant such as a cow, sheep or goat. He is a herbivore existing entirely on vegetation and mainly grasses, like them, but does most of his digesting – at least of the type of fibrous food on which he was meant to live – in his hind gut. Ruminants digest fibre at the front end of the digestive tract and actually have a more efficient fibre-processing system than the horse. The horse's digestive system, considering his evolved physique and lifestyle, is the one system which lets him down.

The digestive tract or alimentary canal is like a compartmentalised tube passing through his body, beginning at the lips and ending at the rectum. Food and other substances (such as medicines or 'undesirables') which enter the tube do not actually get into the body but simply pass through it, being treated and processed on the way by various chemicals and living creatures (digestive juices, enzymes and micro-organisms), pummelled about by the muscular movements of the tube, relieved of useful parts the body needs and left to void the undigested remnants out of the end of the tube.

The object of it all is digestion which enables the body to absorb the goodies. Large, complex molecules in food are broken down into smaller, simpler molecules capable of being absorbed. Proteins are broken down into their component 'building blocks', amino acids, and starch to sugars, mainly glucose. These and other nutrients and substances (medicines etc.) pass from the gut into the capillary network in its walls and so enter the blood and lymph for distribution around the body or for storage.

Structure and Function
Mouth
The horse first selects by smell the food he wants, the very mobile, sensitive lips sort out even single grains or blades of grass which the horse may then eat or spit out again. The incisors crop off grass or grasp leaves, hay or grain and the tongue

and cheeks take it into the mouth and manipulate it into convenient positions for the cheek teeth to grind up. It is soaked with saliva simply to soften and moisten it before swallowing.

Oesophagus
This is the gullet or food pipe which lies beneath the trachea. To prevent swallowed food getting into the latter, the epiglottis closes up like a lid over its entrance during swallowing, and the food passes to the stomach.

Stomach
The main feature of the stomach is the very acid nature of the digestive juices which start work on the food although the stomach protects itself from this acid by secreting some mucus as well. Enzymes speed up the chemical reactions and start to break down the food, the stomach walls helping with the mixing process. There is a very small amount of digestion by micro-organisms in one part of the stomach.

The stomach's main role is preparation, not absorption of nutrients: it stores some food should supplies cease, warms the food, mixes it and releases it in small amounts to the next section of the tract. It also has a safety function in that its acid juices kill most pathogens which may enter with food. However, this is not an excuse to feed food of doubtful quality as the horse's digestive tract is very sensitive and easily upset.

Small intestine
This is the next part of the tract and is subdivided technically into the duodenum, the jejunum and the ileum for ease of identification. This is where the horse's concentrates are digested and absorbed, principally starch. To facilitate this, its inner surface area is greatly increased by the presence of countless tiny projections (villi), inside each villus being a very dense network of blood and lymph capillaries.

There is a loop formed by the duodenum in which is the pancreas, a large gland one of the many functions of which is to secrete into the duodenum alkaline juices to counteract the very acidic stomach juices soaked into the food.

The wave-like contraction of the smooth muscle in the gut wall, which pushes the food along, is called peristalsis.

Liver

Absorbed substances passing into the blood from the small intestine travel in the hepatic portal vein to the liver although some is carried by the lymphatic system. The liver has *many* different jobs among which are the secretion of bile into the small intestine for fat digestion, the detoxification of poisons, drugs and other non-nutrient substances and the processing, storage and regulation of sugars, proteins and lipids (fats).

Large intestine

The large intestine which forms the horse's crucial hind gut is the equivalent to the rumen in cattle, sheep and goats. It consists of the caecum, the colon with large, transverse (very short) and small sections, and finally the rectum.

This is where countless billions of the famous microscopic creatures, collectively called micro-organisms, live and work. The most important part of the horse's food is fibre from straw, hay, haylage, grass and so on. The cell walls of this fibre are composed of cellulose but mammals do not have enzymes capable of breaking down cellulose molecules. Therefore, the micro-organisms or 'bugs' wreak extensive chemical changes on the food (whilst taking their share in payment), breaking down or fermenting cellulose, hence the colloquial name 'fermentation vat' for the caecum: this produces substances called volatile fatty acids (high-energy sources) which can be absorbed here.

Microbial digestion and absorption of nutrients and water continue in the large colon. The small colon continues to extract water and by the time the unabsorbed remainder of the food reaches the rectum, which pushes out this valuable organic resource to soil boxes and paddocks and break so many people's backs, it is of a moist solid consistency with which we are so familiar.

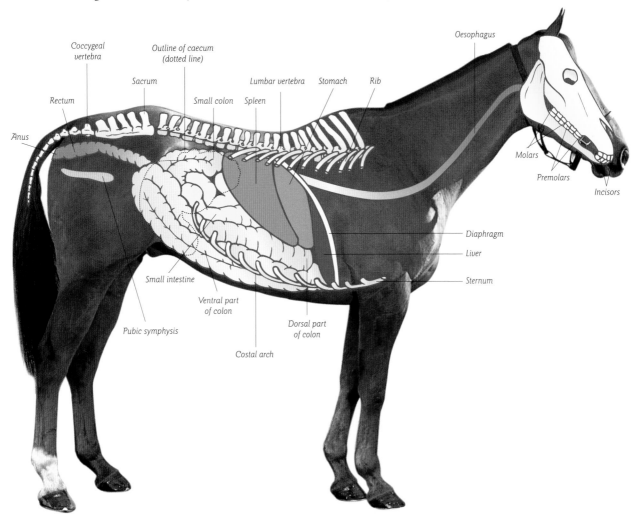

Food for Life

It will be clear from the previous section that the horse is not adapted to eating large amounts of concentrates yet it is this category of feed which seems to so fascinate owners and is given so much emphasis in equestrian marketing because of this. It is true that some categories of horse (old horses, hard-working horses, breeding stock) may benefit from moderate amounts of concentrates depending on their environment and management but the old, traditional, large amounts are now known to actually hamper the functioning of the digestive system, favouring the development of digestive and metabolic disorders and reducing the horse's performance levels.

Nutritional Needs of Horses

The horse's basic nutritional needs are similar to our own. He needs water, carbohydrates, proteins, fats (lipids), vitamins, minerals and trace elements (micro-nutrients). Most foods contain varying amounts of the first four and some of each of the last three but no single food contains all the vitamins, minerals and trace elements a horse needs.

Water

Often overlooked as a nutrient, this is probably the most important and urgently needed of all. The horse will die in a very few days (even less in hot weather) without water but total lack of food will take a few weeks to kill him.

The body is roughly two-thirds water and it is found everywhere in the body – inside the eyes and ears, in nervous tissue, every body cell and between them as well, in the blood and lymph, milk, bone, digestive juices, sweat, urine *ad nauseam*.

Water is needed for digestion itself, and lack of it can cause life-threatening dehydration. A horse working in hot weather or simply kept in a hot, and particularly a humid, environment could need up to about 50 litres or 12 gallons of clean water a day.

Carbohydrates

These are starches and sugars found mainly in cereal grains (oats, barley, maize/corn) but also in fibre and some roots, particularly sugar beet. They are a source of energy and warmth.

Proteins

These are capable of providing energy but are a nutritionally expensive way of doing so. Their main role is to provide the materials from which to build and replace body tissue and they are the only nutrients which can do so.

Fats/lipids

Although the horse's natural food, grass, contains very little fat, horses can digest it quite well and it is most useful as a concentrated source of energy (it is about one and a half times as energy-dense as carbohydrate). It certainly improves the skin and coat and helps make them more water-resistant; it also enhances stamina.

Vitamins, minerals and trace elements

This is a large category of nutrients which are needed in varying amounts, the trace elements, as their name suggests, being required in tiny quantities. They work together and all foods contain some vitamins and minerals, which are all responsible for many different, complex functions in the body.

Water is the most important nutrient of all, yet is often disregarded by owners. The facility to drink clean water more or less at will is essential to contentment and health

1 Rolled oats are a traditional feed, a cereal concentrate, used for hard-working horses and which most of them love. Cobs and ponies, however, should only be fed very small amounts, if any

2 Bruised barley, another cereal concentrate, seems to suit good doers, cobs and ponies better than oats in practice but, again, should be fed very circumspectly as it is a high-energy feed. It should always be fed bruised or rolled, never whole unless cooked, as the grain is very hard and not always chewed properly

3 Flaked maize (corn) is another cereal concentrate and very high in starchy carbohydrate and should form only part of a horse's diet, being deficient in other important nutrients

4 Horse and pony nuts (pellets/cubes) are a popular, convenient way of feeding concentrates and contain several different ingredients. There are several types designed to suit different animals doing different jobs. The so-called 'complete' nuts are said to need no accompanying roughage feed (hay etc) but, in practice, this is not so in the author's experience

5 Coarse mix (sweet feed) is another concentrate feed which horses love. Again containing several ingredients, horses usually love these feeds most of all!

6 Dried sugar beet nuts (a grey colour) should never be confused with other nuts (usually green to beige in colour). They must be soaked in cold water for 24 hours before feeding to swell them, otherwise they will swell inside the animal and could kill it

7 Whole linseed is not mixed with feeds but is boiled to form linseed tea or linseed jelly which is rich in oil and protein. It must be soaked overnight in cold water and boiled hard for at least 20 minutes before mixing with feed, otherwise it is poisonous

8 Dried alfalfa, long or short-cropped, is a very nutritious forage feed capable of replacing top-class hay, haylage or even concentrates, depending on the horse and his work. It tastes rather strong and can be sweetened by mixing it with soaked sugar beet pulp

9 Molassed chop is not recommended by many nutritionists now as too much added sugar is felt to be undesirable. Lightly molassed chop, though, may tempt a finicky horse to eat

10 Carrots are the favourite root (succulent) feed of most horses. They could be fed, with advantage, much more than they are. For instance, a 16hh horse could have up to 10lbs or 4.5kg per day, but more might overdose with Vitamin A. Check with a nutritionist

69

Metabolism

Metabolism means the outcome of all the physical and chemical processes which go in the body during life – the creation and maintenance of body tissues and the provision of energy. The digestion of nutrients has been basically described. The body 'knows' what nutrients it needs to absorb, which it will store and which are for immediate use.

Water is present all over the body and, in times of shortage, the body will draw on its existing water, depleting the tissues, reducing urination and the amount of water passed out.

Carbohydrates are broken down and stored as fat in various fat depots of the body, or they are broken down to sugar (glucose) and either used or stored as glycogen in the muscle cells for immediate energy when needed, and in the liver.

Proteins can be stored but only as fat, losing their tissue-making properties in the process. They are broken down to their component amino-acids which the body selects, reassembles and uses for maintenance or the 'building' of new tissues.

Fats are a valuable energy source and are broken down to fatty acids (organic compounds of carbon, hydrogen and oxygen) and glycerol (a substance used in glycolysis, the anaerobic breakdown of glucose to create energy during very fast work). Fats can be stored in the fat depots and liver if not needed immediately.

Many body tissues are selectively permeable, that is, only certain substances can cross back or forth across them, through membranes, cell walls and so on, in either direction according to the structure of the tissue and to the body's requirements.

Nutrients and other substances not used, stored or required are excreted in the breath, sweat, urine or droppings. Because the horse does not extract nutrients from his fibrous diet as well as some other animals, his droppings are still fairly rich in nutrients when voided and are a good organic fertiliser.

Energy

Energy is created in the body mainly from carbohydrates and fats. Aerobic work is fuelled by energy produced in a different way from anaerobic work, as discussed, and can continue for longer. Anaerobic work results in the production of lactic acid, a build-up of which can be damaging to the muscles. However, even during work, if the speed and pressure are lessened a little, the bloodstream has a chance to clear away the lactic acid and provide more oxygen so the horse recovers and can continue.

In racing, there is a term which describes a horse as 'getting his second wind' and this is what it relates to. If a longish race has been run at a fast pace, lactic acid may have built up and, by easing off the horse, the jockey gives him time to recover, 'get his second wind' and speed up again. Many a horse has won a race because of this process.

Because the horse is adapted to live mainly on fibre, he must obviously obtain a good deal of nourishment and energy from it if of adequate feed value. From the viewpoint of energy, microbial digestion of fibre (cellulose) produces, among other items, volatile fatty acids which have high energy value. The horse has several ways of obtaining fuel for, and creating, energy, and it is the energy content of the diet which should receive most of our attention when choosing or formulating a suitable diet, not the protein level.

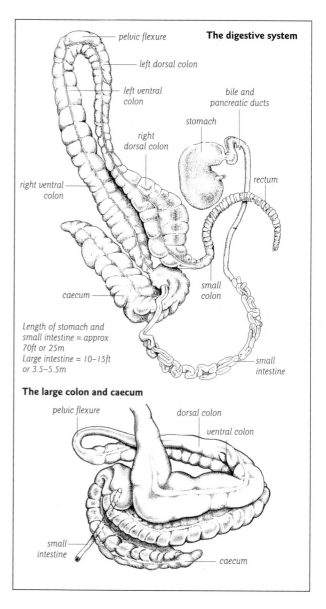

The digestive system

pelvic flexure

left dorsal colon

left ventral colon

right dorsal colon

right ventral colon

caecum

bile and pancreatic ducts

stomach

rectum

small colon

small intestine

Length of stomach and small intestine = approx 70ft or 25m
Large intestine = 10–15ft or 3.5–5.5m

The large colon and caecum

pelvic flexure

dorsal colon

ventral colon

small intestine

caecum

The Genito-Urinary System

The urinary system is the body's main means of regulating its water balance, maintaining its chemical balance (between acidity and alkalinity) and also supports the other excretory organs (skin, lungs and bowels) by filtering from the blood plasma some excess nutrients and, particularly, toxins, especially nitrogenous waste (urea) created in the liver from the processing of protein. These substances are excreted in the urine around four to six times a day and a horse may pass about 10 litres or 18 pints of urine a day – although it seems a lot more when you are mucking out!

Structure and Function

There are two kidneys which are placed in the lumbar or loin region just behind the saddle. They are actually outside and above the abdominal cavity, below the spine and surrounded by thick pads of fat; the muscles of the loin area also protect them so they are not as easy to injure as is commonly imagined. However, care should still be taken when grooming or massaging this area and there should certainly be no pressure here from saddle or rider. The structures involved in the urinary system are the two kidneys, each with a tube called the ureter passing from it to the bladder from which, in turn, leads another tube, the urethra, to either the penis or the vulva.

All blood has to pass through the kidneys for filtering, entering through the 'dimple' on the side of the kidney, called the hilus. Nerves also enter here plus lymphatic vessels, and the ureter leaves the kidney at this point.

Beyond the hilus is a collecting area called the renal pelvis. Surrounding it is the inner area of the kidney called the medulla which contains collecting tubules called nephrons radiating through it to the outer part of the kidney, the cortex. The cortex contains very many filtering capsules called Bowman's capsules. Blood capillaries pass into and out of each capsule, each accumulation of capillaries being called a glomerulus. The combined structure of Bowman's capsule and glomerulus is called the Malpighian body.

Blood passes in and out of the capsule and substances for excretion are filtered out of the blood and pass down the tubules. The tubules loop in and out of the cortex and medulla, surrounded by capillaries, whilst unwanted products are filtered from the blood plasma and other, useful ones, reabsorbed.

The tubules empty into collecting ducts which, themselves, empty into the renal pelvis. From here the unwanted products, in their watery vehicle called urine, pass along the ureter to the bladder for storage until the horse stales (urinates).

The technical word for urination is 'micturition' and depends on how full the bladder is. The pressure caused by fullness stimulates nerve sensors in the spinal cord and the muscles in the bladder wall are then instructed to contract and empty it.

Control of Body Fluids

The kidneys are remarkable in that they can normally keep the body's fluid balance constant despite large fluctuations in the amount the horse drinks. However, if the horse is seriously short of water for whatever reason, then the kidneys will have to hold back a good deal of water and the amount of urine will be reduced but have a higher concentration of toxins.

As you may guess, this function is under hormonal control, the hormone concerned being anti-diuretic hormone or ADH, which is released by the pituitary gland. Over 80 per cent of the liquid filtered and passing through the nephrons is reabsorbed. Of the remainder, the kidneys will retain or excrete it according to the body's water content – dehydrated body = water retained: normally or over-hydrated body = excess excreted.

Practical Implications

The horse has a good deal of control over whether or not he will stale. Most horses prefer to stale on soft ground, grass, sand, woodchips, or bedding, especially when it is fresh when the process may also have a territory-marking function. It seems that both males and females hate splashing themselves with urine (who wouldn't?) and most wait until they are forced to 'go', because the nerve messages are just too strong to resist, before they will stale on hard ground, under saddle or, in some cases, away from home.

TRAVELLING

Because of the motion of a trailer or horsebox, most horses also will not stale whilst travelling which is at least one excellent reason for reasonably frequent rest stops. Your horse may need unloading before he or she will stale.

Rubber stable matting is very popular these days and, if you can find the right sort for your circumstances, it can be a good investment. However, even staling on rubber matting will create splashes so it is important to ignore the manufacturers' marketing ploy of claiming you can save a fortune on bedding because you can't. My experience of several types is that bedding is definitely still needed for the horses' physical and psychological comfort and reassurance. The value of such floorings seems to be in the increased warmth and in the foothold the mats provide. (The management of stables with rubber matting is dealt with in Section 5.)

The Female Reproductive System
Ovaries

The two ovaries are sited just under and slightly behind the kidneys, with a convoluted oviduct or Fallopian tube leading from each one to the tip of its associated uterine horn. The ovaries' main function is to produce ova or eggs plus the hormones oestrogen, progesterone and relaxin, so they form part of the endocrine system. The ova develop within follicles and the number a mare has is fixed at birth.

The oviducts capture the egg released from its follicle into the shield-shaped fimbria or infundibulum and whilst on its way down the tube it will probably, if the mare has mated, meet up with the stallion's sperm and fertilisation of the egg will occur. The oviduct then transports the embryo to the uterine horn by means of peristaltic (wave-like) contractions of its wall. Unfertilised eggs die and decompose in the oviduct.

Uterus and cervix

The uterus has two fairly short horns and the main body. The uterus, oviducts and ovaries are suspended from under the spine by a membrane of connective tissue. The uterus has walls of smooth muscle, its lining, the endometrium, containing glands which secrete various hormones including the pregnancy hormone, progesterone.

At the opposite end of the uterus to the ovaries is the cervix, the muscular neck of the womb which is tightly closed to maintain womb hygiene, except when the mare is in oestrus (to permit the entry of sperm) and during foaling.

Vagina and vulva

The cervix leads to the vagina which is a muscular tube ending in external lips, the vulva, which should act as a seal against the access of pathogens. In older broodmares, however, the lips become

---

HORMONAL CONTROL

As the mare's oestrus cycle was described in The Endocrine System, we shall just mention here that the stallion is also subject to the influence of hormones and day length. GnRH (gonadotrophin releasing hormone) travels from the hypothalamus to the pituitary gland which then produces the same hormone, luteinising hormone or LH, as in the mare but in the stallion it is called interstitial-cell-stimulating hormone (ICSH) which stimulates the production by the testes of testosterone, the male hormone. This is involved in sperm production, the development of the foetal reproductive organs, the descent of the testicles in the colt and the process of puberty. It also produces the stallion-like characteristics which differentiate the entire horse from the gelding.

---

stretched and the seal is not so close as in younger mares. The urethra, the tube from the bladder, also enters the vagina for the voiding of urine.

The Male Reproductive System
The testes and epididymis

The two testes or testicles which produce the sperm hang inside the scrotum (a sac of skin with an internal division to separate the testes). Each has a coiled tube, the epididymis, with a head lying on the top of the testis, a body and a tail and contains more, finer tubules. The immature sperm collect in the head of the epididymis and gradually mature as they travel along in the fine tubules; they are almost mature by the time they reach its tail where they remain until ejaculation. Their final maturation occurs after ejaculation, inside the mare.

The vas deferens

This is a tube which carries the sperm from the tail of the epididymis up through the inguinal ring or canal, an opening in the abdominal wall. In the abdomen, it turns backwards into the pelvic cavity, enlarging to form the ampulla. This is one of the accessory sex glands (the others being the seminal vesicles, the prostate and the bulbo-urethral glands) which produce the nourishing and protective fluid carrying the sperm. Here, the vas deferens also meets the urethra, the tube carrying not only the stallion's ejaculate but also urine from the bladder through the penis.

The penis

Normally soft and lying up in its protective sheath or prepuce, the only times the penis is usually seen are when the stallion is staling and when he is hoping to serve a mare. The penis engorges with blood during sexual excitement, which produces an erection enabling the horse to enter and serve the mare. Its tip ends in a cap-like structure called the glans penis through which the urethra projects for a few millimetres.

Pregnancy

Pregnancy lasts about 340 days in the mare, give or take about 20 days either way. Whilst in the womb, the embryo, later foetus, is entirely dependent on the mare for supplies of oxygen and nutrients and the removal of its waste products.

Evolution developed a brilliant system, common to all mammals with individual species variations, of having the foetus develop inside two specialised membranes – the placenta which is attached all over to the endometrium, and the amnion which directly surrounds the foetus, contact between dam and foetus being through the placenta and via the umbilical cord. Through these means, the foetus's needs are met. The cord carries blood to the foetus although the blood supplies of dam and foetus do not actually mix, simply exchanging 'goods' and 'waste'.

Between placenta and amnion is the allantoic fluid consisting mainly of waste products from foal and placenta, discharged by the urachus, a duct in the cord which closes when the cord breaks after birth.

Foaling

Although the mare can control her time of foaling to some extent, it is the foetus which decides to be born. As it grows bigger and bigger it becomes more and more uncomfortable and it is this foetal stress which causes the foetus to send out hormonal messages to the mare which gradually trigger foaling or parturition. Most foalings take less than an hour and, contrary to popular opinion, rarely go wrong.

Lactation

Changes in hormone levels trigger lactation. Progesterone falls, oestrogen rises and allows the production of prolactin which, in turn, initiates milk production. The removal of milk from the udder stimulates the production of more, supplies peaking at two months after birth.

73

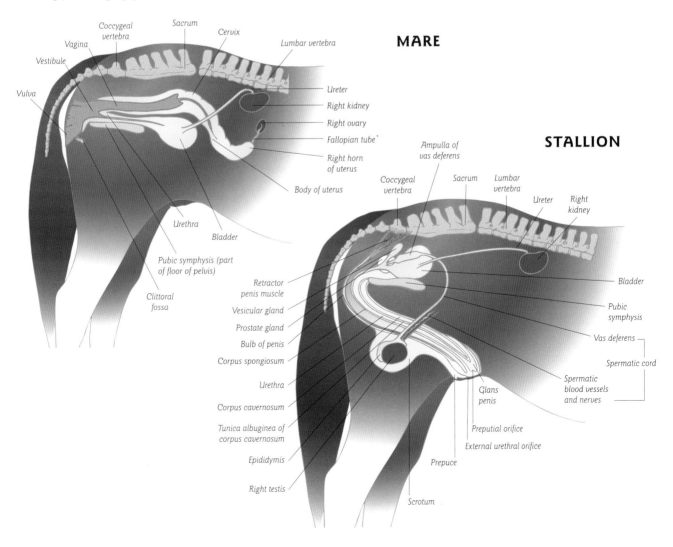

MARE

Coccygeal vertebra
Sacrum
Cervix
Vagina
Lumbar vertebra
Vestibule
Vulva
Ureter
Right kidney
Right ovary
Fallopian tube
Right horn of uterus
Body of uterus
Urethra
Bladder
Pubic symphysis (part of floor of pelvis)
Clittoral fossa

STALLION

Ampulla of vas deferens
Coccygeal vertebra
Sacrum
Lumbar vertebra
Ureter
Right kidney
Retractor penis muscle
Vesicular gland
Prostate gland
Bulb of penis
Corpus spongiosum
Urethra
Corpus cavernosum
Tunica albuginea of corpus cavernosum
Epididymis
Right testis
Scrotum
Prepuce
External urethral orifice
Preputial orifice
Glans penis
Spermatic blood vessels and nerves
Vas deferens
Spermatic cord
Pubic symphysis
Bladder

Nature versus Domestication

Wildlife programmes are among the most popular on television and those featuring *equidae* have their share of the wildlife slots. Reintroduced herds of Przewalski horses have been shown galloping their ancestral lands and the amazing horses of Trakehner origin, in southern Africa's Namib desert, have been shown surviving the appalling hardships of living and procreating in a place where even zebras would find it hard to survive.

Feral herds all have in common an alpha breeding stallion, maybe one or two younger or, at least, non-breeding, stallions, mature mares and youngsters of varying ages. The Namib herds are extensive, surprisingly, but, of course, the Przewalski herds are much smaller, nearer the normal wild size of less than a dozen animals. It seems that the size of a herd is mainly determined by the available keep in their environment and also by the number of mares a stallion feels he can keep tabs on and service.

The way of the wild

Left to themselves, wild *equidae*, including feral horses and ponies wherever they are, follow the picture painted earlier in A Horse's Year. They gear up for mating in spring, the mares not conceiving until they begin cycling and ovulating regularly, normally in late spring or even summer. Their conception time will also depend on when this year's foal is born, if they are pregnant, and they by no means breed every year, as we expect horses to do.

The stallion, detects that one of his mares is in season and starts showing more than a friendly interest in her. An experienced suitor may not try to mate until she is fully ready, towards the end of her season, but a younger one might, and be shown a hard pair of heels for his trouble.

The honeymoon

The pair will spend several days together, courting, licking, playing, nibbling, smelling, maybe lying down together, certainly grazing very close or touching, all of which is important in their bonding process. Herd members, including youngsters, will take some interest in their affair and this is a valuable learning curve for them. It probably also reassures them that all is normal in the herd.

When actually mating, a sensible stallion, no matter how willing the mare seems, will approach cautiously from the side, watching her expression and those heels, asking if the mare will accept him. She will stand for him and, even so, he may mount from the side of her hindquarters to be on the safe side. He will serve her and she will stand for him, and the process may be repeated several or many times for a day or two.

When she goes out of season (pregnant or not), they lose sexual interest in each other whilst remaining friends, and his attention is diverted to another ripe lady.

The Ways of Man

In domesticity, things are very different unless the stallion is running free with his mares – not unusual, if not common, on pony studs but very unusual with horses which are often

This feral Dartmoor pony mare stands quietly and willingly for her suitor

regarded as too valuable to be allowed to do things their own way in case one of them, usually the stallion, is seriously injured.

The most extreme and unnatural method, apart from artificial insemination, is that practised on many Thoroughbred and competition horse studs. The mare has been tested by the veterinary surgeon as having a ripe follicle in her ovary, due to ovulate and, therefore, ready to be served. She will probably also have been 'teased' in hand, separated by a high, strong, padded barrier called the trying board, by a 'teaser' stallion who probably knows even better than the vet whether or not she is ready for his colleague's attentions but, sadly, not for his.

Dressing the part

She will be prepared by having a bridle and maybe also a headcollar or cavesson fitted, she may be fitted with a leather neck protector to save her from the stallion's teeth as he ejaculates, she will wear heavy, padded boots on her hind hooves to protect him from possible kicks and may also be hobbled so she couldn't kick anyway. Finally, she may be twitched to keep her as still as possible and quieten her down. She will have at least one attendant and usually two or three.

The stallion is led to the covering area by his man, wearing his stallion bridle and bit for control. The pair are not allowed to court or even to meet. The stallion is brought behind the mare, encouraged in his erection by his handler, if necessary, and mounts and serves her with no niceties allowed. A sensible handler will let the horse dismount in his own time but often the horse is pulled off almost as soon as he has finished. Warm water will be thrown on his penis to 'clean' it before he draws it up again – and he is led away.

The mare will have her paraphernalia removed and be walked around to prevent her 'straining' and discharging the semen. And that's that.

Compromises

In between the above method and that of stallion and mares running free together in paddocks, there are various other methods.

In the running-free method, a mare once served a time or two (obviously observation is needed) may be removed to divert the stallion's attention to other mares. If not actually living together, the stallion and mare may be introduced in hand, then, if the mare is fully ready, may be turned loose together to do what comes naturally, then be separated again.

In studs where stallions do their own teasing, the pair may at least have already met before actual mating, and some studs adopt the system of having the stallion stabled in the same yard as his potential mates, rather than in a separate stallion yard which is obviously totally unnatural. Sometimes, stallion and mares are in paddocks sited where they can see each other but this method can result in seriously injured horses as they try to get to each other. Mares are not always kitted out as described above and, frankly, if the mare is really ready for mating this is hardly necessary. It is simply that some

This domestic mare would probably do the same as the Dartmoor mare opposite if only she were given a chance – provided she is fully in season and ready. At least she is not twitched

people will not take a tiny chance to at least let the mare be comfortable, so valuable are some stallions.

Tide of opinion

There are many breeders, vets, experienced horsepeople and behaviourists who insist that the kind of stress that our methods impose on horses, particularly in the first method described above, is not only morally unjustifiable but detrimental to successful conception. Certainly, trials done at Ireland's National Stud in the 1970s with a relatively cheap but nicely bred Thoroughbred stallion running free with a herd of 'no-hoper' broodmares (as far as getting in foal was concerned) resulted in all of them conceiving, a big improvement on normal results in the Thoroughbred industry and the commercial horse world in general.

Manipulation and Compromise

Newcomers to an established herd can be chased off and battered if they are not correctly introduced as is happening to this piebald

Having painted the picture elsewhere of wild herds, their structure and how they live, let's consider whether or not this natural situation can be reproduced to any extent in domesticity. The previous section considered alternatives to the extreme in-hand method of actual mating practices. Now we'll consider more natural lifestyles in domesticity.

'Natural' Domesticated Herds

In the UK, the source of this book, it is extremely unusual for horses, as opposed to ponies, to be bred in anything like natural conditions. True, they all have paddocks and pastures as well as being stabled and the larger studs necessarily have many acres or hectares of land over which their horses can roam. Even the system not uncommon on the continent of Europe – yarding the horses for part of their time in large, covered barns and running them on pasture for the rest of the time – is not usual in Britain.

Because the large, commercial studs do have the land to do this, shortage of space is not the problem: it is purely tradition and convention which continue to be firmly upheld in many sectors of the horse world, often for no real, good reason. Many people still feel that stallions are not to be trusted out loose with their mares and that the mares may kick and fatally injure the stallion who may be the sole horse on which the stud's reputation depends (broken legs being the most feared injury). Practice does not confirm this to be likely. Even in studs with floating populations of visiting mares, experience and

opinion shows that the running free method can still be used provided new mares are introduced to the existing broodmare band and to the stallion whilst they are out of season, with normal care, gradually and selecting grazing mates likely to be compatible until the new mare finds her feet (she is normally away at stud for several weeks, anyway).

The best way to introduce a new member of the broodmare band to a 'free' situation is to do so in the dead of winter when all the mares are anoestrus (not cycling). This way the other mares' sexual jealousy is not aroused and it is simply like introducing a mare to a mixed group of other horses at a livery yard, for example. The stallion's active sexual interest will be non-existent and, again provided normal precautions are taken, I know from my own experience that there is only the usual amount of squealing and jostling for new friendships, the stallion usually being kept in order by the senior mares, anyway.

Fairly permanent herds with mixed-age and mixed-sex youngsters can also be beneficially brought up together, and are in a few establishments. The common practice of separating the sexes at puberty or even at weaning is psychologically bad for the horses, some experts believe, because the youngsters receive no natural education, social mores or unmistakable discipline from their elders. It is no use traditionalists claiming that we must take the part of the older herd members: this is ridiculous.

For a start, we do not live with them twenty-four hours a day and, most importantly, no human can mete out discipline to a young horse like another horse. Peer group 'discipline' is not discipline but competition, even bullying, which can easily result in maladjusted horses. Youngsters brought up in mixed-age groups with adults are easier for humans to handle and train. They are calmer, know their place in the scheme of things and are more accepting of human ways. The Lord of The Flies is an example (the principle of which is not fictitious) of what happens to young humans without leadership and control from their elders. Two examples from the animal world involve (1) a herd of elephants in South Africa put together as youngsters with no adults, who turned, as they matured, into aggressive monsters rampaging their park, wrecking villages and fighting among themselves and (2) a pack of young African hunting dogs, raised by humans and returned to the wild, again with no elders, to repopulate an area, who had no idea how to hunt, how to structure and manage a pack or how to deal with marauders. They all died.

Weaning

The practice of weaning foals from their dams at the unnaturally early age of six months or so has had its denigrators for years and is gradually receiving wider, serious consideration. Briefly, not a few experts believe that the psychological pain and scars, particularly for the foal, caused by early separation (except if necessary for the health and wellbeing of dam or foal) last a lifetime and cause behavioural problems throughout a horse's life. Mares in domestic circumstances on modern diets can very easily stand to suckle a foal for longer than six months and, in any case, foals take little milk after that age: they simply need their mother for reassurance, guidance and the odd comforting suckle. In nature, foals are normally rejected at around nine or ten months, anyway, but still stay friends with Mum.

Castration

Few 'ordinary' horse owners are prepared to take on a stallion and most 'ordinary' livery yards refuse to take them, anyway. In practice, stallions correctly brought up (which may be beyond many owners) are not sex maniacs, habitually aggressive or prone to breaking down fences and kicking their way through to mares in season. It may well, however, be very unfair to keep an entire horse in the presence of in-season mares without allowing him to mate (studs do this with their teasers all the time) but, in the wild, only the herd's alpha stallion (who is not

These handsome, well-grown youngsters on a Thoroughbred stud will grow up better balanced, psychologically, if they are mixed with older and younger horses

always the only sexually mature male in the herd) gets to breed unless one of the others sneaks in a quick assignation.

Ethologist Dr Marthe Kiley-Worthington had a vasectomised stallion on her farm for some time living with mares, with the result that 'everyone got lots of sex but we had no unwanted foals, so everyone was happy'. She maintains that most animals probably want and need sex as much as most humans and we do not have the right to deprive them of it. Certainly, her entire competition horses are as well behaved as geldings in mixed company because they have been raised in a balanced way.

Castration will go on and in some cases it is probably necessary because of the inability of many owners to cope with a sensitive, possibly domineering, entire horse. It should be remembered, though, that it is estimated that over half of geldings retain sexual desires and stallion-like instincts regardless of when they were castrated, are capable of achieving an erection, sometimes mount mares and have occasionally been reported as serving them without, of course, ejaculating sperm. Such horses are not necessarily actually rigs (where one testicle remains up in the abdomen) which is the usual unconsidered cry, and I hope owners of mares, particularly those with gelding friends, will not deny them access to geldings at liberty because of this!

From Conception to Middle Age

Horses have a short foalhood and adolescence relative to their lifespan, a long adulthood and a fairly rapid decline into old age and death. Ponies seem to grow old more slowly. It is difficult to answer the question often asked by non-horsey folk: 'How long do horses live?' In the wild they will be really old at fifteen. Domestic statistics indicate the average lifespan is about twenty years but much older horses have been known. Old Billy, a Victorian farm horse turned barge horse, lived to be sixty-two. A great deal depends on good care, correct nutrition and reasonable work, all of which should extend the horse's life.

Foals and Youngsters

The foal is one of the most precocious animals on earth. It has to be because it needs to be able to run with the herd away from danger within a few hours of birth. This is why most foals are born at night, to give them time to get up, suckle and obtain some immunity from the diseases in their environment from their dams, and learn to cope with those long, buckling legs which will be nearly mature length at birth. The newborn foal weighs about a tenth of his mature weight and this will increase to about half his adult weight by seven or eight months.

Foals look 'all bottom' and this is appropriate because the hindquarters provide the power for galloping. The neck is very short (all right, because he does not need to get his head to ground level to graze – although he will turn himself inside out

trying) and his head and jaws are short as his baby teeth take up relatively little room. He feeds from Mum roughly every 30 to 45 minutes, at first.

Foals are inquisitive and playful, gently stressing their bodies and learning how to use them. They need a lot of rest and should not be exposed to harsh weather (cold, windy, wet or hot sunshine) for their first few days.

Growth of Ages

A horse's skeleton is not mature till the age of five, the back being the last to mature. By six to nine months the growth areas in the bones (epiphyseal plates) will have already become inactive in the pasterns and fetlocks, those below the knees and hocks by around twelve months, those above the knees by about twenty-four to thirty months; these are the critical plates often X-rayed by racehorse trainers to see how their two-year-olds' legs are maturing and, hence, how much work they can do.

Adolescence

A horse's adolescence ranges from his yearling stage to four or five depending on his breed (some mature mentally and physically sooner than others) and, at five, he is a young adult. Flat racehorses will start work at around eighteen

This older foal has the proportionately long legs needed to keep up with the herd but his neck is still relatively short

This youngster is showing more mature balance in his development, with his lengthening neck, head and body

The mature horse shows the longer head and neck and longer, bigger body and muscular development of the adult

months, others usually at three years, but all horses should be educated from birth to be well mannered. The still-common method of not handling them much till the time comes to back and ride them does little for their mental development. Leading them around the place, teaching them simple commands, to be regularly handled and brushed, feet picked out and so on, makes for a more mature youngster who is easier to work with later.

Forward, well-developed youngsters, particularly if becoming a little exuberant to handle, can well be backed and ridden lightly for a very few weeks at two years which has a disciplining, maturing effect on them if properly done.

By three, they can be doing light ridden work and, with advantage, loose work (not too much on the lunge) and the competition horse world is increasingly expecting youngsters to be jumping sizeable fences without a rider at this age, although many feel this is asking too much at three years old. By four, your youngster may start competing in ridden classes at shows, and be working lightly a few days a week. Many horses are ruined at this age by doing too much too soon because they look much more mature than they really are, physically or mentally.

Young Adult

At five and six, your young adult horse is physically mature but will still have a youngish outlook. He cannot be too worldly-wise at this age but should be becoming experienced and sensible if he has had a careful, varied upbringing. Again, care should be taken not to overwork him as he

can easily be soured by overwork and being overfaced by work he finds stressful and taxing.

The Prime of His Life

From seven to about twelve, a horse is in his prime. If he has been correctly 'done' all his life, he will be sound, tough, and able to 'work like a horse'. He will be capable of the hardest work he can ever do but it is to be hoped his people will remember he is flesh and blood, susceptible to injury, illness and mental stress, too.

Middle Age

You may not notice a decline in your horse's powers till he is fifteen or older, but very gradually, and inevitably, he will become middle aged with all the niggling little aches and pains that brings. Many horses continue to work hard and well at fifteen and thereabouts, but it is as well to be aware of his 'senior management' status and to keep an eye out for little signs of possible deterioration – a little stiffness, the back possibly starting to dip, one or two grey hairs appearing around the eyes and muzzle, a little more sensitivity to extremes of weather and to flies – that sort of thing, and to make allowances for him. Mentally, older horses often change a little, either becoming more tolerant of irritating circumstances and humans but sometimes showing an increasing tendency not to suffer fools gladly. Study your middle-aged horse and treat him accordingly and considerately.

The Age of Wisdom

If your horse has been worked wisely and cared for well all his life, there is no reason why he should not live well beyond the average age of twenty for a domesticated horse. Few horses, though, are with the same owner all their lives and many are certainly not wisely worked or well treated, sadly. Most buyers, too, don't want a horse who is middle aged or actually old: they usually want one who will be able to 'do something', one they can work for several years, perhaps build up a lasting relationship with, one who will have a fair resale value or one who is not going to force them to make that final decision they would rather someone else made.

I feel this is a very short-sighted view. Older, even downright old, horses can be wonderful friends and unless you want to work a horse regularly in one of the most strenuous equestrian disciplines, you don't need a youngster or a horse in his prime. Older horses are cheaper, any minor physical defects they have picked up over the years rarely matter for any but the most demanding jobs and the old chestnut (no pun intended) about older horses being crafty, lazy, ring-shy and possessing all sorts of unpleasant tricks and foibles can apply just as well to youngsters as many of us know to our cost. Good and bad horses come in all age groups. Good, older horses can be worth their weight in gold. They are used to dealing with humans and have learned our language to a large extent even if we haven't learned theirs. They look after novices and idiots and work well with the more experienced and empathetic. They are actually more willing to build up a strong partnership with deserving humans than youngsters who have still not learned to tolerate us. You should have no more difficulty in finding a good old horse than a good younger one.

Physical and Mental Changes
Skeletal changes
The bones of older horses are not only fully mature but will become more brittle, although normal work rarely causes problems. Joint problems due to wear and tear (usually involving damaged cartilage) and slight, chronic ligament weaknesses may occur if the horse has worked hard galloping, jumping and doing intensive schooling on the flat. Adjusting the type of work he can do, on veterinary advice, usually makes it quite possible for you and him to cope well with such changes depending on their severity.

Osteoarthritis
Osteoarthritis can develop just as easily in old horses as in old people and dogs and, of course, humans and animals can get arthritis at any age – it just seems more common in older bodies. Although conventional veterinary medicine can only treat the symptoms of arthritis, some complementary therapies seem to have success in halting, and sometimes actually reversing, its progress at any stage and can be used with conventional medicine. Like most conditions, arthritis is best caught early. Frequent, moderate exercise plus weight control, medication and avoiding cold and damp are the pointers to coping with osteoarthritis. A varied wardrobe of well-fitting lightweight stable, exercise and turnout rugs is a real boon for any old horse. Long periods of stabling with only short periods out on the move (not standing huddled in a corner waiting to be brought in or, conversely, being drilled on the lunge) are exactly what older horses do not want.

There is also nothing at all wrong with giving them a helpful level of painkillers and keeping on working them wisely and considerately (you'd do it for your old dog or yourself, wouldn't you?) In fact, this is probably what should be done, under veterinary supervision.

There are also increasing numbers and types of

Many older horses develop a sunken back due to its supporting ligaments 'softening' and offering less support. This is less likely to happen in a horse who has been correctly ridden all his life – and, health and physique permitting, it is never too late to start, gently

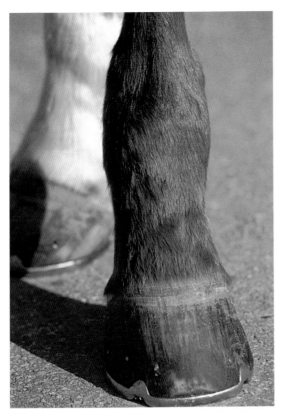

Arthritic joints may well be a sign of a lifetime's hard work. Depending on veterinary advice and treatment, it is often advisable to keep such horses gently exercised to maintain their comfort, mobility and strength

therapeutic feed supplements available to help the greater number of older horses kept in work nowadays, and some seem very effective. Magnetic therapy leg wraps and boots seem to help in some cases, too.

Teeth

The teeth need more care in old horses, as detailed earlier. They should be checked at least every six months and, if they are 'growing out' exposing the roots, rasping should be judicious and the diet may need adjusting to highly nutritious but softer feeds.

Shoeing

If the horse is finding it difficult to tolerate shoeing, try to find a really understanding farrier who will give him time to adjust his legs and joints, who will not force his legs into extreme and unnecessary positions and who, if necessary, may be able to work with your vet to provide special shoes to counter any limb and joint problems.

Death in the Wild

Most wild creatures die terrible, natural deaths. *Equidae* die slowly and agonisingly from starvation as their teeth grow out or due to other dental problems, or because of drought and lack of keep in their region. Most don't become old as they are killed by predators as soon as they start to slow down or show any sign of sickness or injury (or even before then), either being suffocated to death or started on before they are even dead. Infectious disease does not seem to be a common cause of death in wild and feral *equidae*.

Death in Domesticity

Most domesticated horses in developed countries are euthanased (put down) for economic reasons, usually because their owners cannot afford some expensive veterinary treatment which has become necessary. Some are put down simply because they are surplus to requirements or because they can no longer perform the work required of them. Some have incurable conditions (diseases or injuries) for which the only humane answer is destruction. Although there are stringent rules about the euthanasia of horses and disposal of the body, your veterinary surgeon will outline the options.

As far as the method of destruction is concerned, the usual methods are by humane killer (a device with a captive bolt placed against the forehead and ejected into the brain with a hammer) or by intravenous injection of a lethal drug.

At the time of writing in the UK, the practice of giving the horse an overdose of anaesthetic which some horses fight against has been largely superseded by the use of more potent drugs, also given intravenously but specially developed for euthanasia rather than anaesthesia. With this method, the horse becomes completely unconscious almost instantaneously as the drug reaches his brain, there is no gradual 'passing out', dizziness or struggling and the horse dies within about ten seconds.

The horse's incisors normally cause less trouble than his cheek teeth. This set will obviously be capable of cropping grass for many years to come

81

Outside and Inside Influences

Horsey Priorities

As we have said several times, the horse is a prey animal, and unique at that. The horse's priorities are to survive and reproduce. Everything revolves around these two things.

Horses are different

There is no other group of animals physically and mentally resembling *equidae* (horses, asses and zebras). All the other large, herbivorous prey animals have a readiness to fight, although their flight instinct is strong, too.

    Equidae, however, run first and think later. By nature, they are non-aggressive animals: they only fight as a last resort. Flight is their main survival mechanism and it largely governs their body plan and its specialisation for speed and stamina: it certainly governs their mentality. The horse's mind

is also fixated on eating because of the way his digestive system evolved. Whilst other herbivores can spend less time actually eating, can lie down, chew cud and get more out of the food they take in, horses must actually eat for several more hours a day and take in more food to obtain enough nourishment. The horse's mind does not recognise that domestic food is often more nutritious than wild food so that, in theory, he does not need so much. Because the quantity may be smaller than he would eat at will, his mind tells him he is hungry and must eat for most of his waking hours so that is what he wants and tries to do.

The horse's viewpoint

Other aspects of how horses see life include the following:

- The horse is a social animal and although some cope leading fairly solitary lives, the massive majority need other horses around to feel secure and, therefore, relaxed.
- Most horses are followers, not leaders, and need leadership from some other horse, or from us probably in addition to the Field Leader.
- Horses have an extremely strong sense of self-preservation. They particularly want the freedom of their heads and feet so training from us and trust from them are essential for them to permit control of their heads and

---

OTHER INFLUENCES

The drive to reproduce has been dealt with earlier and is a major driving force which influences the horse's mind. Apart from these three aspects, a horse's behaviour is also governed by:

- Hormonal influences about which he or she can do nothing.
- Past experiences (including training) which are usually emblazoned for ever on his memory.
- His environment and management.
- His temperament and individual attitude to life.

handling and, especially, shoeing of their legs and feet.

- Horses are highly perceptive and sensitive. They notice the slightest signs from all other animals, including us, and minute changes in their environment. They are highly sensitive to 'vibes' and pick up each others' and our moods, impending weather, earthquakes and volcanic eruptions and changes in their herd structure, yard inmates and equipment.
- They have a social hierarchy which may be more structured in domesticity than in the wild, and we should work within and around this to a large extent.

Boredom? That's only half the story

Even in previous decades it was admitted that 'vices' were caused by boredom and wise horsemasters gave their horses plenty to look at, enough hay to eat, a lot of gentle exercise and liberty as well as harder work, company and so on, to keep them occupied and interested. Boredom is an obvious result of inadequate management but, in view of the enlightened assessment of the true nature of equine mentality and psychology, stereotypies are now considered to be due to tension, frustration and distress caused by a lifestyle which does not suit, indeed is damaging to, the individual horse performing one or more of them.

Stopping the rot

Although well-established stereotypies cannot yet be fully remedied, their performance can be greatly lessened by giving the horse a more acceptable lifestyle which usually means a more natural one. More real social contact with other horses (simply being able to see them is inadequate) and plenty of exercise, a lot of it at liberty in congenial company, is the main two-pronged attack on this unhappy situation.

Other steps include a more fibrous, time-consuming diet (see 'Feeding' in Section 5), being stabled as little as possible and next to, or with, friends and certainly not near enemies, handlers and riders the horse can trust not to hurt or overstress him, an interesting but relaxed, peaceful environment in the yard and work which the horse enjoys.

Opposite: These feral Australian Brumbies show all the behaviour patterns of their distant, wild ancestors. They descend from settlers' imports and contain much Thoroughbred blood. Although finding ideal surroundings in Australia, they are not indigenous and are criticised for damaging the natural environment

STEREOTYPIES

Stereotypies is the technical word for what are more familiarly known as stable vices. The word 'vice' is not appropriate because it implies the horse is doing something wrong. A dictionary definition of the word 'vice' is 'evil especially grossly immoral habit or conduct, particular form of depravity, serious fault, defect, blemish, (of character), fault, bad trick, in horse etc.' This is, indeed, how vices – stereotypies – were thought of until fairly recently and some more moribund horse people still use that expression.

The reason attitudes, and word usage, have gradually started to change over the past decade or more is because it is now widely accepted that we are the cause of these repetitive, unproductive movements like weaving, box-walking, crib-biting, wind-sucking and other abnormal behaviours not 'officially' called 'vices', like wood and tail chewing, head and neck twisting, scraping the door with the top incisors, frequent door-banging, kicking the walls and (in a naturally peaceful animal) threats and aggression.

I'll make him stop it!

There are various means of physically stopping horses performing stereotypies none of which stops the horse *wanting* to perform them. Fitting muzzles, cutting neck muscles, scattering straw bales around the box, hanging bricks in the doorway and fitting electric wiring over bite-able surfaces are *not* the answer and are grossly unfair to the horse. Research from the USA indicates that stereotypies are an outlet for a horse's distress and those allowed to perform them were better able to cope with life than those prevented from doing so. We are the cause of 'vices' so it is up to us to improve the horse's quality of life, not distress him even further.

Learning and Memory

All creatures have to learn how the world works. We are all born with certain instinctive behaviours and inclinations which help us to survive but the things that happen to us teach us what the world is likely to either throw at us or present to us on a plate. Learning, therefore, goes on all the time. Horses learn very quickly because in the wild their lives depend on it, and usually they learn for a lifetime. Horses never forget but, surprisingly, they do not always act on their memories as we might expect.

Learning is not, then, only what we teach a horse in our training or schooling although horses pick this up quickly provided it is correctly presented to them. When schooling, for instance, you need to have the horse in such a physical position that he not only finds it easy to do what you ask but almost impossible not to do it. You have to use simple, clear requests or aids (physical and vocal), repeated identically several times so that the horse associates that specific sound or physical feel with the action required and you have to praise and reward the horse when he gets it right so that he understands that it was correct and will be pleased to do it again.

Lungeing on one rein is an established, traditional way to school horses in so-called English-style environments although the French invented it (hence its other spelling, 'longeing', meaning to work the horse on a long rein)

84

THERE'S NO EXPLANATION FOR THIS!

We all know of horses who become dangerously traffic-shy because of one accident or near miss but, strangely, not all bad experiences affect the horse's future behaviour even though he must remember them. Horses do have horrific accidents whilst travelling, for instance, yet some load up again next time with no problem.

I've done this before

An instance of how horses remember early learning for a lifetime is shown by an ex-racehorse who had been lunged and backed by one of the best horsewomen in the UK in preparation for his first, two-year-old season. She had a particular way of lungeing which she knew no one else would know about so, when the horse returned to her in his twenties to live out the end of his life, she thought she would just see if he remembered it. In front of an audience of visitors, she lunged him for the first time for twenty years and he performed as though the last time had been yesterday. I could quote many more similar instances.

Having said that, horses usually show a disappointing lack of recognition of former owners, breeders and riders unless they have had a very strong bond, but seem to enjoy meeting old horse friends again. Some have an excellent memory for old stamping grounds – and some don't, or at least they don't show it in any way we can recognise.

Many ex-racehorses, after a period of several months' let-down and psychological relaxation, make excellent mounts for other disciplines. Correct basic dressage schooling promoting engagement of the hindquarters and self-carriage equip them for other careers

Mark, learn and inwardly digest

It is also known that repeating a particular training exercise three times within seven or eight days reinforces it soundly in the horse's brain. Once a week is nothing like as good. But once the horse has learned something well, he will never forget it. If a youngster is given a few weeks backing and riding away in the autumn then left all winter to be brought back into work next spring, he will take tack and rider again like an old hand. Unfortunately, this phenomenal memory applies to both good and bad experiences so, when training, we have to be sure we train well or we may spoil the horse.

New techniques

If a horse has been badly trained, allowed to get into 'bad habits' or been roughly treated and learned to react accordingly, it is usually quite possible to retrain him and give him new experiences. He cannot 'unlearn' the training/experiences he has had but horses of any age are always open to learning, which is what all training and life experience is.

Older horses retiring from one job, say racing, can certainly learn a new job or jobs. Can you imagine two more different ways of going than racing and dressage, yet it is perfectly possible for ex-racehorses to become dressage horses, given correct re-schooling, the right attitude on the part of the trainer and the necessary physique and soundness in the horse.

Different Types of Learning

The two ways in which horses learn are by:

- Classical conditioning in which you obtain a response from the horse to a certain action or cue. For example, when the horses see lights go on in the house in the morning and hear the door or yard gate open they expect to see people. When they hear the feed room door open and buckets banging about, they expect to be fed. They respond by looking expectant and maybe banging their doors if you keep them waiting.
- Free operant or instrumental conditioning.in which horses learn to do something either for a reward or to avoid punishment. (Reward training is now much more in favour than punishment training and results in more trusting, co-operative and relaxed horses. Horses have been proved to respond very well to reward training but poorly to punishment training – not surprisingly.) The horse eventually makes a conscious choice to do something in order to get the reward or avoid the punishment. His action is 'reinforced' accordingly, that is, if he behaves as desired and receives his reward, this is positive reinforcement but if he misbehaves or does not do what is wanted and is punished, this is negative reinforcement.

Obviously, negative reinforcement or punishment training is a very risky procedure because the horse may misunderstand a poorly-given cue or aid, behave as he believes is correct, but is actually 'wrong', and is punished. This is a sure-fire way to create sour, embittered horses. It is also absolutely essential that the trainer's response (reward or punishment) be given immediately and not longer than two seconds after the horse's response, otherwise his brain will not connect the trainer's response with his action, he will become confused and learn nothing. Also, if you reinforce late, you may be reinforcing the wrong action.

Habituation

Habituation is a branch of learning by which we accustom horses to a particular object or circumstance by constant repetition. For instance, we accustom young horses to being groomed by persistently doing it.

REWARDS

Titbits are doubtful reward tools because it is not usually possible to give them quickly enough for the horse to class them as an actual reward. As horses are so sensitive to our tone of voice, an appropriately-spoken 'good girl' or 'good boy' works better. Horses also regard rests as a reward – walking on a long rein with no pressure, or standing still for a few minutes, maybe with the rider dismounted, is appreciated.

85

Attitude is Everything

Predator or Prey?

Most people who associate with animals probably associate with more than one species; many horse owners also have dogs and cats and many people are used to other species, too. All animals are either predators or prey animals and quite a few are both, with differing outlooks on life. Sorry to have to say this again, but the horse is purely a prey animal. His predators in nature come mainly from the dog and cat families. Zebras are preyed on by African hunting dogs working in a pack and by lionesses: male lions are usually too heavy, lazy and slow, and not culturally conditioned by life as a lion to do much hunting – the only time they get out of a trot is when chasing an in-season lioness. Zebra foals may be preyed on by cheetahs who are not heavy and strong enough to bring down and kill a healthy, adult zebra.

Feral horses in North America may be preyed on by cougars and Australian Brumbies by dingoes. In the UK, our feral native ponies no longer have any natural predators big enough to kill them although the odd one has been reported as having been taken by the 'big cats' which, in very small numbers, seem to be roaming the wilds of Dartmoor and elsewhere, probably escapees from safari parks, private collections, circuses and the like.

It depends how you look at it

The differences in attitude to life and its situations between animals with a true prey mentality, like the horse, and those with a predator outlook, like dogs and cats, is considerable. Horses, by their nature, are alert, easily startled and, even though grazing and socialising in a relaxed way, usually have half an eye out for danger. Not for equines the confident luxury of sleeping off an orgy of meat and blood for 22 hours at a stretch as does a sated lion pride: the only thing that will move *them* is a herd of elephants treading resolutely and unwaveringly through their 'camp', knowing the lions will scatter even though their leaders, or an arrogant, ignorant youngster or two, may tough out the confrontation till the last second, eventually escaping with an outraged roar in a cloud of dust. Although feral and wild equines eat steadily for most of their time, they don't 'sleep it off' in a stupor but must stay reasonably alert for danger, sleeping for only short spells.

Large predators do not themselves have predators as such although others may scavenge on their dead and dying bodies. They are not prone to looking for danger but more for seeking out opportunities for a kill, and only then when they are hungry for, as true creatures of nature, they only take from the world what they need when they need it. Faced with an attack, predators will turn and fight in defence. Faced with an attack, a horse will turn and flee in defence. If a horse is actually caught by a predator he will fight back to try to shake it off and get away, and sometimes this works.

Vive la différence!

Predators, then, can be said to have the traits of cunning, deviousness, the ability to plan well ahead (when setting out specifically for the purpose of hunting, for instance), the ability to act on memory and local knowledge of where prey might be, co-operation when hunting in a group (wolves, hunting dogs and lions hunt this way, for example, but most cats are mainly solitary) and tenaciousness in the hunt.

Prey animals can be described as, in general, alert, always ready to flee from danger and sometimes to fight depending on the species (horses only when necessary), wary and suspicious, quick to learn, highly social and with a very keen sense of self-preservation. Equines, too, act on memory and local knowledge as when trekking to distant watering places but whether they actually plan ahead is doubtful, and they are not always too hot on co-operation (for example, if one is attacked others will not usually come to the rescue, with the exception of a foal's dam).

The Ultimate Predator

Then, of course, we have man, the ultimate predator and the only one which habitually takes far more from the environment than he needs. Very often, he does not even take for food and shelter but for sheer acquisitiveness and self-aggrandisement. Man would farm the whole world if he could and his taking and abuse of land and its bounties, plus his pollution of the air above it and his alteration of even our planet's weather systems, are the major cause of the extermination of thousands of species of plants and animals. He is the only creature which commits genocide, which

Play fighting this may be but these Grevy's zebras are also honing their skills at fending off predators. A well-aimed kick can prove fatal to the attacker

abuses and kills not only other species but also his own merely for apparent pleasure and whose combined actions have wittingly brought to the verge of extinction life on earth as we know it – and still he goes on. Maybe Homo Sapiens, the species, is inherently suicidal!

How strange it is, then, that this deadliest, this most lethal of predators frequently forms such a strong psychological alliance with the ultimate prey animal – the horse. It is true that some humans, the more insecure and inadequate, simply want to possess and dominate something covetable, something bigger, stronger, more powerful and more beautiful than themselves. They want his power and beauty to rub off on them, to make them feel good and look impressive to other humans.

For thousands of years man used and grossly abused horses' attributes of speed, strength and co-operation simply as a war machine in both defence and aggression; thankfully this use is now superseded by insensitive, real machines. Other people want to use this power, strength and speed to carry them to glory in competition, again as a self-enhancing power-trip. There are many, though, who have no ulterior motive in their association with horses, who genuinely care about them for their own sake, not because of what the horses can do for them, but who admire, respect and love them and who want them to be content, comfortable and with an interesting, stimulating life which they can share in an equal partnership.

I am sure there are more of this sort of human than we are aware of simply because they are not well-known or in the public eye and, therefore, their actual numbers cannot be known. It is sometimes difficult to achieve a rewarding, lasting partnership (with animal or human!) but thankfully the human species is sufficiently varied to have enough members who keep a horse or horses on a largely altruistic basis (who on earth mucks out on a pitch black, freezing or soaking wet winter's morning for glory or self-aggrandisement?) but also for the great pleasure such a partnership brings – and thankfully, despite the two being such very different animals, their horses seem quite happy about it, too.

Equine Society

$\mathbf{E}$quine relationships in natural conditions and also so-called herd hierarchies seem to be subjects of continuing fascination for horsepeople and animal scientists.

Hollywood hero

Those who do not live near wild or feral herds may have taken as their image of a wild herd the Hollywood depiction of mustangs roaming the prairies of North America. There would be a beautiful stallion who was the herd leader, often shown rearing and pawing the air on high ground, master of all he surveyed. The other herd members would do as he told them, accepting his wisdom and dominance. He would protect them from predators, including man, would know where the best food, shelter and grazing was to be found and would provide his herd with security and guidance as a sort of equine father figure. Well, this may be a glamorous, reassuring picture but it was manipulated by the (male) movie moguls to promote and fit the wild, free, male-dominated image of the Wild West – and is not how it was, or is.

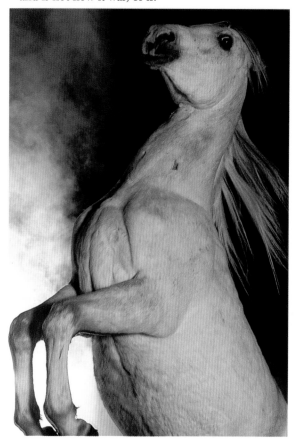

INTRODUCING NEWCOMERS

$\mathbf{D}$omestic herd newcomers may have nowhere to run to if existing members initially reject them so it is safest (especially if they are all wearing shoes) to turn the new horse out with a quiet, friendly one separately from the main herd, gradually introducing others into the spin-off herd to get to know each other, until all can be mixed.

Always try to ensure that the new horse can at least see his new friend/s, ideally being next to one of them, and is certainly not next to a less favoured inmate because, notwithstanding the stable wall between them, each knows it is in the other's personal space and, in horse society, this sort of forced confrontation is one of the most stressful situations you can have and one which has to be endured for many hours out of twenty-four. No wonder so many horses develop stereotypies.

What's it really like?

Horses are not obsessed with dominance: most just want a quiet life with someone else making the decisions. In naturally structured herds, researchers report that there is often hardly any hierarchy, more defined friendships.

Equine society, too, is definitely feminist. The leader is nearly always a mare who makes the major decisions and the females often stay congenially together for life. The stallion is a lodger and when he is ousted or too old or infirm to perform his sexual purpose, a new stallion takes over and the mares just accept him.

Stallions may kill a previous stallion's foals so that they can mate the mares and pass on their own genes instead. Young males are usually kicked out at puberty but fillies, too, leave if a herd is growing too big or if another stallion steals them. The stallion will not protect the herd from predators or police its members, and the herding he does is usually to keep his mares together in the face of competition from another stallion. It is the lead mare who will lead her herd to fresh grazing and water, discipline weaned youngsters and so on.

Social acceptance

Because horses are herd animals, they want to belong and social acceptance is important to their

The 'Hollywood Hero' – the proud, white stallion – would be too visible to survive long in the wild

88

sense of security. In the wild, the newcomers are usually born into the herd and a new stallion will fight for takeover unless a herd is without a stallion, in which case he'll hang around on the fringes in spring, spot who is the Boss Lady and make up to her. If the post is vacant, normally there's no problem.

If a young male is forming his own herd, the females sort out among themselves which mare is going to run the harem and the rare one with the leadership qualities usually gets the job, most horses being followers.

STABLING

There is a strange view in some quarters of the horse world that horses should not be allowed to make friends as it adversely affects their concentration on work! In fact, one of the most distressing things you can do is to stable a horse next to a non-friend and particularly one with whom he or she does not get on. Friendships must certainly be nurtured indoors and out if you want normally settled, relaxed and psychologically balanced horses. Owners must become friends of a different species with their horses, then there will be no problems separating equine friends during work. If they know from the start that work is human time and that they will be reunited later (and sometimes work together, say hacking), there will be no problems. Think of the Three Fs – Firmness, Fairness and Friendship.

Horses approach strangers normally by drawing themselves up to look as big and imposing as possible unless they have submissive natures

Rolling is used to coat each horse with the communal herd smell – a mixture of all members – and so often takes place in designated rolling places

Bonding behaviours

Horses cement relationships with various behavioural acts such as all rolling on the same patch to acquire the herd scent, mutual grooming, manure and urine marking (more common among males) and acts of submission (see 'Getting Through').

Friends firm-up relationships by standing and grazing very close together or touching. Mothers and daughters often become good friends but outside mares brought in by a stallion can find their place and make friends, too.

Unlike the society of some other social animals, it is not only an alpha pair which may mate, with the non-breeders 'auntying' the offspring. The stallion will mate all his mares as they become ready. Both male and females know when the time is right.

Mares bond extremely strongly with their own foals and defend them against all comers, equine and other, but can be even lethally aggressive towards other mares' foals especially if suckling their own. A rejected or orphaned suckling foal in a wild or feral herd is usually under a death sentence. Even the stallion does not usually defend his own foals, so he is no legendary father figure.

Domestic Pressures

The natural picture spills over into domesticity but with noticeable changes due to our manipulations and restricted, unnatural accommodation.

Owners of domestic horses are often interested in the clear herd hierarchy frequently followed by horses in domestic paddocks which seems to arise in artificial, relatively cramped situations. Horses have a variable personal space around them with invisible boundaries about 3.5 to 4.5m (12 to 15 feet) away which only friends and other honoured herd members are allowed to breach. Feral horses naturally respect these boundaries but domesticated ones often have no choice but to cross them and skirmishes and jockeying for position can then occur, with the emergence of a hierarchy.

All Boys Together

Bachelor Bands

Bachelor bands, as herds of all-male horses are called, are equivalent to a men's club or a band of teenage boys, perhaps with a few older members. Apart from crude or sexist jokes (which horses may or may not tell!), their behaviour is rather similar. They rib each other, have mock fights, show off in boisterous behaviour aimed at confirming to the other members what a lad they are and 'not to mess with me even though I want to be in with the in-crowd'. They form friendships and mere colleague-ships, just as mares and fillies do and, of course, all their other equine instincts as regards flight-or-fight are firmly intact: it's just that there are no females around and no sex.

These Dartmoor ponies in a domestic paddock show the boisterous 'boy-gang' behaviour common in bachelor bands in the wild

There's more to life than this

Of course, in the spring a horse's fancy certainly causes much disruption in natural horse society. In any favourable horse-country, there may be several small herds plus a bachelor band or two, all roaming one region, perhaps several or many miles square, depending on the country. The hormones all start to rise in these herds about the same time and they become restless.

A stallion's lot

Established herd stallions must now be on the lookout for not only mares requiring attention in their own herds but also young male members of them becoming too interested in his mares for his liking. Out they will be kicked if they put a hoof wrong, and maybe even if they don't, to pre-empt any hassle. As if courting and mating his mares and kicking out resident pretenders to his throne (sons or not) were not enough, the stallion must also be on guard, like any horse, for predators and also for marauding bachelor bands or lone stallions trying to pinch his mares to form herds of their own. He may even find himself being propositioned by a strange mare wanting a home.

It is not surprising that some stallions just can't cope and are overthrown or relieved of a few mares. If they do manage to juggle so many projects successfully, they usually end the breeding season sadly thin (despite all that spring and summer grass – eat? who's got time to eat?) and really need the autumn flush of grass to build themselves up for a harsh but more restful winter.

The pretenders

From the bachelors' points of view, life among them can become quite competitive. Having spent a calm, friendly winter together with no female distractions – even those they came across were uninteresting, being anoestrus or not sexually active – they must now succumb to the call of nature. Civil war is declared: they often fight mercilessly over any spare mares or fillies who may be around having suddenly found themselves herd-less, or actively try to filch mares from other herds and challenge existing herd stallions, particularly older, sick or injured ones, or those obviously over-worked who can't be everywhere at once. New herds are formed thus and life goes on.

The Entires' Club

In domestic establishments where colts and stallions are habitually used such as circuses, racing yards and many dressage yards (stallions having that extra presence and oomph required in the dressage arena), there are hardly any problems in keeping entires together provided everyone knows what they are doing.

Horses are basically peace-loving animals, as mentioned, and stallions normally only fight when there is something worth fighting over – an in-season mare. Circuses rarely use mares and most dressage riders don't seem to care for them, either, so in a mare-free yard there are no intoxicating

pheromones to distract the stallions and there is no problem. The only normal thing that isn't done is to turn the entires out together, but it is perfectly all right for them to be turned out (as they should be) individually or with, say, a non-breeding mare. The Arab stallion Scindian Magic was not the only one to be taught his manners this way. His companion, the pony mare Glenda, kept him firmly in his place from youth and he had the benefit of her company for years.

Mixed company

Some other yards, particularly flat-racing yards, do have mixed company in residence but fillies and colts are often stabled away from each other and kept separate, as described previously, during work. Entires not used for breeding are normally discouraged from showing any sexual interest in females and come to realise that it is unwanted behaviour. When they later go to stud, if they do, it can be a little while before they relax and realise that this is now exactly what is wanted. There's nothing more contrary than humans. Stallions which do stud work and are also ridden and/or driven are, again, no problem if well-handled and their guidelines made crystal clear. They soon learn, for example, that one set of tack, and especially one particular bit, is used for serving, and a different one for other work, they know what is expected and although their heart rate will shoot up in the presence of a tempting 'bit of stuff', they usually

Lone colts and stallions feel vulnerable and normally try to establish a new breeding herd or to at least secure the company of other males, forming a bachelor band

behave. Neither do they pick fights with geldings. An equine charity was once asked to take in a small herd of stallions which had been brought up together from foalhood. They were all firm friends and provided no strange horses were brought into the herd peace reigned.

Keeping entires on a mixed, non-professional yard could certainly cause trouble even if the staff and owner were competent and trustworthy enough to manage them. It would probably be the other horse-owners who caused the problems by teasing the poor stallion with their in-season mares parading past his box or putting them in the neighbouring paddock. The temptation would be more than a saint could bear.

PERMISSIVE SOCIETY

The subject of vasectomised stallions has been raised elsewhere. Although such horses are frequently used on studs as teasers, it would take an extremely forward-thinking and sensible crowd of horse owners on a mixed yard to allow their mares to be turned out with such a horse and allow them to have fairly normal sex lives! It would also be necessary to separate the geldings for their own safety. I should love to hear from anyone who has kept horses this way.

Girl Talk

Horse society is matriarchal, very definitely an equine version of The Sisterhood. Mares form firm friendships with other herd members and their own offspring. Although colts seem usually to be turfed out of a herd by the stallion, under natural conditions, some research workers, behaviourists and the like believe that mares would form as strong bonds with their sons as with their daughters, if the sons were allowed to stay.

In domestic conditions, there is a surprising number of people who separate mares and geldings during turnout time. Not having been brought up this way, I found it quite illogical and incomprehensible the first time I encountered it. I have never been given a satisfactory answer as to why some people do this. One comment was: 'You have to remember that mares are entires, like stallions, and they cause a lot of trouble in mixed company.' What rubbish! Certainly mares are entires, having their full complement of sexual organs and resulting hormones, but I have never yet met a mare who gratuitously caused trouble in mixed company.

With any group of horses, all male, all female or mixed, there will be a certain amount of squealing, snorting, stamping, mock kicking (usually just bottoms up) and so on when they are first turned out in the morning or evening and have a chance to say a proper horsey 'hello' to each other. Anyone stupid enough to just bundle a strange horse, mare or gelding into an established herd is asking for a lot more than this, including broken bones.

The experts' choice?
Many expert horsemen and women prefer to ride mares than geldings. They feel mares are more loyal, build stronger relationships with their owners, that they are more intelligent, sensitive, courageous, that they give more and like to live life to the full. Of course, gelding and stallion fanciers always counter with the accusation of 'mareish' behaviour and claim that you cannot plan any sort of competitive programme with a mare because, when in season, she will be completely unreliable and it will be a waste of time taking her anywhere because she won't win anything. She's embarrassing in company when in season and makes up to

anything that moves, won't concentrate on what she's doing and does silly and potentially dangerous things. Surely a middle road is more logical. In any case, all temperament differences come down as much to individuality and breed as to gender.

The in-season mare
The mare's hormonal processes during her oestrus cycle, which continues for probably just over six months of the year, have already been detailed. The mare herself has no control over these and can't help feeling the way she does. It is, therefore, very foolish of owners to punish her for behaving as nature tells her to.

Most horse owners and stable staff are female these days, and should therefore have more understanding of the way the mare's cycle affects her and be sensible about it. Like humans, some are more affected than others and if you really cannot stand the way your mare is during her seasons, bearing in mind that you are going to have to put up with it every three weeks for six or seven months, perhaps you should let her go to someone with more

Herds are a matriarchal society, headed by a lead mare, with youngsters of various ages. Stallions merely come and go, conquering and being defeated, whilst the main herd maintains its family core

empathy towards this type of natural occurrence and buy yourself a gelding.

Therapy

If you are certain that your mare's 'difficult behaviour' coincides with her season (keep a diary to be certain), you could discuss with your vet the possibility of treatment with Regumate. This is a synthetic hormone similar to progesterone which, therefore, acts contrary to oestrogen and prevents the mare coming into season. If you compete with your mare, you would have to check with your administrative body as to whether or not they permit drug treatment of this nature.

Another topic to discuss with your vet could include ovarian tumours which can result in mares being anoestrus, in oestrus most of the time or behaving like stallions, according to which hormones the tumour cells are producing.

Some owners report a significant improvement in their mares' behaviour when treated by various complementary therapies such as herbalism, radionics and homoeopathy. There are many herbal 'calmers' on the market now not all of which are successful or appropriate to in-season mares. If you wish to try a herbal product to help with this problem, look for one which is specifically geared to helping mares during oestrus – or rather helping

IT'S UP TO YOU

Mares can certainly be ridden and worked when in season, of course, and competed with as well. If you really feel that you don't want to compete when your mare is in season, then don't: you should have a fairly precise idea of her cycle and when she is likely to be 'in' and can avoid entering events on those dates. Horses are not machines and even geldings and stallions can have their bad days, if for different reasons.

Basically, the solution to this 'problem', which is probably only a problem to the owner and not to the mare, is to employ a good deal of empathy and understanding when mares are in season or, if the owner is a serious competitor who does not want his or her programme disrupted by a perfectly natural process, to compete on a gelding, or stallion, instead.

their owners! It is important to remember that the mare is behaving quite naturally and probably feels fine. There are moral and ethical considerations involved in preventing any animal's natural behaviour (which we do all the time when keeping horses, not least by stabling them) and, although extreme measures such as surgical removal of normal ovaries just to stop a mare coming into season might be suggested, such a drastic measure, which involves the expense and stress of a major operation, would not be considered by conscientious owners or vets.

Something's Missing!

The castration of domestic animals has been going on for thousands of years. Some people believe it to be morally wrong and although they have a valid point of view it has to be said that many castrated animals appear to be much more content than they would probably have been had they been left entire with no chance to live a normal life or even a contentedly domesticated one.

From the point of view of geldings, more 'ordinary' horse owners seem to buy geldings than mares and certainly than stallions because they are easier for them to handle, accommodate and manage than most stallions and, of course, they do not come into season like mares.

How is it done?
Castration is, obviously, the surgical removal of a male horse's testicles. It can be performed at any time when both testicles are descended but is normally performed between the ages of one and three years, usually in the spring when the weather is kind and there is little chance of flies contaminating the wound and introducing infection. It should also ensure that the horse can be turned out to exercise naturally which will help minimise any swelling of the area.

Basically, the colt can be castrated standing up under sedation and local anaesthetic or lying down, unconscious, under a general anaesthetic. The operation involves the removal of all the testicular tissue which prevents the production of male hormones and sperm. Some owners like to leave male colts entire until their three-year-old spring as they believe this encourages more muscular development, more of a crest to the neck and retains a prouder spirit which is fine provided you have the skill and facilities to cope with a big, boisterous, probably unbroken colt for so long. It seems, though, that leaving a male entire does result in a horse who does not reach

the height he would have done if castrated, but this may be debatable.

Removing the problem?

Despite the fact that gelding (castration) does remove the problems of both hormones and sperm, it is estimated that over half of all geldings retain some stallion-like behavioural traits, particularly if they were gelded late (say at three years) and especially if they had previously served a mare.

I bought a gelding who had only been 'cut' (gelded) in his three-year-old spring, a few weeks before I bought him, because he was seen serving his two-year-old sister (who did not conceive). He was running with his sister, his yearling entire brother and his dam who was due to foal again. He had stallion-like characteristics all his life.

Geldings who do show stallion-like behaviour do things like herding mares into one half of a field using the normal stallion technique of driving them with head low, ears back and using a snaking, side-to-side motion of the neck. They may then

Castration invariably 'quietens down' male horses although many geldings retain stallion-like inclinations

stand between the mares and any other geldings, keeping the two 'herds' apart, getting little grazing done themselves! They sometimes strike out with a foreleg when talking to other horses and they may form firmer friendships with mares than other geldings. Some can obtain an erection and some attempt to mount mares. I have never seen a gelding actually enter a mare but some people have.

However, such geldings do not seem to be prone to biting and nipping (definite stallion behaviour) or to kicking, are not abnormally aggressive towards other geldings and are much more 'toned down' in their general behaviour than stallions. Certainly, my horse, mentioned above, had the sweetest imaginable temperament of any horse I have known.

Rest assured

To reassure potential purchasers who do not know whether to buy a mare with all her oestrus 'problems' or a gelding who may be a pseudo-stallion (in fact, they are often called 'false geldings' even they are certainly true geldings), such behaviour is most common in newly structured herds or when horses are newly turned out after a winter mainly stabled. It usually wears off or greatly decreases after a couple of weeks and is, in any case, nothing to worry about.

Why all this should happen, though, can surely only be due to memory, so perhaps, if you want to be fairly sure of removing all stallion characteristics, it would be as well to have your colts castrated early in life.

NEITHER ONE THING NOR THE OTHER

Rigs are another matter. The terms 'rig' and ridgling are the colloquial ones for a cryptorchid, a male horse with one or both testes still up in the abdomen. Such animals maybe fertile, behave like stallions and can be extremely dangerous because they are sold as geldings to unsuspecting amateur owners who simply cannot handle them.

Your vet can take a sample of blood from any horse you suspect of being a rig and test it to see whether or not he is producing male hormones. If he is, the vet can perform an operation to remove one or both testes, as the case may be, from the abdomen or inguinal canal, wherever they turn out to be. This is a fairly major operation but is a sure-fire cure. At worst, you will be left with a false gelding and at best an ordinary one! Your horse will be infertile and your problems will be over, although with any freshly castrated horse it takes a few weeks for things to damp down.

Getting Through

orses and ponies communicate with each other and with other species mainly by sight and body language, the most minute change in posture and way of movement being noted and assessed by an observer. Horses the world over use the same language and they are consistent so it is not difficult for us to learn to speak what has become known colloquially, mainly through Monty Roberts' efforts, as Equus to any horse wherever we may travel and, what's more, to understand what the horse is saying to us.

The human artform, mime, is the same. Anyone anywhere, no matter what language they use vocally, can understand it and could communicate in it. When we British, who are notoriously poor at learning foreign languages, travel abroad, we often

Horses use the most subtle nuances of body language to communicate with each other, often unseen by and, in any case, unintelligible to humans

find that mime, gesticulation and also drawing which is also universal, help us to be understood. The pathetic trait the more stupid of us have of shouting at non-English-speaking foreigners *in English* simply hinders understanding – understandably! Shouting at horses, in any language, often fails to work but positioning ourselves and perhaps the horse in the correct way usually does. There is a qualifying comment on the use of Equus: it has been noted by more perceptive people that horses who have associated with a variety of humans for many years use only a

restricted version of Equus to us (and us alone) and exaggerate the simplest aspects of it because they know that this is all that is likely to sink in and hopefully produce a response. Non-human species don't have this problem. How perceptive horses are!

Body Language

So, the main key to understanding and communicating with horses (and other animals) who are within sight is what is now known as body language – position, posture, movement. We firstly have to understand what we are dealing with, what our partner is communicating to us, what mood he or she is in and, therefore, what response we are likely to get.

General impressions

A horse who is feeling well, confident, interested, outgoing and so on will have an alert look to his whole body, his eyes will be soft and interested, his ears will prick readily in the direction of what is interesting him, his head will be held up normally, he will stand square or maybe with a hind leg relaxed, tail mobile and relaxed and maybe up and out a little. He will usually want to sniff us and will either approach us or stand still when he sees us. Aggressive or very assertive horses may put their ears back in warning or attempted intimidation and may approach us with head down, muzzle outstretched and an expression in their eyes varying from warning to vicious. Their nostrils may be wrinkled up and back and their teeth may even be bared. The tail will be up or may be switching around and the general message is, but not so politely, 'you're not welcome and if you stay remember I'm the boss'.

Horses who are simply super-self-confident may not show aggression but will stand their ground when you, say, enter their box, refusing to move over or may even try to shove you out of their way, may not co-operate in mucking out, grooming or tacking up and may only show interest at feeding time, then not waiting for you to deliver the goods but taking it themselves.

More submissive horses, often youngsters but some others, or those who have at least learned that it does not pay to trample over certain humans, will usually move back or over when asked (provided they understand, as youngsters may not) when you are moving around their box, will not grab food before you have put it in place, will co-operate during grooming, mucking out and tacking up etc. They will show interest without over-assertion, mobile ears, carefully enquiring muzzle and will pay attention to where you are in the stable and what you are doing.

Very submissive horses, almost always very young ones to older ones and to most humans but also some in-season mares to stallions, often show the classic mouthing, snapping movement which says: 'I am completely submissive to you. Don't hurt me.' This movement involves the horse snapping his mouth open and shut, usually about a couple of times a second, with head down, ears forward or to the side but not usually with any sign of fear. Actual fear would promote a flight response and the horse would be trying to get away.

Horses who are feeling sick, depressed or very bored are often difficult to differentiate between. Usually an empathetic owner or human will sense the situation and checking the vital health signs will also help. The head will be level with the withers or lower, the ears will be flopping to the sides or maybe slightly back, the eyes will be dull, the horse may be resting a hind leg or maybe a foreleg if this is causing discomfort although this is not an infallible sign. The tail will be drooping between the buttocks and the horse will have a general air of unease or misery.

Human-to-horse communication

Anyone taught to lunge knows that positioning yourself towards the horse's forehand will slow him down or stop him and putting yourself at his hip will speed him up. These basic principles work in

This mouthing, snapping action (horse on left) is typical of submissive youngsters and often of in-season mares to stallions. Young or submissive horses may also do this to humans

By adopting a non-aggressive, even submissive, stance, you tell a horse that you are not a threat to him and welcome his friendship

the round-pen system of training used by some trainers now: you can work a horse loose, change gait, stop, back and turn him round, just by positioning yourself in front of or behind him.

But to give the horse a hint of your mood, your position in the hierarchy, if you like, you can adopt an aggressive or friendly posture. Looking the horse in the eyes with a staring, assertive expression, squaring your shoulders to him and maybe raising your hands and arms usually stops and sends him away: conversely, standing sideways on to him or at an angle of about 45° with your shoulders drooped and relaxed, head down a little and not staring at him indicates that you are not aggressive and are willing to let him approach and be friendly. Many people find that eye contact in general is not aggressive, it is the expression in your eyes which the horse picks up on and recognises, believe it or not, combined with your general body posture and attitude.

The other senses

Horses also recognise and bond with each other by means of voice, smell and taste, and a good deal by touch. The tone of voice, the familiar smell and taste and the touching, nibbling and grooming actions carried out by horses to other horses and animals and to humans, combined with body language recognised by vision, are all part of the extremely complex but effective language of Equus, one which we would probably all be better off learning to both understand and 'speak'.

The Equine Language

Learning to understand Equus is much easier for us than learning a human language because the horse's natural language, which has provided him with nearly all the communication he has needed over many millions of years, is mainly one of actions, postures, signals and facial expressions. You can learn to speak and understand it fluently and to feel comfortable with it in less than a week if you are really interested in what horses are trying to say. Different parts of the body can be used for several different meanings and, combined with other parts and the horse's general attitude, will give a very clear picture of the horse's meaning.

The head and face

Horses use their whole bodies to communicate, but the face and head are particularly important.

Ears

The ears give you a reliable idea of how the horse may be feeling and where his attention is directed.

- Ears pricked sharply forward and up indicate attention focused directly ahead on something interesting, amazing or alarming.
- If held to the side and relaxed, the horse is relaxed and maybe dozing, feeling off colour or listening intently to something but the direction of which he cannot determine.

Thinking of two things at once (and probably more). The left ear is keeping tabs on the photographer whilst the right one is indicating the horse's attention on something in front of him

- If pointing loosely backwards, the horse is either paying attention to something (not necessary audible) behind or on top of him, or could be feeling ill. If the ears are clamped hard back and down, the horse is signalling aggression, pain or is trying his utmost at the task in hand.

Eyes

A friendly, relaxed horse will have a soft look in the eyes; a bright, alert look shows interest and a good mood whilst a dull appearance and sunken eye shows illness or pain. Aggression is shown by a hard look to the eye but not necessarily with the white showing, nor does the white showing necessarily indicate anger.

Nostrils

- Flared, open and circular nostrils indicate great interest, alarm, excitement or fear.
- Relaxed, semi-open nostrils show a calm attitude or dullness and boredom.
- Nostrils drawn up and back and wrinkled at their tops indicate aggression, pain or severe distress, boredom or frustration.

The head is turned slightly to the right and the ears both pricked forwards, indicating that this horse's full attention is on something in front of him to his right. The eyes and nostrils are wide to take in other information

Position and movement of the head

The horse needs to position his head in certain ways in order to see, so this is not always a reliable indicator of language. However, combined with expression and other body signs, things suddenly become clearer, as explained in Combined Signals.

The legs

- standing with one hip 'dropped' and the corresponding hindleg flexed and resting on the toe. After a minute or so, they will often swap sides. Standing with a hindleg in an awkward position, though, and frequently shifting the weight, indicates pain in that leg, hip or back.
- If a horse often stands with his forelegs unlevel, one in front of or behind the other which is in the normal, straight up position, he is signalling pain in that leg.
- Horses stamp any leg to dislodge flies and may kick at their own bellies if the fly is hard to reach otherwise, although this can also mean pain.
- They paw the ground to prepare a place to roll or lie down, or to signify abdominal pain or frustration.
- A foreleg strike-out is an offensive warning, common in stallions and assertive geldings or even some mares, although in the latter it is usually restricted to a firm stamp.
- A hindleg waving in the air, particularly if the horse is looking in a particular direction (not necessarily by turning the head but simply tilting it so he can see behind him), says clearly that he intends to kick and is either warning or actually taking aim. Be warned that not all kicks are preceded by this warning! Some just happen like lightning.

The tail

- Held high and tight it indicates great interest or alarm. High and swaying from side to side means the horse feels good and perhaps exhilarated.
- The tail clamped between the buttocks shows aggression around the rear (watch for kick signals, too) or pain and/or submission.

If a horse makes a face at you (although this one's owner seems to feel he is playing) raising a hand may stop him in his tracks although he could throw up his head and bang his poll on the top of the door jamb

- A tail being swished or thrashed (called 'switching') around indicates severe displeasure or distress, pain or significant irritation from insects.
- A relaxed tail means a relaxed horse.

Combined signals

Probably aggression or friendliness are the two messages people need most to understand so here is their combination of signals:

Aggression

The horse's ears will be back, his head may be fairly low with the muzzle extended or turned towards the object of his aggression. He will have an angry look in his eyes, his nostrils will be drawn up and back and show wrinkles and he may even be baring his teeth or opening his mouth to bite. His tail may be thrashing angrily and he may be raising and waving a hind hoof in preparation to kick. All this may be accompanied by an equine swear word or two. Message: 'Get outa here – quick!'

Friendliness

The horse will have his ears pricked in a relaxed way towards the object of his affection (a friend, welcomed visitor or human with titbit). The head will be neutral or down slightly as he sniffs and nuzzles. All his feet will be on the ground and his tail hanging loosely. His eyes will have a soft, interested look and his nostrils may be flared or just relaxed and semi-open. Message: 'It's really good to see you; let's spend some time together.' And, if the friend is human, maybe: 'You don't happen to have anything good to eat, do you?'

Most mares will not entertain the attentions of anyone else's foal. The mare on the left has put her ears back and made an unwelcoming face at the little foal on the right whose dam would doubtless step in if things hotted up

How Do You Feel About That?

When riding, we cannot see our horses' expressions. The backward-pointing ears of this pony could indicate anger, fear or simply that he is trying hard to go fast at the request of his young rider

Whenever the subject of equine emotions comes up during conversation amongst a group of horse people, it is often accompanied by a number of blank expressions, shrugs and a noticeable lull in the conversation. The reason is that equine emotions are not at all easy to recognise unless you are really tuned in to your horse.

You can often get a fair idea of how a horse is feeling in general, and will be left in no doubt about strongly expressed emotions, but those little nuances and changes of mood can be very hard to absorb. When we are riding our horses it can be even more difficult as we cannot see the horse's face which, as in any species, usually informs observers of how he is feeling. We can feel the horse's body tone and movements through our legs and seat, though. It is amazing to remember that it is only fairly recently that it has been widely accepted that horses do have emotions and feelings. Older books on training, with some notable exceptions, concentrated almost entirely on getting the horse to do what humans asked or demanded with no

questions asked and no consideration for whether or not the horse wanted to do it let alone whether he felt able to or what kind of mood he was in. Opinions have changed and more and more people are now interested in the horse's psychology, behaviour and in his soul or spirit – in the horse as a sentient being. The more perceptive and caring horse people invariably say how sensitive and observant the horse is and it now seems to be only the really hidebound who pay little or no attention to the horse's feelings.

Because horses are such gregarious, social animals, it is important to them, in their natural life, which spills over into domesticity as the only life most horses have ever known, to be able to recognise how their herdmates and other associates are feeling and to convey how they themselves are feeling.

It often seems to work out that particular

emotions create different effects on the muscles. It is obvious why fear, suspicion, anger, anxiety, nervousness and excitement, for example, make the horse's muscles tense and stiff or actually hard because all these emotions could result in the horse having to prepare for action and run away. Muscle tone increases, the horse gears up for flight, or for fight if flight is impossible.

The emotions of sadness, depression, peacefulness and calmness, conversely, result in loose, slack muscles because the horse is not gearing up for action. States which cannot be classified as actual emotions are tiredness and sickness or pain and will result in loose muscles for the first two and tense ones for the latter. Although not strictly emotions, they affect how a horse is feeling and will be expressed by him.

An ex-jockey friend of mine says he always knew when a horse who was being difficult over something (passing through a gateway, loading into the horsebox etc.) was being awkward or was genuinely frightened. He claimed that if the horse was just being bloody-minded the muscles in his neck would feel normal or soft but if he was frightened or worried they would be tense. I also have found this to work in practice, but when bloody-mindedness turns to anger, you need to look for other signs so that you know how to react!

The late Dr Moyra Williams, co-founder with me of the Equine Behaviour Forum, said: '… in general, pleasure causes relaxation and displeasure causes contraction of various muscle groups affecting the position of the head, the ears, the eyes, the nostrils, the legs and the tail, while tension further alters the rate of breathing which may be evident in calls, snorts, squeals and gasps.' Obviously, the heart rate will also change, an increased rate indicating highly charged emotions such as fear, anticipation, anger and nervousness, whilst a lower rate will mean happiness, contentment, co-operation, sadness, depression and so on.

We reproduce here Dr Williams' chart, originally published in my book *Behaviour Problems In Horses*, published by David & Charles, as it is a very valuable diagnostic aid to anyone interested in recognising and understanding equine emotions.

SIGNS OF EMOTION

Sensation	Ears	Head	Eyes	Jaw and mouth	Tail	Legs	Muscle tension	Breathing	Voice
Pain	Back	Flat	Shut	Stiff	Flat	Stiff	Tight	Heavy	Silent
Fear	Back	Up	Wide open directed to cause	Stiff	Flat	Stiff	Tight	Gasping	Squeal
Anxiety	Sideways	Up	Wide open directed to cause	Stiff	Raised slightly	Stiff	Tight	Gasping	Silent
Apprehension	Sideways	Up	Wide open directed to cause	Stiff	Raised slightly	Braced	Tight	Blowing through nostrils	Silent
Anger	Flat back	Pointed out	Looking back	Showing teeth	Whisking	Braced	Moderate	Fast	May squeal
Anticipation	Forwards	Up	Directed to cause	Stiff	High	Moving	Moderate	Moderate	Nicker
Peace	Sideways	Loose	Half closed	Relaxed	Loose	Still	Slack	Slow	Silent
Happiness	Sideways	Up	Half closed	Relaxed	Loose	May move loosely	Moderate	Moderate	Nicker
Enjoyment	Sideways	Loose	Half closed	Relaxed	Raised	May move slightly	Moderate loosely	Slightly faster	Silent
Excitement	Forwards	Up	Directed to cause	Tight	High	Moving	Stiff	Blowing	Silent
Exhaustion	Sideways	Down	Closed	Relaxed	Loose	Flagging	Loose	Heavy	Silent
Submission	Side to back	Pointed out	Half closed	Lips snapping	Flat	Braced	Moderate	Normal	Silent

Distant Cousins

Horses' instinct for mixing with others extends far beyond their own kind although most horses do prefer other horses and ponies to other species. In nature, like all wildlife, they are part of a rich species mix comprising other herbivores large and small, carnivorous predators, not all of which prey on them, birds, reptiles, insects, amphibians, and water life of various sorts, and take them for granted.

Probably one of the most famous wildlife spectacles in the world is the cyclic migrations of zebras and wildebeest up and down Africa's Rift Valley as they move to and from seasonal grazing grounds, being drowned and/or preyed upon by crocodiles in the treacherous river crossing, by carnivores lying in wait en route and, those who don't make it, being finally finished off by hyenas and vultures.

Zebras and wildebeest, horses and cattle and, to a lesser extent, sheep, make complementary grazing partners. Zebras habitually take the more fibrous stalks of grasses whilst the wildebeest opt for the juicy leaves and flowering or seeding heads and both species are frequently seen with birds riding on their backs ridding them of skin parasites.

In domesticity, cattle are ideal to cream off lush, rich grass, the horses can crop their leavings quite satisfactorily, grazing with or after them, and sheep can do a short-shear job after the horses, although both horses and sheep can clip grass down to the soil. The parasites of each species are killed when ingested by another, unnatural host so mixed grazing is a big, natural help with parasite control.

NATURAL JUSTICE

A particularly aggressive cockerel at a yard where I once kept my mare found her long, old teeth snapping at him an easy match for his hostile attempts to peck her out of his way, so he would jump up and down underneath her instead, pecking her belly out of spite and evading her kicks. Sadly (or happily, whichever way you look at it), some mink got him one night – and Sarah could eat in peace.

If you have a rough patch of land that really wants rooting out and grubbing up but you don't want to plough it (not usually recommended for horse paddocks as it destroys the springy carpet of old turf roots which protects the legs of boisterous, galloping horses), you could do worse than put pigs on it to really clean it up and clear it out before reseeding.

House guests

Many domestic horses share their boxes with other species – the stable cat jumps in and out at will, wild birds nest in the rafters and share horses' concentrates, and hens not only invade horses' mangers but find their backs warm, safe places to

perch and roost. The horses don't usually mind the latter at all but I have known a few be put off their food because some bossy hen was sitting gorging herself in the manger.

Owners who leave old banks round the sides of their horses' beds will often find a corner taken over by a hen or cat bringing up her family there. Wildlife occasionally move in but not where humans are constantly coming in and out, and in many stable yards there is a frequent problem with those not-so-welcome visitors – rats.

All tarred with the same brush

Despite their generally social natures, horses do not like or get on with every other sort of animal they meet: the common aversion of many horses to pigs is well known and lots of horses seem afraid of donkeys despite others having valued donkey companions.

I once had a gelding who, after being bitten on the nose by a Great Dane, developed a hatred of all small animals of any species except children, including little ponies. He was once demoted at a livery yard because he leaned over his stable door, picked up the owner's Afghan Hound by his back and threw him across the small stable yard.

It often seems to be the case that the species horses come across when young are accepted but maybe those they do not encounter till later in life pose a threat or just come into the category of 'unfamiliar therefore dangerous' in the horse's mentality. I have often wondered why my gelding Royal's being bitten by a dog led to his hating all small animals, not just dogs.

But humans are different

Horses do obviously realise that humans are different and seem to separate them quite clearly from other species. In my experience, whereas horses also differentiate between individual humans they do not apply this principle to other species.

We do not spend anything like as much time with our horses as other animals are free to do, even though it feels like it sometimes. Few of us in the western world have our horses sleeping with us

as some eastern peoples are reported as doing. Maybe Romany travellers are the nearest we in the UK get to seeing this.

In fact, the very strong bonds some of us do form with our horses are surely surprising in view of the fact that most horse owners, even those who can keep their horses at home, probably spend no more than an average of 10 to 15 hours a *week* (of 168 hours) actually with their horses, grooming, handling, riding, fussing, not yard chores like mucking out, sweeping up and so on which is not time *with* the horse. It speaks volumes for horses' sociability and accepting natures.

103

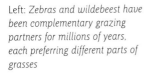

Left: *Zebras and wildebeest have been complementary grazing partners for millions of years, each preferring different parts of grasses*

Right: *Marauding dogs may equate in the horses' minds to a wolf attack. Whilst some horses will run away in panic, others will fight them off, particularly mares with foals*

Do Horses Have a Sixth Sense?

Extra-sensory perception, super-sensory perception, sixth sense, equine intuition, whatever you like to call it, very many people are sure that horses do have some sort of sixth sense. The most famous instance quoted of this is the part of Anna Sewell's *Black Beauty* where Beauty refused to cross a bridge over a river in flood because he knew it was dangerous. Although the book is fiction, most of the incidents in it were taken from life, and this sort of happening is often quoted in literature and legend.

Although we now know that horses can see much better in the dark than humans and this explains the *Black Beauty* incident to a modern horse world (Beauty or his real-life counterpart could probably see the break in the bridge), modern science can still not prove why horses do certain things and sometimes seem to be operating on an extra sense. We are finally accepting that horses are much more sensitive and perceptive than we ever thought they were which explains why they so easily pick up on our moods and actions, and we know their senses are different from and often much more highly developed than ours, which explains a lot even though we shall probably never understand fully how they perceive the world.

Morphic Fields

Dr Rupert Sheldrake has for some time been working on morphic fields in animals, including horses. He has done field trials and various studies and tests of animals being able to 'tune in' to their absent owners. In particular, he has found that dogs really do know when their owners are coming home after an absence: normal times of homecoming were changed in his trials, different cars used and so on, but still the dogs reacted with excitement and pleasure very clearly anticipating their owners' arrival some time later. He has also had some success with horses and morphic fields, and readers are welcome to write to him with their experiences at the address which can be found in the Appendix.

My gelding, Royal, wherever I kept him (always at livery) often used to come to the field gate or, if stabled, start to show anticipation of my arrival, whenever it was, a good half hour before I arrived and the yard owners commented on this particularly.

There is plenty of what scientists call anecdotal evidence (and therefore to be taken with a pinch of salt) about horses refusing to pass supposedly haunted places or those where some disaster involving horses had happened previously. Their ability to predict disasters like hurricanes and earthquakes is probably due to earth vibrations or air pressure, however.

Communication

An interesting story told to me by a very down-to-earth gentleman concerned two horsey friends who were separated when one had to travel to a nearby veterinary hospital for an operation.

On being separated, Cassie (left at home) became upset, sad, worried, whinnied after the horsebox and paced around her box, despite having other company next door. Then, at eleven o'clock, she suddenly calmed down and, although looking rather lost, began eating hay and actually lay down to rest.

A couple of hours later, she suddenly became upset again, pacing around her box, calling, kicking the door and refusing to eat or drink even though it was her normal feed time. It later transpired that eleven o'clock was when her friend, Kelly, lost consciousness under the anaesthetic, recovering two hours or so afterwards. The man who related this incident felt that the communication between the two horses existed even though they were apart and was broken by the anaesthetic which prevented the distant link. Then, when Kelly regained consciousness, the link was restored and she was once again able to communicate her distress to Cassie at their being parted.

Staring Isn't All Bad

Eye contact between humans and horses does not have to be threatening to them as is often claimed. The Equine Behaviour Forum has received several reports from members who habitually look intensely or stare at their horses in a non-aggressive way, thinking pictures of what they want the horses to do, frequently with success.

I saw an acquaintance of mine bring a mare to him from the other side of a paddock by staring at her (she was facing the other way), getting her to turn round to see what he wanted, and then coming over in an interested way. This person never gave titbits to horses. And finally, my old Thoroughbred mare used the same technique on me on a few occasions. We have all had the sensation that someone is staring at the back of our head and this technique is so effective that apparently soldiers are told never to look at the back of an enemy's head when approaching from the rear because it warns them.

The first time Sarah tried this with me I was tidying up my grooming kit just inside the stable door when I felt that someone was staring at me. I turned round to see her standing on the far side of

AUTISM AND HORSES

An early contribution to *Equine Behaviour*, the members' journal of the Equine Behaviour Forum, from Mr Joe Royds who did a lot of work for the charity Mencap, told the story of horses being used for autistic children. The children seemed able to communicate with the horses in a way they never could with humans and, apparently, the finer-bred and fitter the horses (fit Thoroughbred racehorses were best, it seemed), the better horse and rider got on. One little boy spoke his first words ever from the back of such a horse and Mr Royds felt it seemed to be something to do with the electrical brainwaves of autists being on a closer wavelength to horses than to non-autistic humans. The horses recognised the autistic children and people as buddies whereas other humans were more of a threat.

her box, her head turned towards me, ears pricked and staring hard at me with a very intense look on her face. As soon as I made eye-contact with her, she turned her head back, dipped it into her empty haylage tub, raised it again and stared pointedly at me in the same way. She had attracted my attention and then asked me as clearly as could be to refill her tub, then stared again to check that I understood. When I returned a minute later with a big armful of haylage she was standing in the same spot anticipating my return but with a relaxed air, confident that I had, indeed, got her message.

Above: Horses often seem to have some kind of non-physical link with distant friends of their own and other species although what form this takes no one can say. Some humans and other animals also have the same ability

Right: Maintaining eye-contact with your horse does not have to be aggressive or even assertive. Your thoughts and feelings as well as your body posture can convey to each other how you feel and what you want

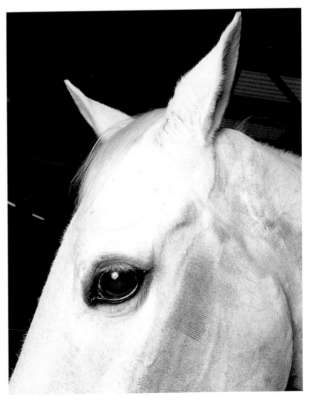

Listen to Me!

Do horses really live in a state of 'learned helplessness'? It is certainly true that the younger handling and training begin the more likely they are to feel that we must be obeyed

This section is entitled Listen To Me! because that is just what most humans have, for thousands of years, expected their horses to do. Relatively few trainers, only the true horsemen and women among them, even considered, until fairly recently, that they might also listen to their horses.

Over the thousands of years that man has been training horses, there must have been many different methods of doing this but I'll bet that the majority of them have involved mostly brute force, fear, pain, domination and a true breaking-in of the horse in that his spirit and will have been broken in the process. The horses were, and in some methods today still are, mentally and/or physically tortured into submission. In many countries and schools of thought, training now involves much kinder methods but inexperience, incompetence and a harsh-minded trainer can change this.

Brainwashing

At a UK conference in the late 1990s, a speaker claimed that most horses today exist in a state of 'learned helplessness'. Like children in an over-strict home or school or prisoners in jail, our horses fit in with the system and co-operate because, strong as they are, they have no choice. We have 'brainwashed'

them from foalhood into thinking that we are invincible – if we have trained them 'properly'.

A similar system involving mental submission was advocated by a person whose name I genuinely forget but who said something like: 'If you want to control the people, give them a conscience.' This strategy has been used with tremendous success for thousands of years in religions and other cultural, social and belief systems. Although horses may not have consciences, they often end up believing that they must do as we wish because this is how they are often brought up, like suppressed Victorian children.

Traditional-viewpoint training

Speaking generally, we have conventionally, in all training, concentrated almost entirely on getting the horse, by kind means or cruel, to understand what we want him to do without question. Only the most empathetic trainers have given the horse any room for coming back with questions, doubts, fears or allowing him time to understand and to make personal decisions about what was being asked.

The most common method in much of Europe and North America, except where traditional Western breaking-in still takes place, is to handle the youngster well from foalhood (although this by no means always happens), to put him on the lunge and/or long-reins at two or three years of age, or younger in Thoroughbred flat-racing, and to train him to walk round us or in front of us, and learn to associate our different vocal sounds with the different gaits and movements we require of him. The saddle and bridle are gradually but persistently introduced, physical aids accompany the vocal ones and then take over largely from the voice and things progress from there. Throughout it all, the horse learns what we are requesting in a one-way communication channel – he listens to us but we very often do not listen to him even if we hear him. Questions or objections from him are taken as difficulties and disobediences to be overcome and quashed.

Really, it can be no surprise, can it, if horses do live in a state of learned helplessness when this sort

Making sure a horse enjoys his training is one way of keeping him fresh. Many horses enjoy loose jumping, if not overdone

of attitude prevails? Horses learn quickly, and learn quickly that humans don't listen. With such a philosophy, horses must feel a level of insecurity and mistrust because they are getting no true leadership from such people, merely domination which is not leadership. They easily become dull, even zombie-like if things are bad enough, and the humans are depriving themselves of a bright, willing partner and performer.

Inside information

One of the things I did a lot of early in my writing career was interviewing notable horsemen and

DISCIPLINE

Being kind to a horse, being his partner even if senior partner, and caring about him does not mean never disciplining him. Horses receive undoubted correction and discipline in a herd not only from their seniors but from their friends. If your best friend started walking all over you, you would soon do something about it, wouldn't you? Horses know that other herd members are to be treated with respect, including equal friends, and that's the way in which many modern horse owners want to be regarded by their horses. With correct treatment, there is no reason why the horse cannot learn to treat you the same way – you are part of his daily life, his herd, after all.

Putting a horse right when he's going too far is only like having words with a human who has treated you badly. There are quite a few horses who will treat you like dirt if you let them. Don't let them.

women for long, detailed articles or series in a professional equestrian magazine and, later, in my own magazine. I visited all kinds of professional and amateur yards, veterinary establishments, studs and so on and, through intensive observation and interviewing over a couple of days to a year, soon picked up masses of fascinating information. I quickly developed a nose for a good place and a bad one, a real horseman and a sham, a partner and a control freak or an outright bully, and soon found I was able to pick up the correct 'vibes' on a strange yard almost within seconds, partly from the atmosphere and the people but mainly from the horses.

I soon found that it is quite possible to be very successful without truly caring about your horses. Several 'top' people I interviewed I would not entrust with my horse for even five minutes!

What I felt really important was that those horses with real horsemen training, handling and working them (for the staff are just as important as the mugwump – that's Anglo-Saxon for 'boss') not only lasted longer but had a fulfilled zest and a relaxed, confident security about them that the others did not. Those fortunate horses whose paths meet people who *do* listen to them, even if also ultimately expecting obedience from the horse, have their problems and difficulties assessed and, where possible, sorted out by those trainers/owners and so have a real chance of a fulfilling, contented life.

Moving on

Let's look next at some of the emerging training methods with non-traditional approaches.

OK – If You'll Listen To Me, Too

It is strange how fashions, fads, beliefs, ways of life and so on seem to emerge, change or die out for no apparent reason. The horse world is extremely conservative and very slow to take on board new ways and discoveries even when people know they are better than the old. It has been said that this is insecurity on the part of those reluctant to change – they cannot be seen to admit that what they have been doing for so long may not have been so wonderful after all and they are going to try something which could be better. But surely, a willingness to be open-minded and to try to improve is at the very root of all true progress, showing intelligence, a caring attitude, modesty (*no one* gets it right all the time), a measure of altruism and sheer common sense.

The growing interest in methods of training which look at things from the horse's point of view, which use his natural language, now widely called Equus, and in which (in order to use it successfully) the trainer has to listen to what the horse is saying is evidence of the fact that very many horse people are looking for better ways of doing things. Some of the trainers using these methods have been using them for many years – one says that his method is 'so old it's new again' – but the time has only just come right for the horse world in general to really start listening to them, let alone to horses.

Common principles
Some trainers use what's come to be called a round pen or a bull pen but the principles of these

methods don't need one, it's just easier with some systems if the horse is restricted in this way. The methods all broadly use (a) the horse's instinct to want to belong, (b) the physical, body language horses use themselves and (c) the fact that most horses are followers, not leaders, and will accept leadership faced with a horse or human they perceive as senior.

Some trainers initially reject the horse (throw him out of the herd) by using an aggressive stance and flicking a long rein or rope at the horse, chasing him away from them till the horse says, by showing submissive movements like flicking an ear towards the trainer, lowering the head, mouthing, licking and chewing, that he will accept this person as his leader if only he will let him back in. Once this is established, the trainer adopts a submissive, friendly stance which interests the horse, who eventually approaches and follows. Once this bonding or 'join-up' has occurred, the horse permits himself to be handled all over, tacked up and ridden with little trouble. This method is the most familiar one in the UK at present, having been introduced by Monty Roberts and used, sometimes with variations, by other trainers, too.

In other methods, trainers use a variety of training techniques and systems, some complicated and some simple, all based on the three criteria given above, using physical signs the horse naturally understands without training, with a view to establishing an Equus-based partnership. Most trainers do aim at being the senior partner but not all – an equal partnership-cum-friendship is the goal of others, like horse friends in a herd.

All the methods I have looked into so far do use principles developed by looking at the process from the horse's point of view using equine, rather than equestrian, techniques, instead of operating purely from what we expect him to learn and getting our own way whether the horse likes it or not.

Someone has to be boss, and it has to be you – so they say
If you mix a lot with horses, sooner or later you will come across a few you know you can't manage.

The use of round pens or bull pens is not essential in training a horse by using his own language – body language – but they make it simpler

Once the horse has been sent away (rejected) by his trainer (herd leader), he usually decides that he wants to belong and will submit willingly, as in the herd. Here, a horse has reached that point and 'joined up' with the human leader, following him quietly

Depending on your temperament, it may take a lot to admit this but in case you are young enough to think there's some shame in this or in losing your nerve (I've lost mine twice and got it back again so it's not the end of the world), the following two tales may comfort you!

First story: Years ago, I interviewed a former top international and Olympic medal-winning show-jumper who also admitted that he had not been able to manage one of his rides. I remembered their short partnership well. This rider had done as well as you can with several other horses before and since this horse but he told me: 'He had me and he knew he had me and we both knew the other knew! I reached the point where I was afraid of getting on him so I told the owner we just didn't click, but the truth was I was frightened of him so I got rid of him before he broke my nerve.'

I thought this superb horseman was probably too much of a gentleman for this particular horse. He was passed on to another rider who certainly wasn't, and they won many major prizes over several years.

Second story: I was interviewing two very competent, professional show riders, husband and wife, (John and Anne – names changed) who were discussing a particularly wilful stallion they were showing in ridden classes for the season. The horse was said to dislike men so the plan was for Anne to produce him. He had smashed up his box twice,

run away with her a few times and she said to John: 'I've told you, I'm not riding him again. We can't afford for either of us to lose our nerve and I can't cope with him. You ride him!' John did, with some success and certainly the horse's behaviour improved. Anne produced in-hand another stallion known for temperament problems, who behaved like an angel with her and the pair won several major prizes.

So – someone has to be boss, but maybe not the same boss all the time. There are lots of safe, effective, rewarding horse/human partnerships which exist on a mutual co-operation basis (like human friendships or living with a dog) where neither is actually the boss. True, horses can make very bad bosses and so can humans. Horses cannot be expected to make decisions about traffic situations, for example, or be allowed to put everyone nearby in danger due to bad behaviour or lack of control. Sometimes the human has to take the upper hand but sometimes the horse is best placed to know what's best. A give and take relationship takes time and effort, intelligence and common sense, but it is the ideal when you can achieve it.

'Into Pressure'?

It is difficult for many people to understand what is meant by the phrase 'into pressure' (as in 'the horse is an into-pressure animal'). As most of us have found out from experience, if you lean on or push against a horse he will push back. He will not automatically move away from you unless he has been trained to do so. This may be difficult for us to understand because, like horses, we have a personal space but our instinct seems to be to move away if someone pushes against us, accidentally or on purpose. We regard it as an invasion of our space and privacy and all but the most assertive, or aggressive, of us will move away.

You would think that, as prey animals, horses would react in the same way but they just push back and some of them actually lean on people or squash them against a hard surface such as a tree or wall as an act of assertion or aggression. Because a horse is so much bigger and heavier than a human, this can be very dangerous.

Lean on this, then
An old cure it is to take into the box with you a strong stick a little longer than the depth of your body from front to back, sharpened to a blunt point on one end. Watch for the horse to make the move, then hold the flat end of the stick hard against the wall with the point towards the horse and let him

When halter-training a foal it is important to overcome his natural tendency to lean 'into pressure'

lean on that while you say 'over' to associate the command with his jumping away. It does stop them after a couple of tries.

If you get caught on the hop, jab your thumb or the ends of your fingers into the horse, hard, quickly and repeatedly, like another horse nipping, and giving the firm command 'over' so he will associate the two in future; a sensitive place seems to be the barrel – flanks, belly or sides – but it works on the chest with a horse who won't move backwards from you. You can also do this on the neck with a horse who just won't learn his stable manners and continually crowds you: you see horses doing this to others in the field, nipping their necks, when they violate their personal space. (One word of warning, don't do it to a horse who has trapped you in a corner with his hindquarters as he will probably kick you and maybe trample you once you are down. The general advice is to squash yourself into the corner and stand absolutely still till he moves. Sometimes, making eating noises or having some paper in your pocket to rustle makes him curious enough to turn round, anticipating a titbit, when you can hopefully make your escape. The moral here is never to go behind a horse you don't know or trust. Some people never go behind any horse.)

Contrary humans
Much of our conventional training actually goes against the horse's inclination to lean into pressure when we want him to move away. How many horses do you know who appear to lean purposely on the foot you are trying to lift? They are doing it from natural inclination although the worldly wise may do it to be awkward! Pushing them with your shoulder is not an effective counter-offensive but, if 'over' does not work, jabbing them in the flank or girth groove with your free hand does (also with a horse who is standing on your foot), as does pinching the nerve which crosses the tendons about a third of the way up from the fetlock. Ask your farrier to show this method.

Pulling power
Horses have to be taught to move away from pressure, either from the leg, a hand on the side or chest, an aid from the bit (which is why the firm contact so often taught today is quite contrary to the lightness we are all supposed to be aiming for), and why a pull on the headcollar of a reluctant horse

usually results in his stopping and pulling back at you and maybe rearing.

Horses who pull back when tied up are responding naturally to this same inclination. They just pull and pull in one steady, sustained effort.

The theory on pulling when ridden is that the horse is pushing against the pain of an uncomfortable pressure in his mouth. (Obviously, he is pushing into it, not pulling.) It seems inconceivable that a horse would give himself more pain but, realising that horses do push against pressure, it makes sense. Horses do run away from pain when they can so pulling back at them usually increases their speed rather than reducing it.

Pleasurable pressure

The type of pressure the horse feels obviously affects his response. We apply physical pressure to horses all the time when handling them, grooming, massaging and so on, and, particularly with the last two, horses can really enjoy it.

They enjoy applying pressure to each other during mutual grooming and respond with pleasure to a similar type of favour from their owners. Some horses offer you the honour of mutual-grooming your back, over your shoulder, in return and people who will not let them do this surely do not realise how confused and maybe rejected the horse then feels. If we're going to learn to use *Equus*, let's do it properly!

Friends mutually groom to please each other but mere acquaintances have been seen to do it, believed to be in an effort to strengthen their relationship. The author believes that humans should welcome this gesture from their horses and reciprocate

---

HORSE, RESTRAIN YOURSELF

There are various types of 'restrainer' headcollars and halters on the market for horses who are bad to lead, who barge off, swing round, run back or rear. They work on some variation of the principle of pressure and release. It seems, again, contrary that a headcollar which exerts pressure will stop the horse pulling you around and if these items are just put on a horse and used without training him in their action, they can actually make things worse. The horse must be trained when he is quiet – and it does not take long – to realise that gentle pressure will be released the instant he gives to it. Then, when he feels the uncomfortable tightening around his head if he is playing up, he stops his antics and comes to hand. Used correctly, these headcollars and halters do work. The horse, in effect, restrains himself.

111

The right reward

Another pleasurable sensation to the horse is being stroked, ideally accompanied by sweet nothings or 'good girl'. Horses do not actually like being patted: they especially do not like being thumped by delighted riders after doing their best for them. You can tell this by the expression on horses' faces as their riders hit them on the neck, or even on the head, at the end of a session or competition in which they have worked well.

Horses equate patting – a sudden, hard, sharp feeling – with being nipped on the neck by a rejecting, aggressive herd-mate – some reward! And *most* confusing especially if accompanied by 'good boy'. What would you make of it if you were a horse?

Living With the Enemy

To recap briefly, we know that the horse is a running, grazing animal, who provides food for carnivores. Because of this, his body has developed as a specialist, fast runner. No one knows why the horse's ancestors did not develop the efficient fibre-digesting rumen of cattle, sheep and goats, but the horse is a sufficiently good fibre-digester to have survived all these millions of years. His digestive system does, however, mean that he needs to actually take in food for much longer each day than, say, a cow so, when free to do so, he likes to spend most of his time with his head down eating and scanning the horizon all around him for trouble.

Although not normally exposed to predators or regular dangers, even the domesticated horse retains the tendency to be easily startled. Not even a police horse or carefully trained military horse is bombproof. We have all seen, in news clips, police horses going berserk under severe pressure, and the occasional mishap with ceremonial horses.

Horses' basic traits of running in defence, needing to eat a lot and needing to be alert to what they perceive as danger are as strong in domestic horses and ponies, under the thin surface veneer of training, as in feral and wild *equidae*. This basic nature cannot be changed.

Feeling Safe

As flight animals, horses' attention is mainly focused in the distance whereas we concentrate most on what is nearer to us. Studies done on horses to check their stress levels in different types of environment,

This horse has lost or unshipped his rider and is galloping off in fear of the unsettling experience – either the rider parting company or whatever caused that initially

Domestic horses can usually drink in peace, but this container, of hard concrete and with exposed pipes, is not the safest source, although it is rounded

involving skin tension, blood chemistry and blood pressure, showed that they were most relaxed and settled where they had congenial company and in environments where they had a distant, all-round view. They were most tense when alone, when separated from close friends and in situations where they could not see around them very well, such as conventional stabling and closed-in stable yards.

Another study showed that, given a choice, horses preferred dim light at night to darkness. Horses living loose in a barn were trained to switch on a light by passing a sensor at a certain point. The light stayed on for only limited periods and, when it went off, some horse or other would deliberately walk past the sensor to switch it on again. These horses were also seen to keep eye contact with each other much of the time. Although they had individual stables into which they could wander at will, they spent well over three-quarters of their time socialising in the communal middle section.

All these findings confirm the expected preferences of an animal which must be on the lookout for danger, which needs to be able to see all around it and which feels safest in a close herd situation.

Drinking

In domestic conditions, we normally keep water with horses nearly all the time. Feral horses' proximity to water will vary according to where they are grazing.

They may not always have water immediately to hand and observations show that, where they have not, they trek to watering places once or twice a day usually at dawn and dusk, drink their fill and trek back to the grazing grounds.

Watering sources are dangerous places in the wild: predators lie in wait there, not always even bothering to conceal themselves, because they know that a meal will definitely arrive before long, all animals being forced to drink. When drinking a full draught of water, which they do not normally do when water is always with them, horses will drink deeply, then raise their heads, have a rest and look around them, then have another long draught. This enables them to let the water 'go down' and also to check their surroundings.

Domestic horses watered at a trough also follow this pattern so should not be taken away when they raise their heads. To be sure they have had enough, it is safest to let them move away from the trough themselves, which they will.

Sleeping

Sleeping is another dangerous but essential pursuit; however, horses have reached the point where they need little sleep although those stabled sleep more than those at liberty, grazing, probably out of boredom.

Horses do not sleep for several hours at a stretch like carnivores and humans. They can rest, doze and sleep lightly standing up because of the arrangement of ligaments, tendons and bones in their legs which 'props' them safely at night. When there is a disturbance because of danger, a predator or whatever, they can be off in a flash because they are already on their feet.

However, deeper sleep is desirable sometimes (although those horses who never lie down manage without it) and for this they must lie flat out. Because

This photo shows the wide range of states in a naturally living herd. One horse is on watch, another dozes standing up, some sleep lightly lying 'upright' whilst others indulge in some deep sleep lying flat out

Friends like close contact with each other and often rest and relax touching each other

of their weight (around half a ton/tonne for the average riding horse), the lung on the ground side becomes squashed and can fill with fluid if the horse stays down too long, so they normally sleep like this for only about twenty minutes to half an hour at a time, then will wake and get up.

Mature horses are rarely seen all lying down sleeping at the same time. One or two always remain standing on watch. When one rises, one of the guards will lie down. This pattern, too, is followed in domestic conditions, when one or two horses in the yard will always be up and awake. Foals at grass, though, can often be seen lying piled on top of each other in what is colloquially known as a 'foal heap', sleeping soundly, their dams grazing around them.

A LITTLE FOOD ALL THE TIME IS SAFEST

One of the Golden Rules of feeding is to always feed after work, never before, as exertion after a full meal could cause colic. The stomach is next to the diaphragm and if strenuous work and breathing is carried out while the stomach is full, not only is blood diverted from digestion to muscular work but also the diaphragm will push on the stomach and interfere with its action.

Obviously, wild *equidae* are eating most of the time and often have to take to their heels at a gallop: if they were prone to digestive disturbance because of this, the species would not last very long. The fact that they never gorge themselves and take in a full meal, as domestic horses often do because of the way we feed them, is a major reason why they can eat and gallop flat out in the same minute without problems.

The 'Flight-or-Fight' Mechanism

The flight-or-fight response is a phenomenon surely all horse enthusiasts are familiar with by now. It is not only horses who operate by this means; it is a self-protection system which is found in all higher animals including humans.

In wild horses it is triggered by the appearance and detection of something the horse sees as dangerous such as a predator but a stallion trying to keep his harem together will experience it at the sight of a rival stallion. Humans will certainly experience it if involved in a fight or other dangerous situation but also if they have a row with someone, especially someone who controls their destiny – being sacked, for instance, is the equivalent of being mugged in the stress stakes.

But let's stay with horses. A wild or feral horse is grazing peacefully with his herdmates when he sees an unusual movement in long grass some distance away. He cannot hear anything and he is upwind of the location (if the predator is smart) so cannot smell anything, either. He stops eating, freezes and may check to see if anyone else is behaving uneasily. His head will come up, ears pointing towards the movement. Other horses will now notice this initial warning if they haven't already. His nostrils will dilate, vainly trying to pick up a scent. He, and possibly some others, will stand stock still, an automatic response to make them less distinguishable to a distant predator.

If there is no more movement, and if other horses do not seem unduly perturbed, he may decide there is nothing to worry about and continue grazing, keeping an eye on the spot. He or a more junior herd member may actually go to see if there really is a problem. If there isn't, all well and good, if there is, the flight mechanism gets into full flow instantly.

On your marks, get set, WHOOSH!

The brain instructs the hormone adrenaline to start coursing through the horse's circulatory system, setting the whole, complex mechanism in motion. The sympathetic nervous system is engaged and all

YOU DON'T HAVE TO BE WILD

These processes happen not only to wild horses being pursued by predators but also to domestic ones being chased by marauding dogs or an aggressive fellow horse in their paddock, to performance horses and hunters when the heat is on, racehorses, pleasure horses and their owners having an informal race out hacking, horses undergoing a stressful schooling session, those experiencing a frightening journey in a horsebox (some transport researchers say that *any* journey entails a good deal of stress), those being clipped or shod if they don't like these processes and a horse who has spotted the vet arriving across the yard or his owner bearing work gear and tack.

Of course, there are various levels of stress and alarm, not all of which induce the horse to flee. Minor incidents, though, such as dressing a painful wound, occurring in an environment from which the horse cannot escape, such as his stable, increase his alarm level. There may be times when you want your horse hyped up, times when you cannot prevent it and times when you want him calm. Calmness from you yourself plus a positive attitude and a mutually trusting relationship going between you will help you both stay in control even when the stakes are high.

sorts of defensive and protective processes start to happen instantly while the horse and his buddies are tearing off like bats out of hell. The blood pressure rises as the vessels concerned with action dilate to carry to the muscles more blood containing glucose, hormones and oxygen whilst those to the alimentary canal constrict, digestion slowing right down. The heart rate and breathing rate increase to deliver the extra supplies and remove the extra waste products faster, the pupils of the eyes dilate to let in as much light as possible for better vision, and glucose is mobilised from glycogen stored in the liver to back up that stored in the muscles.

The horse sweats to help remove toxins and heat, which is rising in the body, and as a nervous response. The spleen contracts to pump large numbers of red blood cells into the circulation to carry more oxygen to the muscles.

An anti-inflammatory hormone called cortisol, the body's own cortisone or steroid, is also mobilised and its high levels act like a natural therapy for moderate damage to joints, muscles and other tissues after peak exertion. This helps prevent the horse feeling stiff and sore so he can run again when necessary. An enzyme called creatine phosphokinase will be released should there be any muscle damage (either from physical injury or due to a build-up of lactic acid in muscles working anaerobically) to facilitate its repair.

Two more familiar substances, endorphins and encephalins, well-known as the body's natural morphine relatives which have a pain-killing, feel-good effect, are released during physical exercise, particularly prolonged or hard exercise, and these will also come into play and be secreted in high amounts should the horse be in pain, perhaps from a wrenched muscle or a twisted leg sustained in his desperate efforts to get away fast. Their pain-killing effects will enable him to keep on running despite his injury, so helping to save his life.

Imagine the horse gets away safely: his name wasn't on the bullet this time. Gradually, much more slowly than it all started, his system winds down as the parasympathetic nervous system takes over, hormone levels return to normal, tissue repair/replacement takes place and energy levels are restored. The horse, his friends and relatives resume eating, their vital support process, keeping a sharp eye out for any further threat. Their number may have been reduced by one. If that one was the favoured companion of our example horse, his or her life may change considerably. If there is now an orphan foal, that foal may die soon, providing food for others.

He'll Fight If He Must

There are times when a horse must fight and although fighting amongst horses is not strictly ritualised as it is in some other animals, like goats and sheep for example, they can fight very effectively, if necessary.

Armoury and Techniques
Kicking

Although horses have no horns and natural hooves are not metal-shod, a kick from a zebra can kill a lioness and a horse could obviously develop even more force. Compounded by steel shoes, a domestic horse prone to kicking can be lethally dangerous and should be managed and worked extremely carefully.

It is often said that kicking with the hind feet is a defensive gesture but this is not always so: mares, in particular, kick out behind in aggression and a well-known trick of nastier horses, actually usually

Horses don't mince their words with each other

ponies, to avoid being caught is to run backwards at a human, kicking as they go.

Zebras are known to form a 'ring of heels', facing inwards with their foals in the middle and kicking out viciously at predators trying to get at the tender, young flesh for a meal. Striking out with the front feet (not regarded as kicking) is certainly assertive or aggressive and stallions frequently do it, as do rigs and the false geldings described earlier. Geldings and mares usually restrict foreleg strikes to a firm stamp. Stallions and rigs often rear and flail their forelegs at any animal or person presenting a threat. They also fight horses and other animals by rearing up and coming down on them with their forefeet. They commonly kill other stallions' foals this way.

Biting

Horses also have strong incisor teeth which, when they have behind them the strength and force of the horse's jaws, head and neck, particularly if his

The horse's teeth are a weapon worthy of respect. These two, though, don't mean business as is evident from their body attitudes

half-ton body is lungeing forwards at the same time, can inflict very injurious bites. Even a warning or playful nip from a horse can cause bad bruising.

A Przewalski stallion in a private safari park killed two strange mares introduced to his little herd by biting their flanks and ripping out their entrails. Another in a public wildlife park killed two pre-pubertal males by getting them down with his teeth and trampling on them. Stallions sometimes bite mares on the neck quite badly during serving which is why leather neck covers are standard equipment for mares at many responsible studs, whether the stallion is expected to bite his mate or not.

Wild or feral *equidae*, say two stallions, will avoid fighting if possible. They usually draw themselves up to their full height, shake their heads, snort, stamp around and run threateningly at each other. When it is clear neither is going to back down, they will fight using various techniques. They rear and 'box' with their forefeet, then one may come down with a leg over the other's neck and biting it, trying to bring him down. They use their teeth freely particularly on their adversary's most tender parts, and a favourite trick is to bite his legs and trip him, to bring him down so he can be trampled. Usually, the weaker horse will retreat when he realises, sometimes badly injured, that he cannot win, and recovers to fight another day – or dies of his injuries, particularly if

they become infected. But fatalities during fights are not unknown.

Fighting People

When truly vicious horses were more common than they seem to be now, grooms were sometimes killed by being trampled on, presumably being grounded by normal kicking first or being picked up and thrown with the teeth. I remember a report in the 1960s of a stallion man having his ear ripped off by the horse he managed and reports of broken arms and shoulders from stallion bites are by no means unknown.

I once visited a Thoroughbred stud to write a feature about it and noticed one of the stallions in a box with a wire grille top door, the others all being free to have their heads out. I asked about him and was told he had come to the stud straight from racing and was extremely vicious. The stallion man had developed an understanding with him and was the only one who could handle him. The horse had been at the stud nearly a year and, although his temper has greatly improved, the man had not taken a day off in that time.

I was assured the grille was only in place when visitors were in the yard (the horse having ripped the back out of the coat of a man standing within reach who had the same regional accent as in the area where the horse had been in training – unhappy associations) and the photograph session we did with the stallion in the yard was the first occasion on which he had been out of his box, other than to graze, without wearing a muzzle.

Why Fight?

Feral stallions fight each other for possession of a herd. Sometimes they even fight off strange mares wishing to enter the herd if they feel their herd is big enough. Mares will fight off strange mares coming into the herd, at least certainly if they are in season. Horses pressed for territory will fight others for grazing and space and horses will also fight if any serious hierarchy differences emerge but these seem quite rare in a natural life where there is usually room to run away.

In domestic situations, stallions will certainly fight over mares if they get the chance. Most stallions kept together with no mares will not normally fight but some will, usually started by younger ones trying their luck in the seniority stakes.

Horses wrongly introduced to each other, particularly one stranger being put into an established herd without preparation, may well fight or skirmish, particularly if the paddock is not large.

There's a Reason for Everything

Any animal which survives in the wild is often living on a knife-edge between survival and death. Although there are times when the living is easy with plenty of food, water, kind weather, a mate, friends and offspring, for prey animals life is never safe. Everything a wild animal does has a real, meaningful purpose from shifting position whilst dozing (to even up pressures on the body) to the most desperate chase (to stay alive). We've looked at horses' flight or fight instinct to avoid being killed but their other behavioural traits also have a purpose which is not always obvious and at which we can sometimes only guess.

What Do Horses Want?

Firstly, they want to stay alive. Self-preservation is key. If enough individuals do not survive, neither will the species. Self-preservation involves (a) avoiding predation, (b) acquiring enough food and water and (c) feeling physically comfortable and mentally safe and content (usually by having shelter, freedom and company).

Secondly, they want to reproduce. A mare can be a good or poor mother and a stallion is no real father at all in our terms, but the instinctive urge to mate and, in most mares, to nurture the offspring, is present in almost all horses at some time. This is key to the survival of the species which is nature's main aim.

Thirdly, they want to socialise and sometimes play with other horses. This is for bonding purposes and is key to being accepted into the protective environment of the herd. How do these needs and wants affect a horse's daily behaviour and life in the round?

Food and water

Horse owners often say of their horses: 'You never stop eating. All you think of is food.' They are absolutely right – that *is* all a horse thinks of most of his time because he is made that way. Knowing how his digestion works and how energy is supplied, it is obvious why he is preoccupied with food. If he cannot eat, he may develop other practices involving the use of his mouth to satisfy the craving to chew such as chewing wood, rugs, his own or other horses' manes and tails, bedding or anything else he can get hold of. The provision of a more or less ad lib forage supply of the right nutritional grade for his constitution and work is the answer to this.

Shelter, freedom and company

Horses may be tough (sometimes), outdoor creatures but most of them hate exposure to extremes of weather and to insects. They will find any shelter they can to remain comfortable, even huddling behind the straggliest of hedges or under a single tree. Failing that, they stand together using each other's bodies as shelter.

In cold, wet and wind they stand with their rumps to the weather to protect their heads and expose a narrow part of their body and so lose as little heat as possible. In warm weather, they often stand side-on to the sun to gather in heat and in hot sun they find whatever shade they can. To protect each other from insects, they stand head to tail, swishing the flies from themselves and each other's heads.

The ideal domestic arrangement to fulfil all these needs is living with other, accepting horses in, say, a large paddock or surfaced turnout area (with constant grass or forage and water) and with a large shelter, covered yard or barn to which they can come and go as they wish.

Reproduction

A mare's temperament often changes when she is (a) in oestrus and (b) pregnant, being quite different from when she is anoestrus and dioestrus. An acquaintance of mine kept her mare constantly pregnant because it was the only way she could handle her! Sweet-natured mares may become stroppy and difficult ones at least co-operative or even positively soppy. Mares with foals, though, can often become very protective of them – just what you want if she is a good mother but not to the extent that you cannot handle her or her foal. Although there is give and take in any good relationship, you cannot have important no-go areas with horses where their and your wellbeing and safety are concerned. Mares and their foals should be regularly, considerately and persistently handled without overdoing it. If amateur owners have problems with dams' natural behaviour, expert advice and on-the-spot help should be sought quickly before the problem escalates.

Reproductive instincts and their resulting behaviour are often a bugbear with 'ordinary' horseowners who are not at all interested in breeding foals or in fulfilling their horses' sex lives. Indeed, most of their horses have no sex lives. This is understandable. They have usually bought their horses to ride, have fun with, often to compete in Riding Club and similar events and the nuisance side-effects caused by their horses' sexual interests, even some geldings, are often not welcome.

Mares' behaviour patterns during oestrus have been

discussed, as have the behaviour of stallions and some geldings. If you really cannot work around the fairly strong, natural behaviours shown by some such horses, it may be best to buy a different horse.

Social interaction and play

It is fairly obvious that horses not free to properly socialise with their own kind and to play as even adult horses readily do, are being kept in a deprived situation. There are many, many horses kept like this in yards large and small, professional and amateur, including those in some of the most highly regarded equestrian establishments in the world. In some countries, once horses are brought up and broken in around three years old, they are never turned free again for the rest of their lives, never allowed to relax, roll, buck, kick and play in even a sand paddock and never allowed anything approaching natural contact with other horses. The fact that, because of horses' great adaptability, they become accustomed to this, like prisoners in strict confinement, and *look* and work well because they are fed, groomed and exercised and worked under constraint does not

Feral horses in the Namib–Naukluft Park, Namibia. Survival for them is a far cry from the cosy existence of our stabled horses. They are of Trakehner origin and so contain a good deal of Thoroughbred blood. They have all the freedom they need but little shelter from the vicious climate of the Namib – and hardly any food. Their numbers have recently been reduced to relieve the pressure on their environment and, hopefully, improve the condition of those remaining. How they survive is a miracle

make it Right. I have never had a horse formerly kept like this but people who have say that the horses are psychologically sub-normal on arrival even if not exhibiting stereotypies. After a few months of fair treatment (psychological rehabilitation) their personalities blossom, they show a bloom of contentment they never had before and they become much more rounded in their attitude to life. Most people who give horses as natural a life as possible in domesticity, and consider their normal wants and needs, find horses even more pleasurable to associate with. From a selfish point of view, this is surely worth the trouble.

But there is much more to life than what *we* want.

Thinking Like A Horse

Having considered the horse's needs and wants, we have a fair idea of his outlook on life. It should not be too difficult for us to 'get inside the horse's head' and view things more or less as he does – to think like a horse – remembering always that he is a running, grazing prey animal.

The Horse's Brain

Traditionally, it has been believed by some that horses are rather stupid (see next section 'Not Just a Pretty Face') and pronounced that, for example, dogs are far cleverer and better at solving problems (always held up as a criterion of intelligence). In fact, dogs have relatively slightly smaller brains for their body size than do horses (although size alone is not the sole relevant point). Also, dogs do not think like horses. It is in their, and our, nature to solve problems in a reasoning, perhaps devious, cunning way because they and we are the horse's opposites – we are hunters. So the comparison is not really relevant.

Horses' early ancestors are known to have had larger brains than other, contemporary herbivores, particularly the part which receives sensory messages and controls learning ability. In fact, today's horses have a relatively large brain for their size, weighing roughly 650g or 23oz, about 0.7 per cent of their total bodyweight.

As part of the Central Nervous System, the brain is, rather obviously, essential to life and, with the spinal cord, is the control centre of everything, conscious or unconscious, that the horse does and all the processes which take place in his body.

Basic structure and function

The brain consists of three main parts:

● The cerebrum or fore-part of the brain takes up the front part of the cranial cavity (inside the skull) and is divided into two hemispheres (right and left) linked by the corpus callosum, an arch-shaped mass of nerve fibres crossing between the two halves. The cerebrum is concerned with receiving sensory messages, with the origination of emotions and the subsequent actions the horse takes in response to how he feels, with memory and learning, with decision-making, voluntary actions and control and intelligence. The surface of the cerebrum is covered in ridges and grooves believed to increase its capacity. Generally, the right hemisphere deals with the left side of the body and vice versa.

At the front of each hemisphere is the olfactory bulb which relays information on smells to the cerebrum. The thalamus, immediately below the cerebrum, relays other sensory impulses, and below this is the hypothalamus which, as we have seen, activates, controls and integrates so many of the body's functions, including the initiation of hormone release by the pituitary gland beneath it.

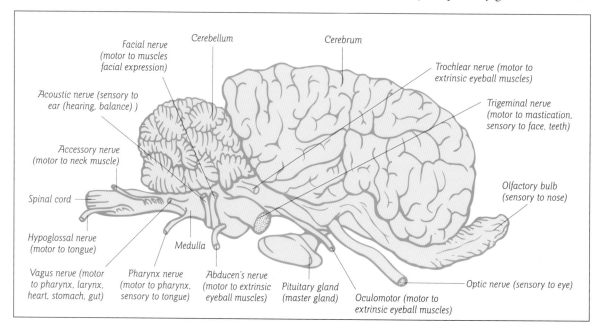

Facial nerve (motor to muscles facial expression)

Cerebellum

Cerebrum

Trochlear nerve (motor to extrinsic eyeball muscles)

Acoustic nerve (sensory to ear (hearing, balance))

Trigeminal nerve (motor to mastication, sensory to face, teeth)

Accessory nerve (motor to neck muscle)

Olfactory bulb (sensory to nose)

Spinal cord

Hypoglossal nerve (motor to tongue)

Medulla

Vagus nerve (motor to pharynx, larynx, heart, stomach, gut)

Pharynx nerve (motor to pharynx, sensory to tongue)

Abducen's nerve (motor to extrinsic eyeball muscles)

Pituitary gland (master gland)

Oculomotor (motor to extrinsic eyeball muscles)

Optic nerve (sensory to eye)

- The cerebellum is the smaller, hind-part of the brain. It has two lobes and a central ridge and is concerned with unconscious control, balance and co-ordination. Unlike the cerebrum, each hemisphere of the cerebellum controls its own side of the body but is, therefore and necessarily, linked to the opposite hemisphere of the cerebrum.

- The medulla is the third main part of the brain, beneath the other two, running into the spinal cord. It is responsible for involuntary and reflex actions such as heart beat, breathing, coughing, swallowing and so on.

Brain disorders and their effects

Mammals' brains are quite well protected inside the bony casing of the skull, but some of the skull's bones are very thin and damage is not impossible. In addition, horses can suffer from brain abscesses and tumours (although they are rare), haemorrhage and parasite damage. The results of diseases and disorders obviously depend on which part of the brain is damaged. Abscesses and tumours may, very generally, result in physical signs like head circling, wandering around and abnormal reflexes in only one eye. There may be drowsiness and inco-ordination and the horse may show marked changes in behaviour. It has been reported that more than one unmanageably vicious horse has turned out, on post mortem examination, to have a brain tumour.

Injury to the brain from severe blows, maybe resulting in fracture of the skull, can result from falling, banging the head during transport or throwing up the head when passing through a low doorway. A kick from another horse could also obviously be a cause. There would probably be haemorrhaging into the brain, and this also sometimes occurs in foals which have had difficult births.

An inflammatory brain disease which can also affect man is equine encephalitis. Treatment is not easy but consists of giving large doses of antiserum: there is a very effective vaccine for prevention.

Because the brain is so complex, symptoms shown by disorders can be very varied. Generally, any change from normal behaviour should not be simply put down to the horse's being 'in a mood'. There may be no need to be overly concerned, but repeated, unusual behaviour, particularly involving inco-ordination, wandering aimlessly around, signs of pain such as the horse pressing or banging its head on a wall or tree, change in personality and so on, should certainly call for veterinary attention.

How Does the Horse Think?

The horse, like ourselves and other creatures, is quite oblivious to how his brain works and how he is enabled to function and survive. The answer to the question 'how does the horse think?' is 'just like any other mammal' as far as the physiological processes are concerned. From a more subtle, psychological point of view, if we want to understand how the horse thinks in the way of what does he think of the world, what is in it and what happens to him, the answer can surely only be that he thinks like a prey animal. He is suspicious of every new circumstance, every new human or animal, every new food, even if only mildly. He has the, to us, strange capacity of not recognising objects out of context, i.e. out of their usual position – also of having to learn everything twice, from each side.

Everything requires investigation...

To us, an umbrella is an umbrella wherever it is: to the horse, it seems to be something grossly horrendous whenever it appears in a new place. Many years ago, members of the Equine Behaviour Forum conducted experiments with their own horses involving placing an open umbrella in various places around the yard, paddocks, manège and so on. Although few horses actually panicked unless a breeze picked it up, every single horse involved, once used to the brolly in one position, snorted and skittered when seeing the identical thing in another. I wonder why.

Not Just A Pretty Face

Intelligence in animals has been argued about probably since man started taking an interest in them. Early man was quick to learn from wolves' and dogs' hunting tactics and social mores and worked out how his prey was thinking when hunting it so must have realised that animals are not stupid. Civilisation somehow seems to have addled his brain, because animals have certainly been thought of by most people as fairly stupid for thousands of years, even though man has, during all that time, used their intelligence to further his own ends. People often say that horses must be stupid to allow us to ride them and do all the things we do to them. We already know that horses are extremely adaptable. We know, too, that there are no wild horses left, only feral ones which exist because man lets them. Is it some kind of innate, even sub-conscious intelligence which has caused the horse to throw in his lot with us, seeing it as a way of surviving?

Many young domesticated horses, if threatened by, say, a dog in their paddock, will run to a human for protection, knowing that the human will usually sort out problems. Horses do soon cotton on to the fact that if they are ill, hurt or in trouble, humans normally put things right and make them feel better. This does not happen immediately, depending on circumstances (for instance, illnesses do not disappear overnight), but the horse knows that the humans are trying to do something about matters.

Intelligence or nature?

It is often said that horses learn by association of ideas as if this does not show intelligence, it is simply a biological process – a particular sound means feed is on the way (classical conditioning), a particular aid means the human wants a particular action (free operant conditioning) – but it takes some intelligence to link the sound (or whatever) and the happening or the aid and the action.

Both kinds of conditioning or learning work with humans, too. When we are learning something, say, academically or in connection with our job, there is normally another human using spoken language to explain what to do. Often we simply have to remember the facts, sometimes we have to put two and two together and get four. But humans who learn well, achieve academic success or get promoted in their jobs because they have learned the company's methods – and politics – well, are

regarded as clever. (The world is also full of brilliant but witless geniuses totally incapable of earning a living.)

When horses do the same sort of thing, we simply say that it is only classical or free operant conditioning – they would learn anyway, this is not necessarily intelligence. We know that horses learn quickly but many people will not admit that this is intelligence, either, merely the way the horse is made for survival. What *do* horses have to do to prove they are intelligent!?

Intelligence criteria

Intelligence can be described as (a) having a high degree of mental ability to learn, remember and understand things, (b) to know one's environment and to deal with it effectively, to adapt to or adjust it and (c) to use reasoning power. Leaving aside for a moment the controversial topic of reasoning power, does any reader feel that the horse is incapable of all that is involved in points (a) and (b) above?

Intelligence, cleverness, is always linked to (c) reasoning power and it has always been said most emphatically that horses have no reasoning power. It still is by many people. Reasoning power, as it relates to horses, can be described as the ability to think out problems and situations and reach a conclusion, possibly expressed by action.

Zoologists and other research and practical workers have, for many years, carried out studies and experiments designed to discover whether or not animals are intelligent beings. Unfortunately, many of their efforts have been directed at discovering whether or not animals are intelligent

ER – I'M LOST!

Studies with most types of animals have involved the still-popular maze tests. They have to find their way to a point in the maze (usually the centre) where there is food, which they then get as their reward. They have to sometimes differentiate between differently coloured food containers and learn that if they turn left or right there will be a container but the blue one will contain no food and the red one will. If the blue one is around the left turn, the animal then has to work out that it must go back and turn right, hoping to find the red one. Horses have been pretty bad at this. I know one thing. If I had to survive by finding my way through mazes I'd soon starve.

when compared to humans. This is not an appropriate standpoint for assessing the intelligence of an animal which has not evolved in human circumstances.

It may be the cowboy who takes all the credit in the cattle cutting competition but a good deal of the skill involved is down to harnessing the natural instincts of the horse. Quarter horses, which excel at working cattle, seem to have a natural 'cow sense' which appears to have been inherited from their Iberian ancestors, still used for stock work today

One man's meat

The true test of an animal's intelligence lies in its ability to survive in its own, possibly changing, environment. What other purpose can there be for intelligence? Horses are superb at surviving in their own environment, point (b), at understanding it, most certainly at adapting to it and sometimes adjusting it *when free to do so.* The problem is that so many domestic horses are kept as prisoners that they do not have much chance to adjust their own environment, although a good number understandably try to adjust their stables!

As only one example, I remember vividly watching my riding school pony, who never left the ground in his life, kick down a fence, not in an angry or frustrated way, to get to his friend on the other side. I thought this was clever then, every bit as clever as our Alsatian who, unprompted, would take the round, wooden knob of our kitchen door in his teeth, turn it, walk backwards with it still turned to open the door, come back for his tin plate, pick it up

and go through the open door to the scullery and drop the plate in the sink.

Bobs kicking down the fence shows (c) clear reasoning power and (b) the ability to adjust his environment. As for point (a), we already know that horses are very quick learners and have lifelong memories for things that are important to them. Bobs understood that if he removed the obstacle he could get to Sunshine.

Call it what you like – the Age of Aquarius with its spirit of harmony, empathy, learning and all that, or a second Equestrian Renaissance which is at last gradually burgeoning in the horse world – the time has arrived for us to be less arrogant, more *intelligent* and accept what many have believed and known for years; that horses have the type of cleverness needed for the kind of animal they are and that they also fulfil our own stated criteria of adaptability, understanding and even – ouch! – reasoning power.

The Survivors

Although the only free-living horses and ponies in the world today are feral, not truly wild, there are still wild *equidae* in the form of zebras in Africa and asses in Africa and Asia. These remnants of what were once large herds are valuable sources of study and information for researchers, behaviourists and others who study the behaviour of wild animals and particularly *equidae*.

Our fingers in their pie

Feral animals are those which have, at some point in their history, been subject to the interference of man. Perhaps they are the descendants of formerly domestic horses, like American Mustangs or Australian Brumbies, or they could be horses, and their offspring and subsequent descendants, of animals such as the Przewalski Horses which have been conserved in safari and wildlife parks and reserves and reintroduced into their former home ranges, or regions very similar where it is felt the climate, vegetation and general environment will be roughly what their ancestors experienced. (It has been interesting to note how quickly they revert to wild ways – a matter of weeks – once living well away from man's influence, a lesser tendency to which is noted by owners of domestic horses turned out on large areas for several weeks or months.)

Although Britain and Ireland's native ponies run free in forests, on moors and in wild, natural country, all of them belong to someone and they are simply the descendants of the indigenous types established here at the end of the last Ice Age around 10,000 or 12,000 years ago. In these cases, many cross-breds have been introduced and the original pony types themselves have often been subject to 'dilution' of type by this means, either by owners who do not care about the indigenous type or in a misguided effort to improve what was already perfect for its environment, with the result that many of the offspring died.

By the grace of man

As far as horses and ponies are concerned, the only reason they exist at all today is because they have been so useful to man and probably partly because there seems to be one of those inexplicable attractions between man and horse, like that between man and dog, which extends beyond pure usefulness. There is certainly something about horses that attracts even the 'non-horsey' and this, plus horses' adaptability and apparent willingness to be part of man's society (otherwise attempts to domesticate him would have been abandoned long ago as they were with the onager, for instance), make them a clear choice to be part of our society.

The humble domestic donkey, the main beast of burden in developing countries, is a descendant of the wild ass of Africa and the Bible. His temperament, like that of the horse, makes him

COMPROMISES

The conservation movement, the increasing interest in wildlife in general and the slowly dawning realisation that the earth does not belong to us has meant that many wild animals have been accommodated in large wildlife reserves; compromises have had to be arrived at where man's needs have been as great as those of the animals. Asian wild asses may well be at risk due to radiation in their ranges from fallout from arms tests in the late 1990s and zebras have been poached for their skins. Kenya's tall, elegant Grévy's zebras (pictured above) with their fine, beautiful striping patterns and a social organisation unlike other *equidae* are greatly threatened by man and his domestic cattle encroaching on to their grazing lands. From a population of 15,000 twenty years ago, they now number 4,000 in the wild and 1,000 in captivity. At this rate of reduction, they will certainly be extinct in a few years as nothing significant currently seems to be happening to preserve them and their lands and their numbers continue to fall at the time of writing.

The Cape Mountain zebra of South Africa, with its unique gridiron pattern on the hindquarters, has only a small population of hundreds remaining but they are under supervision on a reserve and their numbers at least appear to be stable.

Left: *The Somali wild ass is a tall, elegant and highly sensitive equid struggling to survive in its natural environment*

Below: *A female onager and young. The ancient Mesopotamians tried to domesticate the onager, which is inherently bad-tempered by our standards, but gave up*

Bottom: *Przewalski's horses once again roam their ancestral ranges. They do not seem to have ever been widely domesticated*

fairly easy to domesticate. Donkeys are very intelligent: those professionals who work with them say they have much more intellect and common sense than horses. They often face up to danger rather than running, are generally uncomplaining, perhaps excessively tolerant of brutal treatment and are a major economic force to the families who own them, who usually live and work in extreme poverty.

Attempts were certainly made to domesticate the wild types left, the Asian asses and the zebras, all in Africa, but their working connection with man was short lived. Although zebras have been tamed, if not fully domesticated, small numbers having been regularly ridden, harnessed to vehicles sometimes in teams, and worked on circuses, the same cannot be said for Asian asses which, although not so striking in appearance as zebras, are often tall and elegant, very fast but not at all co-operative with man.

Why have Asian asses and zebras, then, managed to survive as true wild animals where horses have not? For one thing, some of them barely *are* surviving. They remain purely because they have been allowed or enabled to do so by man or have been living in areas where man did not want their land. Whenever there is a contest between man and animal for territory, man nearly always wins.

Preserving the gene pools

The protection afforded to animals on reserves and so on, although often not perfect, is well worthwhile if it saves their species. Zoos, safari parks, national parks, reserves and the like, even small private collections, can all, if wisely managed, play a valuable, even essential role in the survival of the few species of *equidae* we have left. It is essential to preserve as much genetic variety as possible. The mating of every Przewalski horse is carefully matched from a genetic viewpoint to try to maintain reasonable diversity from the very

small gene pool the feral herds were started from. Those reintroduced as herds to the wild are carefully assessed genetically to preserve this policy.

The interesting 'reconstituted' Tarpans of Poland, produced by mating together native ponies such as the Huçul and Konig known to possess many Tarpan genes, now run free in the vast, primeval forests of their homeland and are the nearest we shall now get to real Tarpans unless someone comes up with some usable DNA.

The efforts to recreate the quagga, described earlier, are most interesting and in cases like these, the Tarpans and the Przewalskis, it will be fascinating to see what genetic mutations occur and what 'throwbacks' emerge from these efforts to maintain our equine species.

A Place of His Own

Although horses are not so territorial as many other animals, it is generally believed that they have no territorial instincts at all. Observations of both domestic, feral and wild *equidae* has shown this not to be the case. Wild *equidae* certainly migrate around chosen grazing grounds to follow not only seasonal growth in grasses and other vegetation but to move on when they have eaten down one particular area.

As we have seen, the most famous example of equine migration is that of the wildebeest and zebras up and down Africa's great Rift Valley. Other *equidae* in more restricted regions still migrate around, knowing where to find the best grazing, the most effective shelter, the water sources, the safest areas for foaling and so on. Early man's lifestyle became nomadic purely because he wanted to follow the herds of horses and other animals.

When needs must

Sometimes, feral horses and ponies are living in areas not really big enough to accommodate them all. Then, the instinct to preserve territory surfaces and becomes more obvious to observers. The pony herds of Chincoteague and Assateague islands off the north eastern coast of North America are one example of this. Another very interesting observation was made by an Equine Behaviour Forum member a few years ago of feral pony herds on Dartmoor in southern England. She noted that the herds seemed to be mainly in small family groups which had their own clearly marked territories and, so long as family boundaries were respected, there was little trouble.

She also noted that, if general trouble arose, such as domestic dogs running loose on the moor, the little herds would band together in one big one, galloping and milling around like one massive wild herd, perhaps an ancient instinct to increase numbers and, therefore, safety in the face of perceived predation or savaging. Normally, a dog or a group of dogs will single out one particular animal and all converge on that as does a pack of wolves or hunting dogs in the wild. Once the excitement, or danger, was over, the joint herd would once again split into its family groups, each returning to its own territory.

Marking the boundaries

The use of dung and urine in marking out territory is common to many animal species including prey animals, although it is associated in the minds of most people with predators. Stallions will normally dung on top of the droppings or urine of an in-season mare and a potential or actual rival male. They also dung on the outskirts of their herd's territorial boundaries, wherever they are, if land and food are short and they need to stake out their claim during their stay, even if temporary.

Domestic stallions turned out in turn in the same paddock will often roll when first turned out, then make it a priority to go round the paddock sniffing at piles of droppings and urine patches to check which rivals have been turned out before them, then doing a dropping or urinating on top to establish their own superiority. This instinct is used to encourage circus stallions to do their droppings before entering the ring for a performance. A pile of droppings from one horse's stable is placed in a particular spot, then another horse brought along,

BEING KIND TO BE CRUEL

Feral horses do not tend to live near man unless food is scarce or they have found that man is an easy source of it. England's New Forest ponies are a sad example of this: the populations which inhabit the innermost parts of the forest seem to thrive better than those which have chosen to live nearer the roads which traverse it. Motorists habitually park their cars and picnic on the roadsides. They feed the ponies partly to say they have had a 'wild' pony eating out of their hand and perhaps because, as many of them are in poor condition, they feel sorry for them.

Then, when food is not always forthcoming, not only do the ponies turn nasty towards the humans but, still hanging around the roadsides, many are killed by motor traffic every year. Whenever we see signs telling us not to feed the animals, whatever they are, we should obey them.

allowed to sniff the pile, then, positioned appropriately, he will do his own droppings on top to obliterate the scent of his rival, even though he knows him well and works with him. Then another stallion will be brought along, and so on. The first horse, whose droppings were used to start the procedure, is brought along later.

Home, sweet home

Domestic horses often regard their stables as their own territory. This is probably why many of them stale as soon as fresh bedding is put down. They often roll at this time too and although this may be partly for sheer enjoyment, it helps coat the bedding with their own scent.

When moving horses to a new stable or yard, it is always a good idea to clean the box out thoroughly first and disinfect it with a modern, horse-friendly disinfectant, to remove, as far as we can tell, the smell of the previous occupant. This will probably enable the new resident to settle quicker. Although it is important to try as hard as

possible to give a horse a stable he likes and this may involve trying him in a few, generally it is very unsettling for horses to be frequently changed around into different stables on the same yard.

Although we do not normally regard horses as territorial animals, in fact they are, most especially when space and food are at a premium as horses may perceive them to be in conventional domestic conditions. We often put them in small, overcrowded paddocks, by their natural, instinctive standards, in stables which some may want to regard as their own secure territory and certainly to have no enemies nearby, and we give them food when we choose in the amounts we judge sufficient. Under these management practices, the horses may well regard both space and food as being in short supply which can bring out their territorial instincts.

127

An Asiatic Wild Ass in the Hay-Bar Biblical Reserve, Israel. Equids' territorial instincts become more obvious when they are under pressure for space, food, water and shelter

Built-in Disguise

Domestic horses come in a very wide range of colours from sooty black to snow white and virtually all points in between. Some coats have metallic sheens to them which can produce any shade you would expect of iridescence when the light is right. Horses may have coats wholly or mainly of one colour, may have white markings on head and legs, may be parti-coloured (skewbald, piebald, Paint, Pinto), may have spots, splashes, splodges, dapples, brindle effects called roans (an even mixture of white hairs and a colour), and their manes and tails may match, tone or contrast. It's a case of take your pick.

Exmoor ponies show the primitive camouflage colouring of mousy brown, paler underparts and mealy muzzles and eyes

Left: *Although at first eye-catching, broken patches of colour, like the zebra's stripes, actually help a horse blend in to his background*

Wild horses are felt to have had a much narrower range of colours, mainly browns and duns (yellowy beiges) with probably paler underparts, like today's Przewalski horses and some Exmoor Ponies. Tarpans appear to have been a bluey, steel grey. Although grey (white-grey) horses are born black, horses living in sub-Arctic conditions do not change a darker summer coat for a white winter one, like some animals, although some horses' winter coats are slightly different from their summer ones and foals sometimes change colour at their first cast.

Coat colour developed because of its camouflaging effect. Those animals which blend well with their background or have colour patterns which confuse the eye of a predator survive longer to pass on their characteristics. The range of domestic colours we now have is the result of man's breeding efforts and, to some extent, genetic mutations.

Feral populations seem slow to revert to primitive colours. For instance, feral mustangs and brumbies have been running loose for a couple of hundred years or so but still show varied domestic-type colours. The dun with dark list (spinal stripe) colouring seen in some mustangs is a natural one still common in domestic horses. It is not a reversion but has simply carried on through the generations from wild to domestic to feral.

MELANOMAS

Melanoma tumours are due to abnormal formations of melanin and are most common in grey horses who have black skin, because black skin often contains melanin-secreting cells called melanoblasts which can increase their metabolic rate. The resulting accumulations or tumours are at first benign (harmless) and are very slow-growing but once their growth rate speeds up, malignant (harmful) cells invade surrounding tissues which die and ulcerate. Horses live comfortably with melanomas for many years but if their location causes pain or severe discomfort it may be necessary to euthanase the horse. Tumours which are surgically removed seem to regrow more aggressively than before, so the decision is often to leave them alone. The drug cimetidine, often used in humans to treat stomach ulcers and excessive acid production in the stomach, has brought about remission of melanomas and it is well worth asking your vet about this treatment. Homoeopathic treatment is also reported as being successful.

SKIN CANCER

Lack of skin pigment can also result in skin cancer in light or pink-skinned horses. Areas which have little or no hair or melanocytes are most commonly affected, such as mucous membranes, the muzzle and around the tail and genitals, although the disease can occur in areas not exposed to the sun.

The tumours can be removed by surgery, including cryosurgery (freezing), and it is recommended that susceptible horses wear a high-factor sun block.

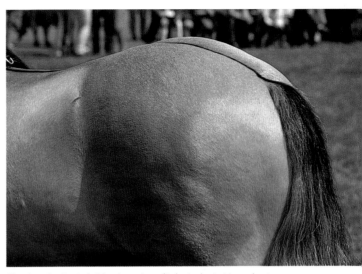

The dorsal stripe is held to be a sign of inherited primitive colouring. It is common in some ponies and cobs, in Iberian horses of dun colouring and in buckskin mustangs and other like-coloured animals of Iberian descent

129

How Colour is Formed

Colouring is due to sulphur-containing, granular pigments called melanins formed from the amino acid tyrosine by the enzyme tyrosinase. They are produced by melanocytes, specialised cells in the epidermal layer of the skin of vertebrates and in the hair which grows from that skin. They are also found in the ciliary body and choroid of the eye, in the pigment layer of its retina and in certain nerve cells. Melanins are black or dark brown and, in different concentrations, give a whole range of colours. They protect the skin from the harmful effects of ultraviolet radiation. This is an important benefit to an outdoor animal like the horse.

Albinism

True albinism is quite rare in horses. It is caused by a recessive gene and affected horses will have white hair, pink skin and colourless eyes which appear pink due to the blood in them being visible. They are extremely sensitive to sun, weather, infection, toxins and other chemicals, insects and are prone to skin cancer. They also possibly have poor eyesight, hearing and weak constitutions. At least they do not get melanomas!

Albinism can be classified as partial, incomplete or complete. Some horses may have white, blue or brown eyes, with white or cream-coloured coat hair on a pink or light-coffee-coloured skin and this latter type of horse may give you all the undoubted glamour of an albino with fewer of the health and management problems.

Markings

Horses may have varied white markings, usually on legs and head, and some excellent animals have been refused breed registry because their markings were not approved by the breed society – such as 'high white' (white above knee or hock) or white on the body. This is said to indicate 'common blood' yet very many high-quality blood-type horses are so marked. Some breeds are permitted no white at all. In practice, white over pink skin can be a nuisance because of the sensitivity of the skin, but it has no effect on the temperament or abilities of the horse.

Other markings may include so-called primitive ones like a dorsal stripe or list down the spine and horizontal zebra-like stripes on the legs.

There are numerous old wives' tales about colour and markings, none of which I have ever found relevant. From the point of view of temperament and performance potential, colour is of no importance at all – it all depends on whether or not you have any personal preference.

Feeding

Feeding is one of those horsey topics most owners love because all healthy horses look forward to feed times and the owner feels he or she is doing something to please their horse. It's an interesting subject and vitally important to your horse's health, wellbeing and comfort. It is not always straightforward, conflicting advice can be confusing, so let's look at the facts.

A Couple of Attitude Adjusters

The main parameters on which to base your horse's diet are the overall energy content and ample fibre of the right sort. The old idea, regarding concentrates as the most important part of the diet and worrying about protein levels, are now known to be not only much less important but potentially harmful.

For a start, the horse is not adapted to eat starchy concentrates (cereal grain – oats, barley, corn/maize). In small to very moderate amounts, these can be used as a booster if necessary; more than that and the starch in them can start to cause problems of metabolism. The horse *is* adapted to eat fibre, and in a big way. Grass and other green herbage, forage feeds, hay, haylage and succulents, particularly soaked, unmolassed sugar beet shreds, suit him down to the ground and he can get plenty of nourishment from these sources for harder work than most amateur-owned horses ever do.

In natural conditions, horses eat almost nothing but grass all year round, keep out the cold in winter and regularly travel around 30 miles a day every day, not to mention indulging in rough horse-play and propelling themselves up to a top-speed gallop and sustaining it for a few miles, when needed. All that on grass – and some owners think stabled horses need bucketsful of concentrates just to carry them round the block a few times a week.

Vote With Your Cash

Good feed manufacturers are sometimes responsible for excellent nutritional research. They publicise their findings and those of other scientists and market feeds in line with them. Today, they recommend, and concerned owners want, less

Virtually ad lib, suitable quality fibre such as hay or haylage is one of the safest, most effective ways of feeding a horse, whose digestive system is adapted to process fibre far better than concentrates. If you must use a haynet tie it at horse's head height. This one is dangerously low

Left: Hydroponically-grown grass is an easy way to give your horse a nutritious, juicy treat outside the growing season

refined sugar, less goo, less starch and fewer artificial additives. In their place we find more fibrous forage feeds of different energy grades made from nutritious grasses, straws and alfalfa, to suit the equine consumer concerned, good haylage (although less hay around in the UK and Ireland), with extra energy, where needed, coming from bagged, branded feeds containing fewer cereals and more pulses, legumes and oils.

Soaked sugar beet pulp, with its high-fibre, high-mineral content, is deservedly being used more as a feed and not just a dampener. We see, and use, a lot less bran and have rightly returned to feeding more chop, often with palatable additives.

Although it is still extremely difficult to buy organic-type feeds for horses, these, too, will undoubtedly become more available provided we keep demanding them. Vitamin and mineral supplements are treated with more caution and care in their selection and concerned owners generally take more care to check out products and feeds in general.

Translating It Into Practice
How much should I feed?
You can calculate your horse's approximate daily weight of feed according to his bodyweight. If you can weigh him on a weighbridge this is ideal. If not, use a length of string and measure him right round his girth, keeping the string straight (vertical to the ground), then use the table on the opposite page to assess his weight.

Measurement/weight tables

Table 1 Ponies and cobs

Girth in inches	40	42.5	45	47.5	50	52.5	55	57.5
Girth in cm	101	108	114	120	127	133	140	146
Bodyweight in lb	100	172	235	296	368	430	502	562
Bodyweight in kg	45	77	104	132	164	192	234	252

Table 2 Horses

Girth in inches	55	57.5	60	62.5	65	67.5
Girth in cm	140	146	152	159	165	171
Bodyweight in lb	583	613	688	776	851	926
Bodyweight in kg	240	274	307	346	380	414

Girth in inches	70	72.5	75	77.5	80	82.5
Girth in cm	140	146	152	159	165	171
Bodyweight in lb	1014	1090	1165	1278	1328	1369
Bodyweight in kg	453	486	520	570	593	611

Tables based on work of Glushanok, Rochlitz & Skay, 1981

- **A daily maintenance ration** for a cob, pony, overweight horse or a good doer should be about 2 per cent of bodyweight daily. For others it should be 2.5 per cent.
- **For lactating or late-pregnancy broodmares, for youngstock and thin horses** (increasing gradually), feed at about 3 per cent of bodyweight daily.
- **For light to moderate exercise** (relaxed hacking) 2.5 per cent of bodyweight daily is correct.
- **For moderate work** (active hacking, Riding Club activities, schooling, half a day's hunting per week etc.) give about 2.5 per cent of bodyweight daily, maybe using higher energy feeds.
- **For hard work** (serious competing, hunting three full days a fortnight, competitive carriage driving etc.) feed at 3 per cent of bodyweight daily and perhaps give extra oil in the feeds (say one tablespoon of corn or soya oil per feed) to provide extra energy without bulk.

Energy

Choose the feeds you use mainly according to their energy content. Energy levels are more significant than protein levels.

For ponies, cobs and overweight animals, an energy content of 7 to 8MJ (megajoules) of DE (digestible energy) per kilogram is quite adequate. For those in light to moderate exercise and for older or thin animals, 8.5 to10MJ of DE per kg is fine and for hard-working horses 12MJ of DE per kg is good enough. Rarely will more be needed.

Feeding hay or haylage on the ground may appear wasteful but it mimics most closely the horse's natural need to eat from ground level and to move gently whilst doing so, which encourages gut movement and promotes good digestion

If you use feeds of a reputable make, the energy content should be on the sack, label or leaflet. If not, ring the manufacturer and ask.

Protein

The highest levels of protein are needed by young foals at 18 to 20 per cent; weanlings need 16 per cent reducing to about 13.5 per cent as they become yearlings and further reducing to 10 per cent as two-year-olds (more if racing). Lactating broodmares in the first third of their lactation need 14 per cent protein, reducing to 12 per cent from the fourth month to weaning. In the last three months of pregnancy, broodmares need 11 per cent protein in the diet. It is not generally realised that mature horses, even those in hard work, do not need more than 8.5 per cent protein in their whole diet whereas many people are still giving levels of 12 or even 14 per cent. An exception to this is old and/or very thin animals who need extra protein as their metabolisms become less efficient or to help replace lost muscle tissue.

The fibre/concentrate split

Equine exercise physiologists and nutritionists are now advising that no less than 50 per cent of the total daily food ration by weight should be given as roughage/bulk/fibre such as grass, hay, haylage or a forage feed, and this is for strenuously working performance horses. For most others in the hard-to-moderate work category, the diet could be split between three-quarters roughage (grass, hay etc.) and one quarter concentrates (oats, barley, cubes, coarse mix/sweet feed). It is also now accepted that horses can work surprisingly hard with no concentrates at all, simply appropriate grass, hay, haylage or forage feed of suitable energy and protein levels.

Understanding Health and Condition

General Signs of Good Health

General demeanour
Horse interested in surroundings (unless sleepy), alert but calm. Should not appear restless unless something exciting happening nearby; should not seem dull/lethargic.

Eyes
Bright, clear, no discharges, swelling, redness, soreness or apparent discomfort (frequent rubbing or closing the eye).

Skin and coat
Coat bright, 'lively', smooth, not dull, harsh or stiff and raised ('staring'). No spots, sores, bare patches, swellings, wounds, raised areas or scabs. Outdoor animals may have some scurf and grease in the coat. Skin pliable and loose, moving easily over the ribs under the flat of the hand. Frequent rubbing or biting the skin is a sign of disorder.

Action
Ideally, straight, even and level, free and confident. A hind leg may be rested but not a foreleg. If a horse seems uneasy on his feet, or joints are swollen or hot, suspect a problem.

Eating/drinking
Study the horse's normal habits so you know when he is experiencing difficulty or discomfort, or is eating or drinking more or less than usual. Excess saliva or froth abnormal.

Droppings
Will pass droppings about every two hours up to about 12 piles in 24 hours. Normal droppings form into apple-sized, oval balls which just break on hitting the ground. Should not be slimy, soft, hard, strong or acrid-smelling or contain blood. Should range from dark green to khaki according to diet, never very dark or pale.

Urine
Clear or cloudy, creamy to yellowish in colour, no bad smell. A male horse should let down his penis to stale (pass urine).

Respiration
Should be silent and smooth. If rapid at rest, or unusually noisy, suspect trouble.

Nose
Very slight watery discharge, particularly after exercise, normal. Blood or excessive or thick discharge abnormal. Yellow or greenish, thick discharge indicates infection.

After rolling
Horse should get up and shake, otherwise it could indicate colic. More rolling than usual can indicate abdominal pain.

Rolling should definitely be encouraged, not denied. Your horse should give a vigorous shake afterwards which indicates that the horse is satisfied and feels good

Dehydration
To check, press thumb firmly on gum immediately above an incisor to create a pale patch. Colour (blood) should return within 1.5 seconds. Also, pinch up and twist a fold of skin on the point of the shoulder: it should fall flat immediately in a healthy horse (see watering pp134–5).

Patchy sweating
Can mean pain and cold sweating indicates fatigue and/or shock.

Temperature, Pulse and Respiration Rates
Take your horse's rates at the same time each day under the same conditions for a week so you get to know his average readings. This takes only about five minutes. Healthy ponies, youngstock and unfit animals have higher rates than horses, old or fit animals.

Average at-rest rates

Temperature: about 38°C or 100.4°F.
Pulse: about 32 to 42 beats per minute.
Respiration: about 8 to 14 breaths per minute (in and out counting as one).

Taking the temperature

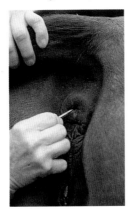

To take the temperature

Buy an ordinary veterinary thermometer from your vet (they are the most accurate type). Shake mercury well down with snapping movement of wrist so it is well below the normal figure. Lubricate the bulb with spit or petroleum jelly and, standing behind and to the left of the horse, pull the dock towards you with your left hand and insert the thermometer several inches into the anus with your right, using a gentle twisting, side-to-side movement. Press gently against wall of rectum and leave in place for at least 30 seconds. Gently remove, wipe clean quickly and read temperature. The average at-rest temperature should be about 38°C.

To take the pulse

Feel where an artery crosses a bone (under jawbone, inside elbow a little way down, above eye and under or at side of dock about a third of the way down). An artery will feel springy under your fingers whereas a vein (which has no pulse) will flatten easily. Leave your fingers in place for several seconds as you wait for the pulse as it will be only about 32 to 42 beats per minute in a calm resting horse. Count, using a watch with a second hand,

The most common spot to take the pulse

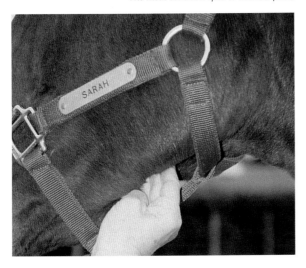

for half a minute, then double it to find the number of beats per minute.

To take the respiration

Stand behind and slightly to one side of horse and watch opposite flank rise and fall (can be difficult to spot). Alternatively, hold a mirror up to a nostril and, once the horse's curiosity is satisfied, count how often it steams up.

Body Condition (Weight)
What to aim for

General healthy bodyweight means you cannot see your horse's ribs but can feel them quite easily. In very fit horses, the last two ribs may be seen and the horse may be lean (but with spine and hips not too obvious) and be well muscled up. In winter, particularly with outdoor animals, you can allow more rib/topline coverage. These criteria apply to all types of animals.

133

Individual type

Some animals are naturally leaner than others, like people. However, the spine all the way down (and the hips/pelvic area) should be well covered with flesh without being podgy or, certainly, having a 'water channel' running down the back.

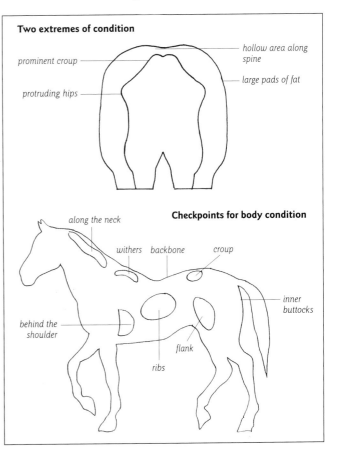

Two extremes of condition

prominent croup

protruding hips

hollow area along spine

large pads of fat

Checkpoints for body condition

along the neck

withers backbone croup

behind the shoulder

ribs

flank

inner buttocks

Watering

We have already seen how important water is to the working of the body. With horses needing up to around 50 litres or 13 gallons of water when working in hot weather or sometimes when simply standing around in a hot environment, the importance of its supply cannot be over-estimated. Although horses rarely drink too much water they often drink too little for various reasons, and this can lead to dehydration.

Dehydration

Particularly in humid conditions, when the horse's sweat does not evaporate effectively into the surrounding air, the horse may sweat even more as its temperature sensors tell it that it is not cooling down. This can easily lead to dehydration.

Another, less expected, situation in which horses can suffer from dehydration is in very cold and particularly freezing weather. Horses hardly ever break even thin ice on their drinking containers and obviously go short of water till some thinking human does it for them. If the horses are only checked and tended twice a day, they may well not drink enough at those times because they never drink as much cold water as they do when their water is a more comfortable temperature, and very gradually dehydration and possibly colic set in. If for some reason the horses are only seen to once a day (never enough) they will dehydrate more quickly.

It is often said and believed that horses will obtain water from eating snow but this is irrelevant: they cannot possibly take in enough snow to provide sufficient water. The old belief that horses should be deprived of water for an hour or more before hard work is now known to be quite wrong. Water passes through their systems very quickly and is not a problem. They should be allowed ad lib water for up to half an hour before hard work. Walking and trotting on a hack is not hard work and you will be warming up before faster work, anyway. Endurance horses are encouraged to drink from any available source en route during competition.

Containers

Whatever container is used must be steady, bite-resistant and safe in case the horse throws it around in boredom. Any wall fixings must, likewise, not be able to injure the horse. Automatic containers should be the type with a meter so you can tell how much or little your horse is drinking as this is a guide to health. They should also have a plug in the bottom for daily draining and cleaning.

Field containers should be sited as far as possible on the highest part of the field, especially if they are

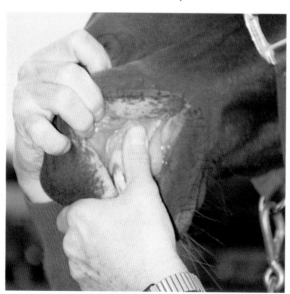

To check for even slight dehydration, press your thumb just above a front tooth to create a pale patch. The colour should return within 1.5 seconds as the blood returns to the capillaries. This is called the Capillary Refill Time test.

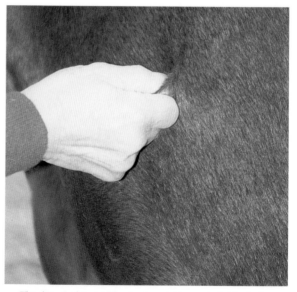

The skin-pinch test will only show fairly marked dehydration. Pinch up and twist a fold of skin on the neck or point of shoulder. If it does not fall flat immediately you let go, the horse is definitely dehydrated and could need veterinary attention

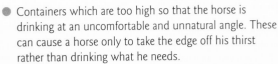

SOME OTHER REASONS FOR INSUFFICIENT WATER INTAKE ARE:

- Water in containers being topped up for ease and quickness, rather than changed. Such water is never properly clean and always contaminated by gases from the stable environment, saliva, old food, bedding and maybe other debris such as dead insects, bird droppings, dust and so on. Some horses refuse to drink such water and their attendants, thinking that the horse has enough water, leave a bad situation to become even worse.

- Containers which smell or taste unpleasant, either because they are not properly scrubbed daily and have become slimy, because they are made of certain plastics or rubber or the water itself is contaminated. Horses sometimes contaminate their own containers by doing droppings in them: they should be cleaned out and disinfected with a product especially for the job which leaves no smell or taste, or one for sterilising baby equipment.

- Containers which are too high so that the horse is drinking at an uncomfortable and unnatural angle. These can cause a horse only to take the edge off his thirst rather than drinking what he needs.

- Containers which move or rattle when the horse drinks can worry him and put him off.

- If away from home, many horses refuse to drink strange water. A large camping container of home water can be taken to mix with 'foreign' water or some product added (to which he is used) to disguise the taste, such as a little peppermint essence. The water in which sugar beet has been soaked is rarely refused by most horses.

- If horses are to be left for several hours without attention, such as overnight or if the owner is at work all day, leave two buckets or containers if they are only normal size to be sure the horse will have enough. Two containers are always a good idea, anyway, always in the same but different corners so the horse can find them in the dark, in case he does a dropping in one.

135

in a fixed position, to avoid as much as possible poaching the ground around them. They should, again, have no sharp corners or edges. Opinions vary as to their siting: I prefer them to be set into a fence along its line between two fields, and not in a corner if the field takes more than a couple of horses.

Large, tough plastic tubs are ideal for providing water if you have no piped supply. They can be filled by hosepipe, stood in large tyres for stability and tied to the fence posts for security. They have the advantage of being able to be moved along a little each day which stops the ground around them becoming poached and worn. Keep them well topped up (and clean) because if they are tall and the water level drops, some horses will not put their heads right down inside to drink as this obscures their vision.

Drinking quirks

It pays to take time to watch your horses drinking so you have a good idea of their personal habits.

If horses are swilling water around

in their mouths without actually swallowing it, this can be a sign of colic and if a horse's teeth are getting worn, or there is some tooth damage, they may not want to drink cold water.

Sometimes horses drink too much water if they are bored. This can result in their passing much more urine than usual.

Do not remove your horse's water during feeding as some people still do. Research has shown that digestion is actually improved if the horse can take a little drink whilst eating, as many do. Having a few swallows after feeding is also fine.

Hot, humid weather adversely affects horses, particularly when competing in strenuous events. To avoid dehydration horses should be allowed to take short drinks at convenient moments – approx a quarter of a bucket (ideally containing electrolytes if your horse will take them)

Grassland – A Vital Resource

If there is one thing horses were meant to do it is graze. Horses love grass. They'll kill for grass. Well, maybe not, but it is probably the most important thing in their lives and the one many horses never get enough of. Some horses, indeed, never get any.

The problem with grass ...

Horses and especially ponies evolved to thrive on poor to moderate grazing. If you live in a dairy-farming area, on rich land producing equally rich grass, and have the most usual sort of half to three-quarter Thoroughbred, warmblood, pony/cob type of animal, it may be no wonder you restrict your horse's grass for fear of giving him laminitis, obesity and all the ills that go with rich grass.

This young foal, who cannot yet eat or digest much grass, can only obtain its benefits from his dam's milk

Horses are better on beef cattle and sheep grazing.

Many premises which have horses, though, have the opposite problem – small paddocks with grass grazed down to the roots, providing nothing but a nibble and a leg-stretch. The bad news is that not only is this sort of grazing boring for the animals (but better than standing in most of the time) but also some researchers, nutritionists and vets currently believe that such overgrazed, stressed grass and purposely maintained 'starvation paddocks' produce substances which actually favour the development of laminitis.

Horse grass

The good news is that it is now easy to provide good *equine* grazing with suitable grasses and nutrient levels for horses and ponies, from laminitics to Badminton contenders. It costs no more to create than looking after any grassland

DRAINAGE

Drainage is crucial to good grazing particularly in wet seasons and on low-lying land. Poor drainage is the reason so many yards close their paddocks in winter so that the horses never get any proper turnout for half the year. How much better it would be for everyone, most importantly the horses, if some thought and financial priority were given to creating and maintaining effective drainage ditches and installing a proper drainage system so that there could be year-round pasture turnout on a rota basis in all but the wettest seasons.

and you do not need to plough up your paddocks or put them out of use for a year: you can gradually change to equine grassland by various means such as thorough harrowing, getting rid of unwanted vegetation, appropriate fertilisers to balance up your soil chemistry without supercharging it and seeding 'horse' grasses into your remaining sward.

There are various firms which will provide free soil and herbage analysis provided you are buying your fertilisers and grass mix from them but don't be fobbed off by sales talk; if they obviously don't produce a specialised equine mix go to a firm which does. There are agricultural consultants, nutritionists and, in the UK, the Equine Services Department of ADAS, the Agricultural Development Advisory Service, which is part of the Ministry of Agriculture. The phone number is in your local telephone book. In the USA, contact the County extension agent.

The right sort of grass for horses will provide them with so much food of the right nutrient content that you will save money on other feeds – and on bedding. Provided you get the shelter conditions right as well, you can leave your horses out for much longer and they will be healthier and more content, too. So you all benefit.

Herbs

Some of the most popular feed additives and supplements today are the herbal ones and, if formulated by a reputable company, they can be beneficial. Most modern paddocks have few herbs because they were eradicated when thought of as weeds and have never been replaced. Now, it is good practice to sow a varied herb strip on the highest, driest parts of paddocks where they will thrive away from competition from grasses.

Horses are believed to have what has been termed 'nutritional intuition' by behaviourist Dr Marthe Kiley-Worthington and studies on feral

equidae seem to confirm that they definitely medicate themselves when the right herbage is available – herbs and a wide range of grasses.

Basic grassland care

Whatever advisor you choose to help with your grassland will give you information on maintaining it, but basically, all land should be rested for at least three continuous months in each year and preferably more. When the horses are taken off, they can be followed by sheep or cattle to eat off the long, ungrazed areas the horses have reserved for droppings, or they can be topped (mown) and the cuttings ideally scattered on the short areas the horses have grazed.

Harrowing should be done, any recommended fertilisers applied and the land rested while the horses are eating off some other land. When that begins to look patchy, the horses should be moved on again, maybe back to the first area or on to a third if you are so fortunate. If you are very short of land, rotate and make the very best use of it during the grazing season, rest it all winter after treatment, and arrange turnout on other areas such as surfaced play areas, outdoor manèges or indoor schools.

One key to good land management, at least on the small paddocks many owners have access to, is removing droppings, and that is dealt with in the next section.

POISONOUS PLANTS

Poisonous plants are a cause of worry and aggravation to many owners. In the UK, ragwort is on the increase and although local councils have the power to enforce its eradication, they do not seem to have the *duty* to do so and so nothing seems to be done about it. Because of constant financial cutbacks, 'spare' areas, roadside verges and so on are no longer cut as they used to be and although this is wonderful for the restoration of wild flower areas, ragwort takes advantage and is proliferating everywhere, seeding itself into neighbouring land. Because of the organic movement, many people do not want to use 'chemical' sprays to kill it but sometimes needs must. The recommended remedy of hand-pulling actually makes the situation worse as it is utterly impossible to ensure that you get out every scrap and the ragwort reproduces like the Medusa from one tiny fragment.

It is worth learning to recognise other poisonous plants so you can take appropriate action and also worth remembering that healthy paddocks with a strong-growing sward stifle most of them. Many, too, taste bitter and horses normally avoid them unless very hungry.

137

Parasite Control

The International Donkey Protection Trust, based at Sidmouth, Devon, England do a great deal of work helping to improve the lot of working donkeys in developing countries. It has found that the single most important factor in maintaining the donkeys' health is to worm them. This caused such a startling improvement in their condition that it is now a major priority in their management and in the work of the Trust.

Owners of domestic horses and ponies may be surprised to learn that even healthy-looking animals can carry a heavy worm burden; also, unthriftiness and low bodyweight are not the only problems parasites cause.

How they work

A major effect of parasites is the damage done to the intestines, as the worms attach to the inside of the

Over-grazed, horse-sick pastures become parasite-ridden, weed-infested and of low feeding value. Picking up the droppings every couple of days will help the parasite problem, if nothing else. Leaving droppings down contaminates the grazing, too

gut, sucking blood, or burrow through the body on the migratory parts of their life cycles, also damaging blood vessels and other internal organs.

There are several types of internal parasites with vary life cycles. They are usually picked up by the horse licking eggs off his forehand or picking up larvae from the grass, bedding or even infected hay, grass, straw, stable walls or floor. The parasites hatch inside the horse, travel around, lodging in the lungs, stomach or intestine, according to species, sucking blood, damaging blood vessels and other tissues and organs, blocking intestines and stopping blood flow, killing the tissues in the area supplied (often the gut) and causing fatal colic.

Natural remedy

Wild and feral *equidae* suffer sometimes from parasite infestation but also often appear to treat themselves with selective grazing and browsing, according to studies. They have a much wider range of foods available to them and vastly greater areas of land to roam than our domestic horses, making

infestation less likely and easier to deal with naturally. On domestic paddocks, horses allocate lavatory areas for doing droppings which is one way to restrict the spread of larvae. The eggs pass out with the dung, hatch and the larvae are eaten by the horse. They go through their life cycle, are passed out again and so on.

What are you dealing with?

Your vet can find out what worms, if any, your horse has by means of faecal counts (counting the number of specific eggs in a few balls of your horse's dung) and by blood tests. He or she can then tell you how much of what drugs to use and when, to get rid of them. Subsequent egg counts done ten to fourteen days after treatment will reveal whether the treatment has been successful or whether 'your' worms have developed resistance to the drug used. (Resistance occurs partly because owners worm without expert advice, using incorrect amounts of drugs at the wrong worming intervals: this creates a 'breed of resistent super-worms' which can cause major problems.)

Worm Medicines

Anthelmintics (anti-helminths, helminths being parasitic worms) used in the UK belong to three chemical groups – benzimidazole, avermectin and pyrantel. They are sold under various brand names, so check on the pack for the drug the product contains. As we go to press a new wormer, moxidectin, has become available. Check with your vet about its use.

General Parasite Control

The kind of weather most conducive to worm production is warm, moist weather. Worm larvae and eggs are killed or desiccated by frost and by hot, dry weather.

Your vet will devise an appropriate worm-control programme for your horse's circumstances but basically, in addition to the treatments mentioned above, bear in mind that (a) you need to dose all horses on the place, appropriately, all year round for effective control and (b) during the grazing season you should dose at the intervals recommended for the drug chosen, using a drug from one of the three drug groups all season, rotating on a three-year rota to a different drug group each grazing season.

Holistic/natural control

If there are few horses on large areas of good grazing, you may not need such a rigid programme but still need to know what worms are involved. You can have worm counts done and worm the horses individually according to the species of parasite present.

Homoeopathic worming remedies are available, as are herbal ones.

Picking up droppings from large areas with few horses is not critical, but it is vital on small or heavily stocked areas: do it at least twice a week during the grazing season and more often in warm moist weather to remove the eggs before they have time to hatch into harmful larvae.

MAIN TYPES OF PARASITE

Small redworms

These cause more trouble than other types because they can delay their development by burrowing into the gut wall in the autumn as larval cysts, then emerging in vast numbers in spring all together, causing gut damage and badly infested pastures. They can cause serious disease and even death, young and old horses being especially at risk. A five-day course of fenbendazole (a benzimidazole) in November and February will cope with this problem.

Ascarids

Mainly a problem in youngsters, older horses can also be infested. All drug groups will deal with ascarids.

Threadworms

Young foals showing diarrhoea, lethargy and poor appetite may be infested by threadworms to which they will develop an immunity at about six months of age. The avermectin drugs will treat threadworms, although your vet might recommend giving fenbendazole at seven times the normal dose rate.

Tapeworm

These belong to two species which affect horses, living in the small and large intestines. They have an intermediate host, the forage mite, which lives on straw, hay or grass and eats the eggs passed in the horse's dung. The larvae are eaten by the horse and mature inside him, sometimes causing internal blockages (manifested as colic). Treat with pyrantel at twice the normal amount, in March and September.

Bots

Not worms but the larval stage of the bot fly, horses lick the eggs off their bodies in summer and they develop into larvae in their stomachs, often causing digestive problems. They emerge about ten months later in the horse's droppings. Treat with ivermectin (an avermectin) in December after the first frost which will have killed any remaining adults; this combined action, if everyone did it, would soon result in the extinction of the bot fly.

Home or Hell?

An ideal establishment for keeping horses happy and healthy is something many owners would die for! By far the biggest majority have to make do with limited facilities and most private owners of horses have to keep them on someone else's premises where they may have very little say in how the horses are cared for.

Having some knowledge and ideas for how to improve your horse's home and care can enable you to improve your own premises and enables you to know what to look for in a rented place or livery yard. Most places can be made more horse-friendly with a little imagination and only moderate expense.

It is wonderful to have plenty of land for horses to run on so that, with the right sort of grazing and shelter, they can be out most of the time and still fit for work. However, vast acres are not essential for horses to be fit and content. The three most important factors in this are:

- ample social contact with other congenial horses,
- the facility to eat (the right sort of food, as described elsewhere) for most of their time and
- plenty of exercise, at liberty whenever possible but not always necessarily.

Horses have been kept for thousands of years in conditions where they receive a lot of work (often several hours a day of moderate, steady work), are stabled in close proximity to others (often in standing stalls/tie stalls) and have diets comprising plenty of bulky roughage (hay, haylage, forage feeds) and they are obviously healthy, content, routined and, therefore, secure and confident. So adaptable and co-operative is the horse that, so long as these three top criteria are catered for *and he is handled properly by people he trusts*, he can, temperament permitting, be quite happy.

Pasture

Being turned out to grass in comfortable weather is seventh Heaven to most horses. An interesting, mentally stimulating paddock, varied grasses and herbs and changes of grazing make life interesting for such an intelligent, perceptive animal. Although they appear to prefer large paddocks (not surprisingly), small ones which fulfil their other needs are fine: what they want is to be free and together.

A generous supply of the right sort of grass is one of the most effective, cheapest, most effective ways of correctly and naturally feeding a horse – mentally and physically. Seventh heaven to most horses!

Non-Grass Turnout

When grazing is limited or non-existent and the ground waterlogged, other turnout areas can give horses that important chance to play around as they wish for a while each day. Outdoor manèges and indoor schools, can be used and most yards have areas which could be safely surfaced, fenced off and made into small 'play' areas. A surfaced enclosure with access to some kind of shed, barn or stables left open, or even just pens built on to the stables, is often all that is needed to take the pressure off confined, stabled horses.

Yarding

Covered yards, ideally opening into an outdoor area, grass or otherwise, are an excellent way of housing compatible horses. Doors, sliprails or gates can be fitted to keep them in, if necessary. Horses are often fed communally in such facilities at least with their bulk feeds and it is no hassle to feed concentrates individually if someone stays to see fair play. If problems are anticipated, the horses can be stabled while they eat their short (concentrate) feeds and this is a good chance for a checkover, too.

FEEDING FACILITIES AND METHODS

In natural conditions, horses have their heads down eating for most of the day and night. Even when standing about loafing, as they do, their heads are naturally held effortlessly, by the ligamentum nuchae in the neck, below their withers. Horses have a long trachea and it is easier for them to keep their airways clear of naturally accumulating debris and mucus if their heads are down most of the time. This is yet another excellent reason to turn them out, and also for feeding them at ground or low level.

Haynets and ordinary racks are obviously out for this purpose: for safety they have to be around horse's head height which is no good from a health point of view; also, horses constantly develop all the wrong muscles as they pull the hay out upwards and sideways, as they do. Long fibre (hay or haylage) can be fed loose on the ground, or in plastic dustbins in a corner or from sectioned-off corners of the box, both of which can also be filled with short-chopped forage feeds. In yards, it can be fed in long, low racks or containers along the walls.

Fixing mangers at ground level can cause problems as horses are likely to get their feet in them so short feeds can be fed from mangers with their tops at the height of the horse's elbow (and with rounded lower edges to prevent knee injuries should the horse stamp or paw whilst eating) or from buckets or bowls on the ground, removed as soon as the horse has finished. Water containers should, likewise, be at low level.

Yarding compatible horses and ponies together is a much more horse-friendly way of accommodating them than individual cells

Below: *The author's old mare, fresh from a day in the field, makes immediately for her haylage tub – still eating head down, as nature intended for comfort and good digestion. Sixth Heaven for Sarah!*

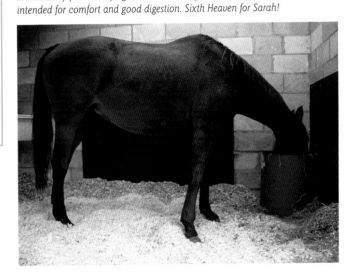

Because it is known that horses are happier and feel more secure when they can see all around them, there should be generous outlook facilities on all four walls, if possible. Just because a building is large does not mean it is well ventilated so this important aspect of housing must receive attention. Ventilation by means of Yorkshire boarding (spaced boards) is excellent, and easy and cheap to provide whether renovating or building from new. Bedding in these yards works best if they are on an earth base, as most are, for good drainage. In practice, if they are properly ventilated, they can then be skipped out daily and the bedding removed mechanically every few months. Some are not even skipped out, just having fresh bedding added when needed and, because of the drainage and ventilation, they work well with no soggy bedding, fumes or smells.

Stabling

The same criteria apply to stables – ample outlook points, good ventilation and (at the risk of my being called mad) the facility for friendly horses to see, touch and communicate with each other through or over the partitions. The film of *Black Beauty* featured ideal loose boxes with interior partitions about the height of horses' backs or just above, with a higher area at the back where horses were fed. Horses kept in such boxes must be friends – but horses should not be stabled near unfriendly ones, anyway.

There are many sorts of stable flooring now available, mainly rubber, a selling point of most being the saving in bedding, appealing, as usual, to most owners' desire to save money! Some work in theory but not practice. One thing is certain – zero-bedding systems for horses do not work. I have found that, to be fair to the horse, generous beds are still needed but the floors do provide a slip-resistant, warmer surface than the usual concrete.

Complementary Health Care

Healing, intuitive, instinctive and purposeful, has been going on probably since life began. The body has its own healing mechanisms but sometimes it needs help.

Animals and primitive peoples always seem to have had an intuitive knowledge of healing, seeking out plants or other substances they felt they needed. Ancient civilisations developed to fine arts various forms of healing, the sort we today call alternative or, more accurately, complementary medicines because they can so often complement, or accompany, what we now accept as orthodox medicine.

Modern scientists (including doctors and vets) often doubt their efficacy because they rightly claim that, in most cases, there is no scientific proof that they work. Although this is slowly changing for some therapies as more conventional (modern) scientific work is done on them, this argument is, to many, insufficient reason to avoid them because there are often vast quantities of documented evidence of their properties and effects, even though we may not know how or why they work. Lack of modern scientific proof that a therapy works does not mean that it does not work. Modern orthodox medicine also uses some substances and methods which are known to work without our knowing how.

Although most therapists who are not also qualified veterinary surgeons may not treat an animal without referral from a vet, at least in the UK where this book originates, small numbers of veterinary surgeons are now qualifying in complementary therapies themselves or involving qualified therapists (non-vets) to consult at their practices and work with them.

Different Philosophies

The main difference between orthodox and complementary medicine (human or veterinary) is that the former tends to target and physically treat specific diseases or injured parts whereas the latter usually concentrates on healing the whole animal or person (hence the word 'holistic' for some therapies) as it usually works on the principle of disease being caused or enabled to develop by the disruption of energy flow through the body. It aims to restore the correct energy flow, encouraging and enabling the body, mind and spirit, as a single entity, to heal itself by stimulating its own healing mechanisms. This is why such therapies are also often called 'energy medicines'. We live surrounded by rays and dynamic magnetic fields which are believed to affect our own magnetic and energy forces for better and worse: energy and holistic medicines are based on restoring and maintaining beneficial states of these forces.

Some Therapies Explained
Herbalism

Medicine using vegetation is probably the oldest form and one that horses use naturally if allowed access to the appropriate plants. Herbalism, probably one of the most effective therapies, emphasises the concept of healing through nutrition and the effect food has on the body. Most importantly, the patient is assessed from a complete

Solaria are used for drying off horses after swimming, as a means of relaxing a horse, giving heat therapy and providing full-spectrum light therapy depending on the types of bulbs used

mind/body/spirit perspective and within a wide context of influences.

Many plants are very potent and must be used with great care. Even though herbal remedies (often sold as feed supplements) are readily available to the general public, owners should discuss their horse's condition with a qualified herbalist and use any remedy strictly as advised.

Radionics

Stemming from the observations of an American neurologist, Dr Albert Adams, around the middle of the twentieth century, radionics or radiesthesia is based on harmonising the mind, body and spirit of the patient by detecting distortions in the unique, individual energy pattern each is believed to possess and treating them by the transmission of energy to the patient (sometimes over great distances) by means of electronic instruments, thus allowing normal function to be restored.

The practitioner needs a 'witness' from the patient – a small lock of hair, a piece of fingernail or horn. This is believed to give out the individual's energy pattern, together with any distortions, which the trained practitioner can assess and treat radionically.

Acupuncture/acupressure

This is an ancient Chinese therapy based on the belief that energy (Qi or Chi) flows around the body on specific routes or meridians. The energy is balanced by the opposing or complementary influences of Yin (= empty or negative) and Yang (= full or positive). Imbalanced energy produces symptoms of illness which is treated by inserting needles into, or applying fingertip pressure to, various specific points (for specific purposes) along the energy meridians which stimulate or suppress the appropriate type of energy – Yin or Yang. The

body's own painkillers and sedatives, morphine-related opiates called endorphins and encephalins, are known to be stimulated by acupuncture and acupressure and this could be part of a modern, scientific explanation of why acupuncture seems to be effective.

Osteopathy

A therapy of body manipulation, osteopathy aims to 'free' or adjust joints and muscles which have become fixed at the limit of their normal range of movement, mainly due to injury (maybe even a very minor injury which has gone untreated) or muscle spasm. Once the pressure and strain on the relevant parts is relieved, it is believed to also relieve stress on internal organs as well as enabling the body to function normally, not having to compensate for pain in one part by abnormal use of another.

Chiropractic

Closely related to osteopathy, chiropractic concentrates on the gentle manipulation of muscles and joints mainly in the spinal area from where the nerves of the peripheral nervous system emerge from the spinal cord. The correction of misalignments by skilled manipulation removes pressure on nerves which may be causing pain or malfunction. The popularity of both osteopathy and chiropractic in the horse world, also physiotherapy and massage, is understandable considering the athletic nature of most horses and the stresses and strains horses' backs experience, even just by standing still carrying the weight of a rider.

Left: A confident, friendly touch from the therapist sets a horse's mind at rest, although this one still looks a little apprehensive!

Below: Various physical therapists use different techniques to help horses, sports massage and chiropractic being two of the most common

Fitness

If you have read this far through this book you will by now be in no doubt, if you ever were, that the horse is a grazing, running animal! His natural life, moving as a matter of course around 30 miles a day sometimes under pressure and sometimes not, is not only good for his physique and metabolism and well within his capabilities but also keeps him mentally occupied and satisfied.

Starting with a Handicap

The contrary side of human nature comes out when we devise careful programmes of increasing feed and work to be carried out under saddle, yet deny horses the freedom to roam on grasslands of poor to moderate nutrient levels, which is what makes feral horses so very fit. Some people even say that once the horse begins a fitness programme he should be denied liberty in case he strains himself. True! If the horse is denied freedom as a matter of policy, he may well go bananas when he finally is turned out, but if his routine involves daily turnout as well as work-exercise there is unlikely to be a problem.

WE'RE FITTER THAN YOU!

On a round-up of some feral mustangs in the USA, researchers accompanying the riders were interested to note that the mustangs could easily out-run the mounted horses far beyond the allowance made for the weight and interference of rider and saddle. The mustangs took fewer, longer strides and, on arrival at the holding corral, were breathing more slowly than their ridden cousins. A few were restrained to check their heart rates and although the readings were raised by fear as well as exertion, they were lower than the researchers expected and, in some individuals, lower than some of the ridden horses.

The normal method of keeping the horse standing around for most of his 24 hours, riding him for a couple of them and perhaps turning him out for one or two, means he is idling for 20 to 22 hours a day – clearly not the most effective way to tone up his skeletal and cardiac muscles, stress his bone, keep his wind clear and his systems working actively.

Beneficial Stress

The body 'gets fit' in response to gradually increasing stress. Stress is by no means always harmful: it is good for humans and animals in bearable doses because it forces the body to respond by strengthening itself, improving its responses and generally becoming a more efficient biological machine.

When a particular level of work (stress) is given to the horse, his body adapts to it so that it becomes strong enough to withstand it next time it is encountered. A slightly higher level of stress is then applied and more adaptation occurs and so on, little by little, until the required level of fitness is reached. Too much stress (over-stress or distress) causes injury: too little does not result in the necessary adaptation.

How Long Does It Take?

A youngster who has never been through a fitness programme will take longer to become fit, as will an elderly horse. Any horse embarking on a fitness programme should have a medical check first, especially older horses.

You can make a completely soft, unfit but healthy horse half fit in about six weeks provided he has been made fit previously. This stage of fitness is adequate for active hacking with mostly walking, some trotting and a little cantering, plus easy jumping, some schooling or instruction, half a day's easy hunting, showing classes and the like. Six more weeks of increasingly demanding work will make a horse fully fit for most pursuits and a sixteen-week programme will take you through a three-day event, ability permitting.

TPR – Temperature, Pulse and Respiration

Knowing your horse's normal, at-rest TPR rates and monitoring how they rise and fall in response to work is crucial to getting a clear picture of how

Fast work is needed to develop heart fitness and optimal lung capacity. It is also good for developing the propulsion muscles of the hindlegs, quarters and loins, provided the horse is ridden correctly

fit he is. The average at-rest rates will be – temperature 38°C/100.4°F: pulse 34 to 42 beats per minute (bpm): respiration 8 to 14 breaths (in and out count as one) per minute, approximately.

Take his at-rest rates weekly and note how they all lower as he becomes fitter. Once you are well into any programme, take the pulse and respiration rates after his normal warm-up period of walk/trot and immediately after fast work. Take them again after ten minutes walk/rest when they should be noticeably lowering and again a further 20 minutes later when they should be back to warm-up levels. If they are not, you are overdoing it and should slow the programme down a bit. If the horse is fully fit for the work you have just given him, the pulse and respiration will return to warm-up level or near within 10 minutes.

Points to consider

Once fast work starts, the heart/pulse rate must be raised above 100 bpm for enough stress to be applied to increase fitness. Once the horse is quite fit, to condition the heart properly, the heart/pulse rate must be raised to 160 bpm and to develop anaerobic ability it must be raised to 200 bpm.

The pulse:respiration ratio will normally be about 2:1 to 3:1. If it ever nears 1:1 the horse has been over-worked, distressed and needs veterinary attention.

DESIGNING A PROGRAMME

If you start in Week I with 30 to 45 minutes smart walking on five days a week and end, say, in Week 12 with two hours daily, five or six days a week of an hour-and-a-half walking with the remainder split into 20 minutes trotting and 10 minutes cantering (in convenient spells), you can easily mark off all points in between with your planned, increasing daily work. The initial walking-only phase should occupy two to four weeks (the fitter you want the horse the longer the walking phase), then introduce trotting, then cantering a week or two later depending on how the horse is responding, some getting fitter quicker than others.

INTERVAL TRAINING

Fans of interval training claim that it produces fitness quicker than traditional methods because the horse is only very slightly more stressed after each work stint (see below) so is not undergoing the greater physical demands of traditional training and is less likely to suffer training injuries (normally of muscles, tendons or ligaments).

Interval training starts at the half-fit stage and is done on only a few days a week. You give your horse repeated short stints of work, letting him recover in the rest interval after each one to *almost* his warmed-up pulse rate before doing the next stint. If allowed to recover fully, his body would not experience increasing stress so would not adapt. As fitness increases, stints are lengthened and the speed increased, the pulse rate constantly being checked. If he has not recovered to a given rate after ten minutes cooling down in walk after his stints, slow your programme down.

Protecting Against Disease

Horses have been endowed with very efficient natural disease-prevention mechanisms as described earlier. Without these, particularly the immune system itself, they would not last long. Conditions in which the immune system is seriously compromised (such as AIDS in humans or CID – combined immuno-deficiency – in some Arab foals) bring home forcefully the importance of the immune system because, although medicine can often help sufferers feel better and delay the inevitable, it cannot fully take the place of the body's own protection.

Vaccination

Vaccination gives a horse artificial, active immunity against a specific disease. Vaccines contain antigens (bacteria, viruses) which can be live, attenuated (live organisms which are altered in the laboratory so that they cannot cause disease) or dead. They all alert the immune system to produce antibodies against the bacteria or viruses involved. Equipped with antibodies, the horse will be able to fight the disease should it arise. Different vaccines against the different diseases offer varying periods of immunity and need boosters at appropriate periods for immunity to remain effective. No vaccine can guarantee that your horse will not get the disease at all although vaccinated horses usually remain disease-free and a few may have a very mild attack.

Homeopathic vaccination

There is increasing interest in vaccinating horses homeopathically although the competitive administering bodies do not currently recognise its effectiveness.

Some homeopathic veterinary surgeons feel that conventional vaccination 'overloads the immune system' and has 'hidden disadvantages' (as they were described to me in an interview) such as lack, and loss, of performance. Homeopathic vaccines are felt to by-pass these problems and to be extremely effective. They are normally given by mouth. It is possible to worm horses homeopathically, too.

Creating a Healthy Environment

Although the horse's immune and other defence systems are very effective, there is a limit to their efficacy. If the horse is in an environment where he is constantly challenged by the presence of bacteria, viruses or fungi or other substances such as excess carbon dioxide and moisture in the air, dust in the stable or working area (outdoor manège/indoor school) or ammonia from rotting excreta and bedding, he is far more likely to suffer poorer health (even if it is sub-clinical – not obviously noticeable) than a horse kept in a good environment. Usually, it is the very sensitive respiratory system which is affected, the very one we cannot actually improve.

Ventilation

Most buildings used for stabling are poorly ventilated and consequently are humid inside, with too much moisture, carbon dioxide and, if the bedding is badly managed, ammonia. Stable dust and fungi from forage and straw make things worse.

The horse gives off water in his breath, sweat, urine and droppings. High humidity creates perfect conditions for the growth of bacteria and viruses, and fungi grow on organic material, so as well as your horse's wellbeing suffering, your buildings rot.

Good ventilation reduces levels of

Yorkshire boarding, as in the upper walls of this covered yard, ensures economical, highly effective ventilation

moisture, gases and airborne contaminants: it also lowers the temperature of buildings (fine for horses) and so discourages pathogenic growth. So-called American barns pose a problem because everyone thinks that there is plenty of air in them but there is probably, therefore, poor ventilation because people think it is not necessary and disease is likely to be more common in the horses.

Even the airflow around your yard can be instrumental in maintaining a healthy environment. All else being equal, openly sited yards provide a healthier airspace than those more closed in, so look round your premises to see if you can perhaps remove any obstructions to airflow provided you do not then end up with a howling gale whistling around the place.

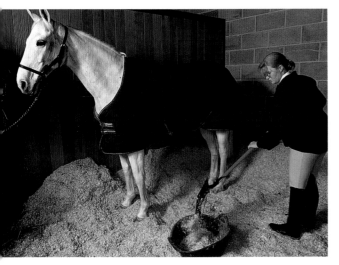

Bedding

Everyone knows how to keep bedding clean but many people don't bother to do it. Whether you use straw, shavings or anything else, it is obvious that leaving in material contaminated with urine and droppings likewise contaminates your horse's environment. Bedding systems like deep and semi-deep litter save us time but they mean that your horse spends most of his time among his own rotting excreta.

Banks around stable walls ('to stop him getting cast') are often left in place for weeks and months, only the central area of the floor being attended to and then often not properly. Such beds are reservoirs of disease organisms and dust, particularly fungi but also of toxic gases if they are wet with urine. This presents a respiratory challenge which any horse, hard-working performance horse or not, can do without.

It is extremely labour intensive to fully muck out stables wash down and maybe disinfect floors daily but this is undeniably the healthiest method for

average, poorly ventilated stabling and used to be standard practice in all well-run yards.

Soaking hay

As we now know that even the cleanest-looking samples of hay (and straw) contain fungi, soaking hay is becoming common policy. There is no need, however, to soak it for longer than five minutes and some researchers and nutritionists say that a really

Change the water in which you soak your hay after each soak

Left: *Properly dust-extracted wood shavings are an excellent bedding for most horses but re-do banks more or less daily to maintain a hygienic environment*

thorough dunking (till it has stopped bubbling) is good enough. The longer it is soaked, the more nutrients leach out of it, making it less and less nutritious. The object is simply to swell the fungal spores to a large enough size to prevent them being inhaled into the tiniest airspaces of the lungs where they do most damage. Let the hay stop dripping before giving it to the horse but do not let it dry out as the spores will shrink again and cause trouble.

If you feed hay in tubs so the horse can eat with his head down, clear out and rinse the bottom daily to prevent an accumulation of wet gunge. Haylage is often preferred to hay, especially in winter when it keeps best, and presents no dust or mould problems provided it is of good quality.

General cleanliness

Keeping the yard and stables reasonably tidy and clean can only help your horse's general wellbeing. Germs and flies do breed in accumulations of organic filth and flies bring further familiar problems. Scrubbing out feed and water containers daily with clear water, plus the use of one of the new horse-friendly disinfectants around the place, reduces the challenge to your horse's system and enables his energy to be put to better uses.

Dental Care

Some aspects of a horse's teeth (mainly structure and function but also some problems that can arise) have already been mentioned in Dentition, but there are other aspects of which it is important to be aware.

Dental problems are often the subject of neglect but can result from malformation or injury.

Signs of Trouble

We are always told that our horses' teeth should be examined 'regularly' and rasped (floated USA) if necessary. But how often is regularly? For mature horses showing no eating or mouth problems, checks should be six-monthly. For youngsters (up to five years of age when the horse should have his or her full set of permanent teeth), six-monthly checks are minimal and they should really be checked more often. This also applies to old horses, say from their late teens onwards, to discover whether or not the horse's teeth are getting down to the roots which will probably necessitate a change of diet.

If your horse starts showing *any* signs of mouth problems at all, leave the bit out and ride him in a bitless bridle, if at all, and suspect trouble with his teeth. Signs may be varied and you need to know your horse's normal behaviour to spot some, although others are so obvious you could spot them in any horse:

- If your horse seems to be eating very carefully,
- If there is a lot of undigested food (grain and fibre) in his droppings
- If he is taking longer than usual to eat up, does not eat up or quids (drops food out of his mouth)
- Any reluctance to eat when he normally would
- playing around with food instead of eating properly
- Snatching movements of the head, holding the head in an abnormal or strange position
- Any strong or unpleasant smell from the mouth

Teeth can be broken by kicks or by the horse accidentally biting on a small stone in his grass or other food. Apart from this being painful depending on the position and extent of any crack or broken piece, the sharp edges so formed can

Foals are born with their front teeth – so it's not surprising that suckling can be an uncomfortable procedure for the mare!

easily cut the cheeks and tongue. Horses which start suffering from weight loss, failure to thrive, colic, impaction, choke or diarrhoea may have digestive problems because they are not chewing up their food properly before swallowing.

Horses who are not chewing their food properly may retain large wads of partially chewed food packed between their cheeks (sometimes on only one side) and the back teeth. Sometimes the cheek/s may appear puffed out and if you try to carefully feel the outline of the teeth through the cheek tissues, you cannot distinguish them. You can carefully bring out any food with the handle

Expert and thorough dental care (not always a popular job with some people doing it and, therefore, sometimes skimped) is essential to a horse's comfort, health and behaviour

149

of a wooden spoon which you slide into the mouth between the cheek and the teeth.

If you find your horse has become difficult in work remember that individuals show pain and discomfort in different ways. Back and foot problems are often suspected but dental ones seem to come low on the list. (As a rather extreme example, I recently came across a horse who was diagnosed as having shoulder lameness but the problem turned out to be a broken tooth.) Always have the mouth examined by a vet or good equine dentist at the first sign of trouble rather than using stronger and stronger bits or getting tough with the horse thinking it is disobedience.

Tooth Abscesses

These are very painful and usually stem from some previous injury around the tooth root which has become infected. There may be a swelling around the root of the tooth: if an upper tooth, this may extend into the nasal sinuses and you will not be able to see it but an abscess on a lower tooth may show a lump on the lower jaw. The horse will definitely show signs of pain and feeling miserable.

The vet can administer antibiotics to tackle the infection although the abscess may burst and pus appear seeping out of the skin on the lower jaw (not to be confused with strangles!) or may come down the nostril on the side of the abscess, if in the upper jaw. The tooth will probably need to be extracted under anaesthetic and the opposing tooth will need very regular rasping down to enable to horse to eat properly.

Crib-biting

As horses who crib bite and sometimes those who gnaw wood excessively often wear down the edges of their incisor teeth, these habits can be detected in a strange horse by a simple examination of the front teeth. The wear does not cause a problem with grazing but you may not want a horse with these two habits.

EQUINE DENTISTRY QUALIFICATIONS

There is no qualification in the UK for equine dentists at the time of writing. However, there is an excellent course run in the USA at the World Wide Association of Equine Dentistry. There is a basic qualification and a Masters qualification. The only training available in the UK is an apprenticeship with a dentist holding a Masters Certification (it takes three years to obtain both qualifications) and all examinations have to be taken in America at present. In the UK, although an equine dentist may rasp a horse's teeth, remove caps and so on, any surgical procedures such as removing a tooth or attending to an abscess can only be carried out by a veterinary surgeon. It is also unlawful for anyone other than a vet or the horse's owner under veterinary instructions to administer any tranquilliser or sedative to a horse to make him quieter to handle for purposes such as dentistry.

Equine dentists who hold the American qualification may work in conjunction with veterinary surgeons in the UK. The veterinary profession is currently looking into the matter of equine dentistry with a view to regulating it. Let us hope that a suitable training course and qualification/s may become available.

Blood Tests and Profiles

The horse's blood is his transport medium for distributing nutrients, oxygen, medicines, hormones and other substances and also for removing toxins and various waste products. However, it can also reveal a good deal about the horse's state of health and fitness by laboratory examination of blood cells (haematology) and of blood serum or plasma (biochemistry). Because blood can change quickly in response to disease, work and stress, nutrition and electrolyte status, it can prove a valuable tool for assessing and monitoring a horse's health and fitness.

Because each horse will have his own normal ranges of values, those working at peak level such as high-level competition horses and racehorses may have regular tests firstly to establish a 'baseline' and secondly so that the vet can assess the significance of any changes.

How Tests Are Taken

A small amount of blood is taken from the jugular vein in the neck and withdrawn through a hollow needle into a syringe containing an anticoagulant to prevent clotting, a second slightly larger sample also being taken into a separate container and allowed to clot. The procedure can cause some little discomfort (as anyone will know who has ever had their blood sampled or given a blood donation) but most horses do not object. Those that might can have a little local anaesthetic at the spot first.

Blood should be taken when the horse is as relaxed and calm as possible: when he is even mildly excited (as when eating), alarmed (at the presence of the vet), has been worked within twenty-four hours or is agitated (at being kept in waiting for the vet), the spleen squeezes out extra red blood cells into the circulation which can mask the true situation. Restraining the horse with a twitch, restrainer headcollar or even a bridle can send up his alarm level and other parameters, too, can rise after such situations. Knowing the horse's normal values within a range means the vet can make allowances for such situations.

The veterinary practice will send or take the sample to a laboratory within a day with a request for whatever profile or test is required. The laboratory has highly trained staff and often extremely sensitive electronic and other equipment and the printed-out test results will be sent to the practice usually within a day or two.

When the results come back, you may have a copy but, unless you have appropriate knowledge, you will not understand it. The vet will tell you what the test indicated and what information it provided, then you can both take things from there.

The Equine Profile

The equine profile is done to check a horse's general health and can be done annually or, more likely, on a new horse in the yard or on any horse believed to be a bit 'run down' or in obvious poor health. If any specific condition is suspected, the vet can ask for relevant extra tests to assist in a diagnosis.

The various parameters listed in the profile result will indicate to the vet such things as whether or not the horse is anaemic, has gut damage (due to parasite infestation), is brewing up an infection and many other factors. If anything specific is suggested by the results, the vet may want a further test or tests to give more guidance and information. Some blood tests (although not all) are very expensive and care is taken to request only what is felt really necessary.

The Fitness Check

Horses working at peak level – three-day eventers, endurance horses and racehorses in particular but also high-performance horses in other categories (including hunters) – can, with advantage, be sampled for a fitness check before performing strenuous work such as a major competition.

Hard work does significantly stress or, if they are not properly fit, distress horses and is asking for trouble in the form of injury. Horses which may be chronically dehydrated, anaemic or incubating an infection, for example, are in no state to be taking on peak work: lasting damage can be inflicted on a

An equine profile should be standard practice before beginning a fitness programme and, later, fitness checks are invaluable for giving you and your vet, a true picture of your horse's fitness. No amount of pulse monitoring or intuitive observation can take their place

horse who is, say, developing a virus infection by stressing him even to levels he can normally cope with quite well, and other incipient problems can be aggravated. You may well see no signs at all of the horse being below par but a fitness check on a small sample of blood may reveal a problem, then you can safeguard your horse's wellbeing and future performance potential by keeping him at home.

Test Results

Haematology

Red and white cells in the unclotted blood are counted and the haemoglobin level assessed to indicate whether or not the horse is anaemic. The PCV (packed cell volume) to check for dehydration is calculated by spinning the blood in a special tube in a centrifuge and measuring the depth to which the cells pack into the bottom. The higher the proportion of cells, the lower the fluid proportion, which will indicate dehydration if the PCV measurement is higher than normal. The unclotted blood is also used to check for some nutritional deficiencies.

Most horses object far less to having a blood sample taken than they do to having an injection

151

The white cells of different types can tell us whether the horse may be suffering from particular types of infection (bacterial, viral or fungal), allergic conditions or parasitic infestations.

Biochemistry

The serum can tell us the protein and enzyme levels in the blood which can indicate the quality of the diet, the state of the liver and kidneys, intestinal and digestive problems, the possibility of parasitic infestation, the horse's level of immunity to disease, the presence of muscle and tissue damage either due to injury or azoturia and the presence of minerals, drugs and other substances.

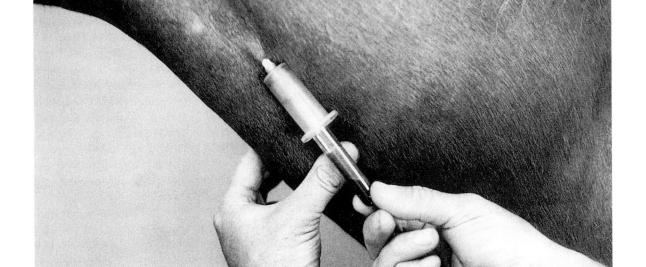

Farriery

Farriery is a very skilled and responsible profession and one which is at last becoming more respected, partly through the efforts of the profession itself and partly because of the realisation of horse owners just how crucial skilled trimming and shoeing are in maintaining a horse's comfort, health and soundness.

Not too long ago, there was a good deal of professional friction between veterinary surgeons and farriers, particularly if an owner's farrier advised one course of action and the vet another: I have known situations where both refused to speak to the other, or to take any notice of the other's opinion, and the poor owner and, worse, the horse needing the attention, were stuck in the middle. Fortunately, this rarely seems to occur today and farriers and vets often work together to the greater benefit of the horse.

Farriery for Foals

When foals are born, they sometimes have apparently serious deformities which often right themselves naturally: for instance, it is not uncommon for foals

Foals should have their legs and feet handled for a few seconds every day more or less from birth in preparation for their first, hopefully uneventful, dressing from the farrier

to be 'down on their fetlocks' at birth, but as the tendons and ligaments strengthen and the muscles become toned up and stronger, the condition often corrects itself.

However, many breeders feel it is worth getting a farrier and/or vet to check over any foal with less-than-normal feet and legs to see whether they are likely to right themselves or whether they will need help. Any faults which develop as the foal grows should likewise be seen without delay.

Foals' bones are much softer and, therefore, more malleable than those of older horses. In fact, corrective trimming to influence conformation is much less likely to succeed over the age of six months as the leg bones are much harder.

Foals will need their first foot trim around the age of two to three months, if everything is normal. Make life easier for everyone concerned by training the foal from early days to have his feet handled, gradually picking them up, holding them in the positions the farrier will use (flexed and extended leg), picking them out and scraping the bearing surface of the wall. Much praise and very short sessions (starting with just a few seconds and building up), done daily, will give you plenty of time

WORKING UNSHOD

If your horse works mainly on soft and/or smooth going and has good hard feet, it may be quite possible to work him unshod. Some horses just are not comfortable without their shoes but many benefit from going barefoot and if your circumstances seem appropriate, it is worth discussing this with your farrier.

The horse will probably need naturally well balanced feet and straight action and his diet must be equally well balanced as far as vitamins, minerals, trace elements and other nutrients are concerned. It takes months for new horn of improved quality, produced from a better diet, to reach ground level so you may need to wait some time before the practice becomes feasible, if horn quality has been a problem.

There are various products on the market claiming to harden and toughen up hoof horn and their differing claims can confuse owners: discuss them with your farrier to see if they might benefit your horse. One product which was formerly believed to benefit horn and which is now generally avoided by the knowledgeable is ordinary hoof oil. By coating the horn with a greasy, impermeable barrier, it can prevent the natural 'breathing' quality of horn and its uptake and release of moisture, both of which can weaken it and, consequently, your horse's feet.

Good feet and action to start with, regular, expert trimming, a balanced diet and sensible work could well mean that shoes no longer feature in your horse's management – provided you are absolutely sure that he is comfortable without them.

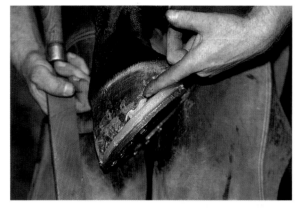

A good farrier, willing and able to carry out surgical and corrective farriery, is worth a horse's weight in gold!

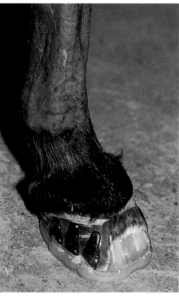

Here a dorsal wall resection (removal of the wall at the toe) has been carried out to enable new, healthy horn to grow after an attack of laminitis. The synthetic shoe has been glued on and will probably be a heart-bar shoe, expertly positioned with the help of X-rays to support the pedal bone

to be able to present a well-mannered and foot-wise foal to your farrier.

Corrective and Surgical Shoeing

Although corrective trimming may be most important for youngsters, the right foot balance to suit the individual horse is vital for the maintenance of correct stresses and forces on the feet and legs. Most of us do not own our horses from foalhood and often have horses whose feet have been inappropriately trimmed and shod and have developed abnormal growth and perhaps lameness because of this.

For instance, it is increasingly felt that the dreaded navicular disease is largely due to horses having been trimmed to have low heels and long toes which increases the pressure placed on the navicular or distal sesamoid bone (which acts as a pulley) by the deep digital flexor tendon running under the back of it before attaching to the pedal bone. As well as drug treatment and appropriate trimming, farriery for navicular cases usually now involves the fitting of heart-bar shoes to help support the heels and the

prognosis (outlook) is good. Horn usually increases where stress is great and lessens where it is slight. Horses' feet can twist, split, grow lopsided, deform and do all sorts of peculiar things if they are not watched carefully and kept 'right', by no means all horses having perfect action resulting in perfectly normal forces on the feet. So, even if a horse with substandard feet is mature, a skilled, concerned farrier can do a lot to improve them.

Sometimes less-than-perfect conformation of feet and/or legs which seems to the owner to have the potential for correction may be accommodated and worked around by the farrier for fear of introducing unaccustomed stresses which may do more harm than good. All good farriery, and perhaps especially surgical shoeing to help improve deformities or assist in foot or leg injuries, is a greatly skilled art and science as well as being hard, dirty physical work. It is always worth learning from a really good, experienced and, just as importantly, concerned farrier who is interested in your horse's wellbeing and not merely in slapping shoes on as many horses in a day as he possibly can. Fortunately, this attitude is much rarer than formerly.

Life With Our Horses

Despite the increasing mechanisation and 'technologisation' of today's world, it is apparent that the horse is as popular as he has ever been, mainly for humans' leisure pursuits and competitive ambitions but also still as a working animal. From being a prey animal and a source of food, bone tools, raw materials such as hide and mane and tail hair for clothing and domestic equipment including tents, through to being a means of transport in warfare, agriculture, domestic life and industry, to his present main jobs as leisure hack and sporting horse, the horse continues to play a big part in the lives of millions of people. To the horse, of course, it is all work although he clearly seems to enjoy some of it and many horses plainly do not want a life of inactivity and feeling cut off from interest and stimulation – not surprising in such a sensitive and intelligent animal.

To many people, a life without horses, at work or play, is unthinkable

Diversity

Imagine the ways we work with horses, from the farmer in eastern Europe, the logger in Scandinavia and Canada, the plough horses still used in some corners of England, the impressive dressage horses and show jumpers of Germany, the High School horses of Iberia and Austria, the zestful show jumpers of France, the ancient, tough hot-bloods of Turkmenistan, Ukraine and their neighbours, the ceremonial horses of England, the terrific eventers of New Zealand and the multiplicity of breeds in America, all with that country's unique stamp of gaits, personality and glamour – it is impossible to mention them all. They all need different ways of training, management and care yet underneath they are all horses and all need their identical needs as a species catering for.

A new regard

It is no longer good enough to believe that we provide the brains and our horses the brawn. Apart from the enlightened attitude which is gradually spreading in the horse world that the horse is much more sentient and intelligent than many people believed, if they ever considered it, respected scientific work done mainly in the USA is showing that horses *are* emotional, clever creatures with very much more going on in their heads and bodies as regards perceiving, assessing and reacting to their world than was dreamed of a decade ago.

Your kind of partnership

The matter of developing a partnership with a horse is as complicated as that involving human relationships. Most horses are followers but that certainly does not mean they are content to live in abject slavery. It cannot be argued that our horses are slaves because we have total control over their lives and deaths. So slaves, yes, but abject slaves, let's hope not, although for some this is undoubtedly true.

Some horses need leadership in almost everything, many are better off with a partnership based on mutual friendship and respect and a few do want to be boss all the time – just like humans. It's up to us to decide whether or not we can get on or whether we should try again with some other horse. You may love horses but you don't have to love *all* horses!

There's only one Horse

The numerous qualities which have made the horse uniquely important to us are not found in any other single animal – size, strength, speed, sensitivity, tremendous adaptability (mental and physical) and willingness, even desire, to co-operate with us or, when necessary, stoically tolerate us. An acquaintance of mine who is into all things psychic and other-worldly believes that it is the task of horses in this life to tolerate humans, to teach us to be better creatures and to help us develop to higher levels of spirituality. The horses will get their reward for putting up with us in another existence! If this is true, they certainly deserve it. I cannot say why people are attracted to and fascinated by horses in such numbers even if they dare not go near them. There is just 'Something' about a horse that no other animal has, perhaps a sort of inner wisdom and generosity. He does jobs that no other animal could do and affects people emotionally in a way

that no other animal does. It seems so little to ask that, in return, we supply their basic physical and emotional needs – yet so often we don't.

The livery problem

Very many people who will be reading this book are forced by domestic and financial circumstances to keep their horses away from their homes, on someone else's premises, either simply renting a stable on a livery yard or paying someone else to do all the work involved in looking after their horse. This can be an extremely frustrating way of owning a horse but, for many, it is either this or having no horse at all.

Human nature seems to be one of the hardest things on earth to cope with, as horses know. A recalcitrant yard owner who refuses to let you put an extra outlook in your horse's stable at your own expense, who refuses to rotate and manage his or her land so that horses can have decent, year-round turnout, who forces customers to buy sub-standard feed and bedding from them rather than bringing in from outside the supplies their horse really needs and who, despite accepting payment, does not perform the tasks for which he or she is being paid, obviously does not deserve to be in business or involved with the care of live creatures. A horse owner who persistently ill-treats or badly manages his or her horse, who makes no effort to get up to date with the latest ideas and research for the horse's benefit, who won't turn her horse out because it will get muddy and who thinks it is all right for the horse to live inside four walls most of his life with little exercise and probably insufficient fibrous food to even keep him physically comfortable, and with no emotional or mental stimulation obviously does not deserve to have a horse, or any animal.

Addresses

The following is a select listing of commercial and non-commercial organisations and individuals which readers may find interesting. They range from traditional to 'new wave' as more and more horsepeople look for a different, more wide-ranging approach to enhance their lives with horses. An SAE will be appreciated and may mean you get a quicker reply! I apologise to those I have omitted due to lack of space.

Association for the Promotion of Animal Complementary Health Education (UK) (APACHE)
Archers Wood Farm, Coppingford Road, Sawtry, Huntingdon, Cambridgeshire PE17 5XT
Helps you find a complementary therapist/practitioner in your area. Seminars and newsletters for professional practitioners and lay members alike.

Association of British Riding Schools
Queen's Chambers, 38-40 Queen Street, Penzance, Cornwall TR18 4BH
Long-established association for riding school proprietors, offering a full range of amateur and professional qualifications. Teaches classical equitation principles, as the foundation of all disciplines. Nationwide riding schools approval scheme.

BALANCE
Westcott Venture Park, Westcott, Aylesbury, Buckinghamshire HP18 OXB
'The Way Forward'. Encourages horse owners to adopt a 'wholistic' system of training and management for their horses and to respect the horse as a teacher and friend. Balance saddling system. Straight-Forward Riding. Feldenkrais for Riders.

BodySense
Cloud Nine, Coppett Hill, Goodrich Ross-on-Wye HR9 6JF
Alexander teacher, Sally Tottle, runs courses and gives lessons, applying AT techniques to riding.

British Equestrian Directory
Wothersome Grange, Bramham, Wetherby, West Yorkshire LS23 6LY
Comprehensive source of information, listing just about everyone, everything, every association and every business you're likely to need in the horse world.

British Equine Veterinary Association
5 Finlay Street, London SW6 6HE
Helps you to find an equine vet. in your area.

British Horse Society
Stoneleigh Deer Park, Kenilworth, Warwickshire CV8 2XZ
Works for all riders, horses and ponies in riding clubs, training and education, welfare, safety and rights of way. Also represents

horse world's interests to government bodies. Qualifications and riding school approvals.

Classical Riding Club
Eden Hall, Kelso, Roxburghshire TD5 7QD
'Harmony in Horsemanship.' Started by classical rider, trainer, lecturer and author, Sylvia Loch, for riders, trainers, students and horse-lovers to promote classical principles of equitation, working with the horse's conformation, physiology and psychology.

Doma Vaquera UK Ltd
Manor Farm, Knotting, Bedfordshire MK44 1AE
Traditional (classical) Spanish horsemanship and horses. Clinics, demonstrations, shows, seminars and competitions plus training videos, equipment, tack and clothing. Informative, instructive newsletters. Trips to overseas shows and schools.

Enlightened Equitation
East Leigh Farm, Harberton, Totnes, Devon TQ9 7SS
'A Kinder Way of Riding.' Courses and lessons from Heather Moffett, teacher, lecturer and author of *Enlightened Equitation* (David & Charles). Remedial students and horses a speciality. School horses for non-owners. Home or away. Saddles, pads and seat-savers.

Enlightened Horsemanship
Parkside, 11 Marlborough Lane, Bath Avon BA1 2NQ
Freelance tuition - classical, simple, kind. Contact Erica Lynall for an explanatory leaflet.

Equine Behaviour Forum
Grove Cottage, Brinkley, Newmarket, Suffolk CB8 OSF
Unique, voluntary, non-profit-making group which aims to advance the sympathetic management of horses by promoting a better understanding of the horse's mind. International membership - overseas enquirers, don't worry about the SAE! Quarterly journal.

Farriers Registration Council
Sefton House, Adam Court, Newick Road, Peterborough, Cambridgeshire PE1 5PP
Helps find a registered farrier in your area.

Hilton Herbs Ltd
Downclose Farm, Downclose Lane, North Perrott, Crewkerne, Somerset TA18 7SH
Suppliers of quality herbal products.

HorseSkills
63 Chaigley Road, Longridge, Preston, Lancashire PR3 3TQ
Freelance horse- and rider-friendly (w)holistic tuition – flat or jumping, private

or groups, talks, clinics and workshops; also, horse management consultancy and schooling. Contact Susan McBane. Classical Riding Club member listed in CRC Trainers Directory.

Parelli Natural Horse.Man.Ship
Rushers Cross Farm, Tidebrook, Mayfield, East Sussex TN20 6PX
The British office of the system of horsemanship devised by American Pat Parelli. Run by qualified PNH instructor Ross Simpson and his wife, behaviourist Heather Simpson. If you fancy doing amazing things with your horse and improving your relationship, contact them.

Reflective Riding
Pound Farm Riding Stables, Old Lane, Cobham, Surrey KT11 1NH
'One Way to One-ness' with Wendy Price. A holistic approach to riding and living. Workshops and courses with the emphasis on the mind/body/spirit approach.

Riding Success Without Stress
Coughtrey House, Gladstone Road, Chesham, Buckinghamshire HP5 3AD
RSWS is Joni Bentley's method of applying the Alexander Technique (and others) to riding. Teacher-training courses, workshops, lecture-demonstrations and lessons.

Monty Roberts/Intelligent Horsemanship
Lethornes, Lambourn, Hungerford, Berkshire RG17 8QS
Monty's British agent, Kelly Marks, (holder of the Monty Roberts Advanced Professional Certificate,) presents the Monty Roberts Preliminary Certificate of Horsemanship course in modular form plus other Intelligent Horsemanship courses, workshops and weekends.

Dr Rupert Sheldrake
20 Willow Road, London NW3 1TJ
Working on morphic fields in all animals (see p104).

Tellington-Touch Equine Awareness Method
South Hill House, Radford, Bath BA3 1QQ
Sarah Fisher, qualified TTeam practitioner, will send you information on how TTeam, developed by Canadian Linda Tellington-Jones, can help improve equine behaviour, and deepen horse/human relationships.

Think Equus
Ambergate Barn, PO Box 230, Kidlington, Oxford OX5 2TU
Michael Peace is one of the élite group of Monty Roberts Advanced Professional Certificate holders. At the time of writing, his Think Equus Approach, developed from Monty's methods and his own techniques, has had a 100 per cent success rate with 'problem' horses.

Index Numbers in *italic* indicate illustrations